Second Edition

Language and Learning Disorders of the Preacademic Child

with Curriculum Guide

Tina E. Bangs

Speech and Hearing Institute
University of Texas Health Science Center at Houston

ANNE MAUZY
Coauthor Chapters 8 and 9

Prentice-Hall, Inc., Englewood Cliffs, New Jersey 07632

Library of Congress Cataloging in Publication Data

BANGS, TINA E.
    Language and learning disorders of the preacademic child.

    Bibliography: p.
    Includes index.
    1. Education, Preschool — Curricula.   2. Learning
disabilities.   3. Language disorders in children.
I. Mauzy, Anne.   II. Title.   [DNIM: 1. Learning disorders
— Therapy.   2. Language disorders — Therapy.   3. Curricu-
lum.   4. Hearing disorders — Therapy.   5. Child, Preschool.
LC 4661 B216Lb]
LB1140.4.B36   1982   371.9   81-5189
ISBN 0-13-523001-2   AACR2

Editorial production/supervision
    and interior design: *Edith Riker*
Cover design: *Carol Zawislak*
Manufacturing buyer: *Edmund W. Leone*

Printed in the United States of America

10   9   8   7   6   5   4   3   2

Prentice-Hall International, Inc., *London*
Prentice-Hall of Australia Pty. Limited, *Sydney*
Prentice-Hall of Canada, Ltd., *Toronto*
Prentice-Hall of India Private Limited, *New Delhi*
Prentice-Hall of Japan, Inc., *Tokyo*
Prentice-Hall of Southeast Asia Pte. Ltd., *Singapore*
Whitehall Books Limited, *Wellington, New Zealand*

contents

Preface   ix

1

INTRODUCTION   1

Definition of Terms   2
Public Law 90-538   3
Public Law 94-142   12
Summary   14
References   14

2

LANGUAGE ACQUISITION   15

Introduction   15
Definition of Language   16
Theories of Language Development   16
Major Components of Language   17
Content   18
Form   19
Use   36
Metalinguistics   40
Summary   41
References   41

3

PREACADEMIC AND AFFECTIVE EDUCATION   43

Introduction   43
Reading   43
Handwriting   50
Mathematics   54
Affective Education   63
Summary   67
References   67

4

LEARNING REQUIREMENTS   69

Introduction   69
Memory Retrieval   77
Summary   84
References   85

5

TESTING   86

Introduction   86
Purpose of Testing   87
What to Test   90
Test Selection   93
Test Environment   103
Scoring   107
Reporting   110
Summary   114
Norm-Referenced Tests   115
Criterion-Referenced Tests   116

6

PROGRAM DESIGN   117

Introduction   117
Educational Philosophy   117
Curriculum Guide   122
Teaching Strategies   127
Program Organization   133
Summary   144
References   145

7

PROGRAM DESIGN PROCESS   146

Introduction   146
A Curriculum-Based Test   147
Developmental Behaviors   148
Class Levels   148
Curriculum Guide   149
Meeting Special Needs   150
Summary   151

8

INSTRUCTIONAL PROJECTS   152

Coauthor Anne Mauzy

Introduction   152
Projects   153
Summary   185

9

CURRICULUM GUIDE   186

Coauthor Anne Mauzy

Introduction   186
Schedule of Events   187
Kindergarten Level Curriculum Guide   190
Prekindergarten Level Curriculum Guide   200
Nursery Level Curriculum Guide   208
Summary   217

10

MEETING SPECIAL NEEDS   218

Introduction   218
Alternate Systems of Communication   219
Technical Aids for Alternate Systems of Communication   230
Criteria for Selecting Alternate Systems and Technical Aids   233
Research   236
Summary   237

APPENDIX 1

DEVELOPMENTAL BEHAVIORS   238

Language Comprehension   238
Language Expression   241
Kindergarten to First Grade   244
Reading Readiness   244
Arithmetic Readiness   245
Problem Solving — Avenues of Learning   246
Problem Solving   246
Avenues of Learning   247
Social-Personal   250
Motor and Self-Help Skills   252

APPENDIX 2

CASE HISTORY FORM A: FOR PARENTS   256

APPENDIX 3

GENERAL CASE HISTORY FORM B   260

APPENDIX 4

FORM FOR RECORDING LANGUAGE SAMPLES   262

APPENDIX 5

TEACHER-MADE TEST   263

APPENDIX 6

BEHAVIOR MODIFICATION PROGRAM FOR A KINDERGARTEN
CLASS   268

APPENDIX 7

HOME-TRAINING ACTIVITIES   270

APPENDIX 8

PICTURE FILE AND OTHER TRAINING MATERIALS   274

Bibliography   *276*

Index   *286*

preface

The second edition of this book has been prepared in response to the increased knowledge of the late 1960s and 1970s in the field of psycholinguistics and of how this knowledge relates to language learning in the preschool years. Furthermore, legislation of Public Law 94-142, The Education of All Handicapped Children Act, mandating early childhood programs in public school settings makes this second edition a timely product. Readers familiar with the earlier version will note that the revised book has been divided into two parts: Part I, Foundation for Instructional Programming, and Part II, Instructional Programming. In Chapters 1 through 6, there has been an effort to include documentation of pertinent clinical studies as they apply to the foundation for instructional programming. Recommended reading at the end of selected chapters has been provided for those readers who wish to obtain further information related to the content of these chapters.

Chapters 7 through 10, include a curriculum guide that has been revised to reflect, even more so than in the first edition, the linguistic approach to teaching children with language or learning deficiencies, irrespective of their handicapping conditions. The curriculum is designed for the developmental range three years to first grade, although pertinent data have been included in the age range birth to three years (Caldwell and Stedman 1977, Bloom and Lahey 1978, and Bangs 1979).

The reorganization of the curriculum guide and the inclusion of instructional projects will provide early childhood specialists with a much simpler approach to instructional programming than appeared in the first edition. Furthermore, the instructional model lends itself to laying out a full year's program. Many of the developmental behaviors listed in the Appendix have been selected from standardized criterion-referenced tests, which are, of course, curriculum based. All in all there is a continuous thread of educational philosophy and basic principles that flow through the book.

The purpose of the text has not changed. The goal is to translate and apply clinical research and teaching experience in such a way as to meet the needs of children who are capable of achieving in a preacademic program but have handicapping conditions, including language or learning disability, mental retardation, hearing impairment, environmental deprivation, and multiple disabilities. It is not the purpose of this text to present remedial programs for the profoundly retarded child who will never reach the preacademic skill level or to attempt to remedy the emotional problems of the emotionally disturbed child. The text presents (1) information related to the developmental scope and sequence of language and learning behaviors in a normal preschool population, (2) the what and how of assessing the areas of language, cognitive skills, and preacademic subjects, (3) an instructional model for program development, (4) a preacademic curriculum guide based on normal development, and (5) a chapter on meeting special needs through alternate systems of communication and technical aids.

The book is written as a text for university preservice training programs that are preparing students to teach language- or learning-handicapped children in the developmental range three years to first grade. The book is directed also to teachers who have been assigned to instruct these children yet do not have all the necessary information and skills to implement and conduct the programs. The text is also suitable for psychologists, physical therapists, social workers, and physicians who wish to gain additional insight into the educational process of language- and learning-handicapped children. Because the contents of the book are based on normal developmental principles, kindergarten and nursery school teachers of nonhandicapped children will find the model appropriate for their instructional programs.

I am indebted to my colleagues who contributed in many ways to the first edition of the book, to Anne Mauzy for being coauthor of Chapters 8 and 9 of this edition, and to the wise counsel and early encouragement given by my late husband, Jack L. Bangs.

Tina E. Bangs

1

introduction

Room 4, Fisher Elementary School: Kenneth and John, both five years of age and enrolled in a kindergarten class, are drinking their milk and obviously are engaged in a race to see who will finish first. They finish at the same time, and John says to the teacher, "Look, me him beat together."

In the same class is five year old Edward who has been given a pair of scissors and a piece of paper with a circle drawn in the center. He is told to cut out the circle. Edward views the drawing from all angles, then asks, "But how can I cut out the circle when all this paper is in the way?"

Room 5, in a kindergarten class for hearing impaired children: Theresa, age five, is asked to retell the story of Hansel and Gretel. She relates it as follows: "Hansel and Gretel eating. They went in the house and were eating. The witch coming. The witch felt the bone. Telled the boy in the cage, 'I will eat that boy.' They came home."

Display case, Fisher School entry hall: Seventeen matchstick-drawings on bright orange construction paper depict the kindergarten class's assignment to "make a house with the matchsticks." Sixteen of the houses are composed of the sticks glued vertically and horizontally to form houses. But the seventeenth composition is a maze of matchsticks which fail to form proper angles, indeed, often fail even to meet. This drawing belongs to Terry, age five.

By kindergarten standards, John and Theresa are delayed in their acquisition of language. And what of Terry's disorganized match house standing in jumbled contrast to the symmetrical constructions of his classmates? And Edward's inability to devise a system for cutting the circle from the paper? Are they running up warning signals that may be diagnostic of specific learning problems?

Educators became concerned about these children and believed that public schools should provide special programs for language and/or learning handicapped children much earlier than age five. Impetus for the development of early childhood programs for these children was also fostered during the late 1960s and 1970s by (1) the impact of research in acquisition of child language from birth to approximately forty-two months of age and of developmental studies in cognition and (2) federally funded projects to develop model programs for identifying, assessing, and training the children. Although research and program development have opened new doors to serve these children, lack of agreement on definitions of language and learning as well as on when these skills are considered deficient has hampered progress.

DEFINITION OF TERMS

For purposes of this text, language is viewed in three dimensions: content (or meaning), form, and use (Bloom and Lahey 1978). Content or meaning includes the knowledge children have about their world, form is the linguistic code used to talk about this knowledge, and use has to do with the goals of language and how children understand and choose certain strategies for meeting their goals (Chapter 2). Children who are deficient in one or more of these areas often are identified by the following labels: language disorder, language disability, language delay, language deficiency, and language problem. To attempt to define these terms often leads to further confusion between description and etiology. A language disorder, for example, is defined as one that demonstrates some kind of bizarreness in language acquisition, while a language delay is one that follows the pattern of normal language learning with late onset and a longer acquisition period. To avoid the issue of etiology, the author has chosen to use these terms interchangeably. To determine when a child is considered to have a language deficiency is another issue. Different school districts have different standards for admitting language deficient children, often according to the criteria designated by their test instrument(s). This text interprets language to be deficient when the language development age is less than the child's chronological age. With this interpretation, mentally retarded children are language delayed as are deaf children who have had insufficient language training. The difference between these categories of children lies in the development of their cognitive skills including perception, attention, memory, retrieval, and central processing (Chapter 4). Many deaf children do not have cognitive deficits that will interfere with academic achievement, but retarded children do have such deficits.

To understand fully the language deficits of handicapped children involves assessment of both language and cognitive skills (Chapter 5). By adding the area of cognition, which is basic to language learning, we again confound the problem of labeling by introducing such terms as learning disabilities, language and learning disabilities, language and learning disorders, and the list goes on and on. For this text the label is not the key to intervention. The key is the identification of the skills that are present, thus providing levels of criteria to enable progression according to each child's rate and style of learning.

Much of the controversy over terminology occurred during the time when federal monies were available for developing model programs for handicapped children. Although standard terminology was not established through these programs, some very good early strategies for intervention were developed and disseminated. Many of these inno-vative model programs, funded in 1968 by the Bureau of Education for the Handicapped through Public Law 90–538, continued to be in use in 1980. Legislation in 1975, Public Law 94–142, provided free and appropriate public school education for a wide age range of handi-capped children including in most instances three year-olds.

PUBLIC LAW 90-538

Public Law 90–538, Handicapped Children's Early Education Assis-tance Act, was signed by President Lyndon Johnson in 1968. This legis-lation provided grant monies for developing, piloting, and evaluating early childhood programs for handicapped children in the age range birth through third grade. Each program was designed to meet the needs of parents and their children who demonstrated deficits in one or more of the following areas: oral language, written language, problem solving skills, motor development, and social and personal relationships. Project directors developed model programs that included such topics as early identification, assessment, intervention, and evaluation. The goals of Public Law 90–538 and the problems encountered in the early childhood projects for handicapped children, referred to as First Chance Programs, should be of interest to persons who are developing programs to meet the needs of their school districts.

Before 1968, very few programs for handicapped children in the age range birth to first grade were available in public school settings. Parents kept their children at home until the school district either accepted them at age six or rejected them because there were no special education programs available to meet the children's specific needs. Parents who were fortunate enough to live in communities where private and community sponsored speech, hearing, and language centers were in operation, enrolled their children for individual or group instruction designed to remedy or circumvent their deficits and keep them progressing at full potential. Unfortunately there were many parents who did not seek out programs or learned that none was available in their community. As a consequence, many handicapped children reached adulthood with no clinical or educational intervention.

With the passage of Public Law 90–538, the First Chance Programs were funded to develop a variety of model programs that would fulfill the needs of all handicapped children in the age range birth through third grade. The goals of these early childhood programs were carefully spelled out by consultants to staff of the Bureau of Education for the Handicapped which was the source for funding. The goals included early identification, a shift of emphasis from the handicapping condition to the educational needs, development and dissemination of the product, parent involvement, team approach, continuing education and accountability.

Early Identification. Over the years, teachers have observed that the older the children are who have problems, the more difficult it becomes to cut through their compensatory mechanisms and to patch up the basic problem. The children who proceed undiagnosed until a relatively late stage in their careers are in severe difficulty. By the time the problem is pinpointed, the children, their parents, and their teachers are confronted with a thorny, many-faceted dilemma.

The first facet of the problem is the children's frustrations in their quest for additional knowledge. If grades must be repeated to correct the disability, the children are denied further pursuit of knowledge while they backtrack to remedy the deficits. If grades are not repeated, the deficiencies must somehow be corrected in order for them to make further progress. In either case, the children are faced with emotional overlay—a keen sense of failure if retained in a grade—or further frustration if they are expected to maintain a standard of scholastic achievement with classmates who do not share their difficulties. Parental concern, then parental pressure, often add to a child's learning problems, and teachers are placed in a quandary as to the successful unthreading of the child's difficulties.

A solution to the dilemma is early identification of children with handicapping conditions. Identifying profoundly deaf children, Down's Syndrome children, or cleft palate children may be accomplished during the first year of life, but the less gross the abnormality, the more difficult it is to identify the problem. Information disseminated from the First Chance Programs has been a boon to developing strategies for locating all handicapped children in order to assure early assessment and intervention programs.

Shift of Emphasis from Handicapping Condition to Educational Needs. The labels deaf, hard of hearing, mentally retarded, learning disability, environmentally deprived, and multiple handicapped are some of the descriptive terms that have been used to designate categories for funding at state and local levels, for placing children in appropriately labeled classes, and for certification of teachers in each of the specialities. Early on, advisors to the First Chance Programs recognized individual differences among children within a labeled population and the futility of teaching in accordance with the label rather than in terms of the preacademic and academic needs of each child. The banner was raised and the phrase *A Shift of Emphasis from the Handicapping Condition to the Educational Needs* became a slogan for many of the First Chance Programs. No longer would there be curriculums that included arithmetic for the deaf or language for the retarded. Baseline information in all preacademic skills would be obtained, and each child would be taught according to his or her rate and style of learning in the scope and sequence of normal development.

Development and Dissemination of a Product. A third goal of the First Chance Programs was to develop a product — a schema for early identification, assessment, and training of handicapped children or perhaps a program that included all of the charges — and a means of disseminating information about the product. From 1968 to mid-1980, over 200 programs have been funded. Information about these projects has been spread through the popular media and scholarly literature and by word of mouth.

A unique method of disseminating information was accomplished by Louise Phillips, project director of a First Chance Program in Magnolia, Arkansas, who had several model classes in one school. She was asked if she would object to having the voting booths set up in her school building on the city election day. Although there is enough activity in a school building during the day without adding the problems of a constant flow of citizens who have come to vote, the project director accepted the request and proceeded to lay out her strategies. With the use of ropes tied to standards, traffic was routed past every early childhood classroom where handicapped children were being taught. Guides were available to discuss the project with the citizens of the community, posters were appropriately displayed, and all classroom doors were open to provide visibility to the program in action.

A standard method of disseminating products of the First Chance Programs has been through text books and assessment tools. In 1968, the Speech and Hearing Institute in Houston, Texas, was funded to develop model programs for the age range birth to three and for the kindergarten level. From this program came the text *Birth to Three: Developmental Learning and the Handicapped Child*, (Bangs 1979) and *Birth to Three Developmental Scale* (Bangs and Dodson 1979). The model program for the kindergarten level was developed by Anne Mauzy coauthor of Chapters 8 and 9 of this book.

Parent Involvement. High priority was given to the goal of parent involvement. Often parents are the first to suspect that their child may have a handicapping problem. Too often they are the last to be listened to by professionals, and frequently they are excluded from the clinical and/or educational management of their own child. First Chance Programs introduced or reinforced the need for parental involvement in the total habilitation or rehabilitation of their handicapped child. Project directors were careful not to frighten parents by presenting the teaching roles for them too soon. They cautiously introduced new teaching concepts that could be carried into the home and practiced by family members during all activities of daily living. Through this professional support parents began to feel competent and effective in reinforcing in their home the skills that had been demonstrated at school. Although there is no simple answer as to how parents can become involved, there is truth to the statement that parents are eager for help both as parents and as teachers of their handicapped children. Early childhood specialists capitalize on parents' needs for involvement and discover ways of initiating programs that are stimulating, alive, interesting, and educational and that can be carried into the home.

Team Approach. Another goal of the First Chance Programs was to involve a variety of professional staff whose specialties were interdependent. These professionals included members of the medical profession, social workers, speech-language pathologists, audiologists, physical and occupational therapists, and psychologists. One or more of these professionals, along with the family members, teacher, teacher aides, and other pertinent persons, constituted a team that provided comprehensive services to meet each child's individual needs. Hayden and Gotts (1977), both of whom were involved in First Chance Programs, discuss the essentials for a team approach and include the following recommendations.

> Leadership style is perhaps the crucial factor in promoting a team effort. A program director who understands team effort to mean, "I make the decisions, call the shots, and you, the staff, carry out my plans" is unlikely

to be able to help a group of individuals begin to become a team. The essentials for developing an effective team approach are discussed briefly in the following paragraphs.

All staff are oriented to the "big picture" of the program. Although roles are differentiated, each staff member needs a general understanding of how the program is operated. The teacher aide, for example, needs to understand how the program fits into the local service delivery picture as well as the major components of the program and its operational procedures. Perhaps the teacher aide will be the one to serve a public education function when everyone else is otherwise occupied and that important surprise visitor arrives for a tour. Understanding the big picture tends to increase the meaningfulness of a given person's work and make for greater personal satisfaction.

Staff roles are differentiated and progessional development ladders are defined. "Team effort" means cooperative effort toward commonly agreed upon goals. A frequent distortion of the concept is that everyone does the same work (or stated differently, all team members have the same or interchangeable roles). The concept of "team" in no way implies that everyone has the same role or that all must be able to do everyone else's work. The team concept works so well because in fact the individuals who make up a staff have many different interests, talents, skills, and capabilities, and these are drawn upon and utilized. Team work does imply that each individual has a clearly defined role to play and that the roles are related to each other in such a way as to ensure the accomplishment of the common goals. Roles that build on other roles (for example, the teacher role is based upon the skills and knowledge of the assistant teacher role) are identified and individual ambition to develop and advance is encouraged.

Staff participate in development and interpretation of major program goals or major changes in direction. Team work is facilitated when staff develop a consensus over the directions and major developments in a program. This does not mean that individual staff members should always be able to block or veto decisions, but rather that, prior to making major decisions, time is devoted to open discussion of the issue. The program leadership then has at its disposal the ideas, comments, and insights of the individuals who will later have to implement whatever decisions are reached and can take action accordingly.

Individual differences and characteristics are valued. A positive contribution to team work is made when the individual qualifications of staff members and their unique potentials for contributing to the program's development are recognized. Efforts should be made early on to identify special talents or skills of staff and to encourage them to use those skills on behalf of the programmatic effort. For example, one of the teachers may have a real talent for drawing. This skill can be given appropriate recognition and directed to program goals if the teacher is requested to illustrate newsletters, brochures, or other program media. Perhaps one of the teacher aides has a penchant for videotape equipment. Such an individual can be encouraged to develop this interest and through technical assistance and perhaps some formal training make a real contribution to the program through videotaping services.

Communication channels are kept open and honest. The key to successful team work is communication. Time must be provided for all individuals involved to talk together and to understand information related to program operations. Written memoranda should be supplemented by face to face contact at least weekly. Every effort should be made to be sure that essential messages concerning program operations flow back and forth in a clear, un-distorted fashion. Leadership personnel should take time to listen to staff concerns. The informal communication system of the "grapevine" may be inevitable, but the state of the formal channels need not cause staff to come to rely on the informal system to acquire basic information about program operation.

There is a real hazard in larger programs that the operational units become so large that good communication becomes difficult. Program leadership should give careful consideration to forming teams and subteams so that the size of the operational team unit is kept between six to eight people. Once a larger group is involved more formal communication is inevitable.

Overall, careful selection of staff in the beginning and the establishment of trust between leadership and line staff lay a foundation for team work. An honestly recognized and openly expressed need to bring to bear the skills of each staff member for the program's success builds on that foundation. The time and effort involved in providing for face to face communication of staff members (including the leadership personnel) will assure the soundness of the team structure being built. Promoting real team effort does take more time in the initial phases of program development, but it pays off in increased individual responsibility taking and heightened commitment to program goals later on. (pp. 248–249)

The joint endeavor of a team will aid in overcoming difficulties that relate to sorting through professional nomenclature, understanding each other's services, and crossing over professional barriers of certification and job descriptions. There has been indeed a forward movement in applying interdisciplinary services to young handicapped children.

Continuing Education and Inservice Training. A graduate from a university deaf education training program once said to the author, "I don't know why you continue to attend lectures. I learned *the* method for teaching deaf children, and now I can put my profession to practice without further coursework, seminars, or workshops." The phrase *Continuing Education* or *Inservice Training* was not in vogue at that time. It is apparent that to this deaf educator *the* method was all that was needed, and there would be no research that could add to or detract from *the* method. It has been said that getting people to accept new rule books when they have memorized the old ones is often asking too much. But for most early childhood specialists keeping abreast of clinical research and adapting findings to ongoing curriculum guides is perhaps one of the most time consuming and yet rewarding experiences. The preparation of personnel in all early childhood professions is continuous with a goal toward providing better services to handicapped children and their families.

Accountability. Last, but certainly not least, was the goal of accountability. In general, project directors were assigned three tasks to assure that accountability was built into each program: (1) specification of desired student performance written in the form of performance objectives, (2) establishment of procedures to monitor the instructional program to determine if objectives were met, and (3) publication of a report relating student performance to the instructional program. When these tasks were completed, teachers would know if what they had purported to teach was actually learned by the children. If so, new objectives would be written. If not, the program would be recycled by the team after determining what steps needed to be altered in order to meet the objectives. It seems a logical next step that every tax-paying citizen should be given the right to review accountability studies in the public education programs in which their children are enrolled.

Meeting the goals of First Chance Programs was a requirement for all project directors, most of whom encountered an incredible number of problems that had to be solved or circumvented. Knowledge of these problems and strategies for overcoming them has helped new project staff in developing their model programs.

Problems Encountered in First Chance Programs

Project directors of the original twenty-three funded First Chance Programs were confronted with problems of locating handicapped children, transporting them to and from the diagnostic and training programs, providing services in remote and sparsely populated areas as well as with problems of attendance and foreign language barriers, to name but a few.

In Magnolia, Arkansas, Louise Phillips was the project director of a planning grant to develop a program for mentally retarded children who resided in remote areas surrounding the city. She discovered that some of the families had not enrolled their normal children in school let alone sought services for their handicapped children. In fact, no special education children had ever been identified in these remote areas. Why? Because parents were found to be suspicious of census takers or any outsider irrespective of the purpose for entering the community. How then did the Magnolia project staff locate the children in need of special services? They found knocking on the doors to be nonproductive; instead they trained and relied on indigenous workers to help locate the children. Perhaps the best person was the letter carrier who had contacts with the majority of families in these outreach populations. He could tell you where the child lived who could not talk, behaved in a peculiar manner, could not walk, or just looked peculiar. He or other trained indigenous workers met with parents of these children and discussed the remedial program available in Magnolia.

Finding the children was not the only problem. Children without transportation had to be bused to the First Chance Program; sometimes the trip took two hours to the school and two hours back to the homes. Rather than waste these four hours of "learning time," a special bus was designed that simulated a classroom. Here the retarded children received stimulation in a variety of language and learning activities, such as counting children on the bus, learning songs and sequence games, story telling, and playing show and tell. Teaching social amenities was also part of the bus ride.

Another group had a grant to train cerebral palsied children under an educational model as opposed to a medical model. Their basic problem was transporting the children to and from the training center. The distance was not great, and buses and drivers were available. The appalling situation was that the ghetto areas where the children lived were overpopulated with drug addicts willing to steal to support their addiction. Picture the problem. A bus pulls up to the door of an apartment in the ghetto. The cerebral palsied child lives with his family on the fourth floor. The mother would like to have her son downstairs waiting for the bus; she cannot carry at one time her child and his crutches down the stairs. If she takes the crutches first, they may be stolen before she gets back up to her apartment and down with her child. She does not want to leave the child alone while she goes back for the crutches. Because of the need for an aide to assist the mother, and the drivers' request for protection, the problem was solved by engaging two drivers for each bus.

The project at the Speech and Hearing Institute in Houston extended its preacademic program to public health clinics in low socioeconomic areas. There dope and robbery were not the problems — attendance was. Project staff found low daily attendance of children and their parents because of the innumerable problems facing the parents. They had to stand many hours in long food stamp lines; when their other children were sick and could not go to school, the mother had to stay home to care for them; cars, if owned, were in constant need of repair; heavy rains prevented walking to school because no family members had rain boots; and the majority of parents, themselves uneducated, were not motivated because they did not understand the need for early intervention. Two strategies were undertaken. Transportation was provided for the child, parent, and other siblings when needed. This increased attendance records. Then a teacher aide (an art major) provided an arts and crafts program one day a week for parents. Their products were always something that could be used in the home. This program increased attendance 80 percent over a three-month period.

The Mount Carmel Guild Diagnostic Center for Hearing, Speech and Communication Disorders situated in the heart of Newark, New Jersey, had a different problem. Dr. John Hourihan, project director, developed a prototype for socially disadvantaged children living in the black and Spanish speaking communities. Many of the children came from homes where the parents used black language or were immigrants from Puerto Rico. Which language should the children learn? Would it be black English, as it was called? Would it be Spanish? Or should it be English as taught in the schools the children would be attending? A short course in black English linguistic structures was given by Dr. Orlando Taylor of the Center of Applied Linguistics in Washington, so that staff would understand the parents of the black children who comprised the largest of the various groups attending the preschool program. Since some of the staff spoke Spanish, no short course in that language was given. The problem of the children exposed to two different languages was a knotty one. Inasmuch as the parents were an integral part of the preschool program, they were polled on their preferences, and the majority opted for the children to be taught in the language of the schools they would be attending — middle class English.

In Alaska a planning grant was awarded to Dr. Helen Byrne, who, with her project director Marion Bowles, developed a program that would provide medical treatment and preacademic and academic programs for children with hearing impairment. In the native population which consisted of Indians, Aleuts, and Eskimos there was a high incidence of otitis media (middle-ear infections) among the children. According to a medical census of 1967, otitis media was the leading disease, and an estimate of 10 to 15 percent of the children would be expected to have hearing loss sufficient to interfere with language development. The problems facing this staff were sometimes insurmountable. First, the area of Alaska takes in about 1.5 million square miles, and scattered within this area were approximately 178 villages which were the homes of about 37,400 natives. Most of the villages are off the beaten track and could be reached only by air and only during certain seasons of the year. It was reported during this period of time that Alaska may well have had more settlements not on any road system than the rest of the United States combined. Only twenty-three of the villages had telephone services, although most had battery-powered radios. There is no need to discuss the problems involved in reaching this population of children. The facts speak for themselves. With improved roadways in Alaska, the results of the planning grant have demonstrated positive changes in what originally appeared to be unmanageable problems. Public information has brought children with ear infections to medical clinics for treatment, and language-training programs for these children have been implemented.

The initial and continuing cost of planning for and operating nationwide programs for early childhood education of the handicapped has taken many thousands of tax dollars. The author believes that the tax dollars have been well spent, in that with the help from these programs many youngsters, who otherwise would be on public welfare as adults, will become full or partially self-supporting tax-paying citizens. Most important is the impetus these programs had on the passing of Public Law 94-142 providing public education for all handicapped children.

PUBLIC LAW 94-142

The Education for All Handicapped Children Act, Public Law 94-142, signed by President Ford in 1975, guarantees the right of handicapped children to receive free and appropriate public education in the age range three to eighteen years. In 1980, the upper age limit was extended to twenty-one years. However, for children in the three to five and eighteen through twenty-one age ranges, the mandate does not apply if such a requirement is inconsistent with state law or practice, or any court decree. The following excerpts have been taken from the government document, Public Law 94-142 (1975).

How are handicapped children defined for purposes of the law?

Handicapped children include mentally retarded, hard of hearing, deaf, speech impaired, visually handicapped, seriously emotionally disturbed, orthopedically impaired, or other health impaired children with specific learning disabilities who by reason thereof require special education and related services.(Section 602)

How is special education defined?

The term "special education" means specially designed instruction, at no cost to parents or guardians, to meet the unique needs of a handicapped child, including instruction, instruction in physical education, home instruction, and instruction in hospitals and institutions. (Section 602)

What is included in related services?

The term "related services" means transportation, and such developmental, corrective, and other supportive services (including speech pathology and audiology, psychological services, physical and occupational therapy, recreation, and medical and counseling services, except that such medical services shall be for diagnostic and evaluation purposes only) as may be required to assist a handicapped child to benefit from special education, and includes the early identification and assessment of handicapping conditions in children. (Section 602)

What is the definition of "free appropriate public education"?

The term "free appropriate public education" means special education and related services which, (A) have been provided at public expense, under public supervision and direction, and without charge, (B) meet the standards of the State educational agency, (C) include an appropriate preschool, elementary, or secondary school education in the State involved, and (D) are provided in conformity with the individualized education program required under section 614.(Section 602).

What is individualized education?

The term "individualized education program" means a written statement for each handicapped child developed in any meeting by a representative of the local educational agency or an intermediate educational unit who shall be qualified to provide, or supervise the provision of, specially designed instruction to meet the unique needs of handicapped children, the teacher, the parents or guardian of such child, and whenever appropriate, such child, which statement shall include, (A) a statement of the present levels of educational performance of such child, (B) a statement of annual goals, including short-term instructional objectives, (C) a statement of the specific educational services in which such child will be able to participate in regular educational programs, (D) the projected date for initiation and anticipated duration of such services, and appropriate objective criteria and evaluation procedures and schedules for determining, on at least an annual basis, whether instructional objectives are being achieved. (Section 602)

Are there procedural safeguards?

Section 615 of the P. L. 94-142 document gives a detailed account of the rights of parents; regarding due process it states "Whenever a complaint has been received under paragraph (1) of this subsection, the parents or guardian shall have an opportunity for an impartial due process hearing which shall be conducted by the State educational agency or by the local educational agency or intermediate educational unit, as determined by State law or by the State educational agency. No hearing conducted pursuant to the requirements of this paragraph shall be conducted by an employee of such agency or unit involved in the education or care of the child."

What are the financial arrangements: national, state, and local?

The law provides specific guidelines for local school districts in applying for Federal funding to meet the needs of higher costs for education of all handicapped children. Federal monies must be spent only for those "excess cost factors" attendant to the higher cost of educating handicapped children. A given school district must determine its average annual per pupil expenditure for all children served and then apply the Federal dollars only to those additional cost factors for handicapped children beyond the average annual per pupil expenditure. Such a requirement does not obtain for the State education agency in the utilization of its allocation under this Act. However, the State education agency is required to match its allocation on a "program basis, " but is not required to match the new monies.

Public Law 94-142 has been legislated to insure for handicapped children free and appropriate education commensurate with their individual needs. The above discussion is only a thumbnail sketch of details that are included in the federal government document and in state and local education agencies' rules and regulations. Educators must be apprised of the facts, for the law is established as a permanent authority with no expiration date.

SUMMARY

Early childhood education of the handicapped had been for many years a major concern of special educators who believed that early identification and intervention in a public school environment would alleviate many of the problems that result in late identification and training. It was and currently is believed that if early training takes place, ultimately there will be a rapid decline in special education classes. Furthermore, less public money will be spent in the wrong places — trying to patch up weaknesses that should have been identified and treated well before six years of age.

Although most parents were concerned about their preschool handicapped children, they were not aware of the need for early intervention or they could not afford the high cost of private practice. In the late 1960s this concern was recognized on a national level, and Public Law 90-538, Handicapped Children's Early Education Assistance Act, provided grant monies, through the Bureau of Education for the Handicapped, to develop model programs for handicapped children in the age range birth through third grade. The next step was to legislate a program that would provide free and appropriate education for these young handicapped children. This was accomplished in 1975 through Public Law 94-142, the Education for All Handicapped Children Act. This law has been enforced and includes children in the age range three through twenty-one. By 1980 over 200 model programs had been funded by the Bureau of Education for the Handicapped, and many of these have become the models for instructional programming in the schools.

REFERENCES

Jordon, J., A. Hayden, M. Karnes, and M. Wood. *Early Childhood Education for Exceptional Children.* The Council for Exceptional Children, 1920 Association Drive, Reston, Virginia 22091, 1977.

Public Law 94-142: The Education for All Handicapped Children Act. For copies of the law and further information write to N.E.A. Instruction and Professional Development, 1201 16th Street, N.W., Washington, D.C. 20036.

2

language acquisition

INTRODUCTION

Human communication is concerned with producing some kind of a response between two or more persons. These persons must, therefore, clearly understand one another, or the response may be far from what is expected. Clarity is particularly necessary in written language, for the writer is seldom available to make explanations. It seems logical, then, that operational definitions of terms employed in this text will help eliminate semantic confusion. Bridgman (1927, p. 25) in his discussion of operational definitions, states:

> Experience is described in terms of concepts, and since our concepts are constructed of operations, all our knowledge must inescapably be relative to the operations selected. Operational thinking will at first prove to be an unsocial virtue; one will find one's self perpetually unable to understand the simplest conversation of one's friends and will make one's self universally unpopular by demanding the meaning of apparently the simplest terms of everyday argument.

Similarly, Whatmough, (1956, p. 104) wrote ". . . it is operational definitions which make science scientific, i.e., productive or verifiable and repeatable results, logically connectable and communicable provided that the conditions of investigation or experiment are not changed."

The purpose of this chapter is to present a summary of the ever-increasing publications concerned with the acquisition of child language to its adult form with emphasis on the age range three to first grade. Topics for this chapter have been selected to provide the early childhood language and learning specialist with linguistic knowledge from which language assessments (Chapter 5) and language intervention programs (Chapters 8, 9, and 10) can be developed. The assessment and intervention programs are directed toward the acquisition of skills that will be needed for academic achievement, namely, oral language, reading, arithmetic, and writing readiness, and affective education (Chapter 3). The scope and sequencing of *oral language* development in normal children, primarily between the age span of three years to first grade, is also identified in this chapter. Such information will provide curriculum data for help with language deficient children who are within the stated developmental age range.

DEFINITION OF LANGUAGE

What then is language? Language in its broadest meaning is the act or acts which produce some kind of response between two or more persons. Languages are composed of a system of arbitrary signs that allow for communication through oral language, written language, sign language of the deaf, Morse Code, everyday gestures like beckoning, and such other forms of semaphore as flag signals, to name but a few. Oral language, as discussed in this chapter, is defined as a structured system of sound sequencing that produces meaningful words (vocabulary) that are used in isolation and in rule-governed phrases or sentences to be spoken or understood between or among speakers and listeners. Both sender and receiver abide by the same set of rules. The words serve as a code that represents the objects, events, and feelings that have been and continue to be experienced through our sensory-motor systems. Oral language, then, represents the knowledge we have about our environment and gives us a medium through which we can communicate with one another.

THEORIES OF LANGUAGE DEVELOPMENT

A review of the theories underlying the acquisition of child language to its adult form is beyond the scope of this text, which is clinical in nature. In passing, however, it may be noted that there are three dominant theoretical positions describing language acquisition: behaviorist, nativist, and cognitivist. The behaviorist position, with Skinner (1957) as its foremost proponent, utilizes concepts of stimulus response, imitation, reinforcement, and practice to account for language acquisition. The nativist position of Chomsky (1965), McNeill (1966), and Lenneberg (1967) holds the hypothesis that humans are innately endowed with a theoretical language acquisition device in the brain, and, hence, language is determined biologically. The cognitivist combines the theories of the behaviorist and nativist but shifts the emphasis to underlying cognitive abilities (Bloom 1970, 1973; Bloom and Lahey 1978; Brown 1973; Bowerman 1973; and Cromer 1974).

In contrast to the behaviorists and nativists who consider the child to be essentially passive in language learning, Bloom and Lahey (1978, p. 267) view the child as an "active seeker and processor of new information selectively paying attention to the environment." Within this chapter and text is the theme that in all activities of daily living children through experiences gain knowledge to store with the old, and they will demonstrate what they know through language comprehension and expression. It is assumed that there is a strong linkage between biological makeup, including cognitive processes, experiences, concepts, and language acquisition. Furthermore, children are not taught the rules of the language they will speak, but, through experiences, concept development, and listening to language, they will discover the rules. Language learning is a discovery process.

MAJOR COMPONENTS OF LANGUAGE

Bloom and Lahey (1978) identify three major components of language: *content, form,* and *use.* This three-dimensional view of language plus cognitive development (see Chapter 4) is basic to describing acquisition of child language to its adult form as well as to understanding deficiencies in the language of some children. *Content* relates to the knowledge and ideas children have about their world or the semantics of language. *Form* is described in terms of phonology, morphology, and syntax. The phonological features include articulation, voice, rhythm, and stress. Morphologic features, or the units of meaning that make up the grammar of the language, include the child's lexicon and grammatical morphemes (inflections) that are attached to nouns, verbs, and adjectives such as *s* (boy–boy's), *ing* (walk–walking), *est* (heavy–heaviest). These inflections by inclusion or exclusion can change the meaning of what is being said. Another way in which the form of a sentence can be varied is by changing the prosodic features including pitch, stress, intonation, loudness, and pauses between words. A rising inflection, for example, generally indicates a question form. The *use* of language includes the reasons for speaking, the strategies used to obtain interaction and control in a speaking situation, and the listener's interpretation of what he or she heard.

Although it is expedient to study the specific linguistic components of content, form, and use, it is apparent that there is an interlacing among these components which makes it difficult to ferret out clean examples of each language feature of a child's or an adult's utterances. The current trend is to investigate the interaction of these three components in both normal and deficient language populations. This involves research entailing the interaction of what we say (content), how we say it (form), and our reason for saying it (use). The early childhood specialists who are concerned with the language deficient child, cannot, however, stand still while scientists seek answers to the multitude of questions being asked. The clinical and educational specialists must develop workable constructs that they can apply to their assessments, curriculums, and teaching strategies.

CONTENT

The content of language is the knowledge or concepts children have about the world in which they live. Concepts, which are nonlinguistic categories, are developed from experiences, become the representations of our experiences, and form the content of language. In a diagram of language content Bloom and Lahey (1978, p. 12) include three major categories: object categories, object knowledge, and object relations and event relations. From birth on children perceive who and what is in their environment, and they have knowledge of such objects as mommy, daddy, Joe, Rover, the name of a city as well as other objects that remain constant. In addition, children through environmental experiences gain knowledge about classes of objects: boys, girls, dogs, balls, pencils. Not only do they know about these objects but they also perceive object relationships. Children observe that objects may exist, disappear, and recur and that objects have distinctive properties. These observations lead to the development of such concepts as color and size and qualities of softness or hardness. Children come to know that objects have relationships of action, location, and possession — a ball can bounce, a ball may be in a box or out of a box, it may be John's ball and not Sue's ball. With regard to the relationships of objects to events we know that children develop concepts of time, and in the primary grades understand the purpose of a calendar. They have concepts of causality and can answer such questions as "Why do we carry an umbrella?"

Children all over the world talk about the categories of objects, actions, and relations, but the topics within the categories may be different. For example, children living on a farm may talk more about cows, horses, and tractors than do children in the city. During the winter months in the north children may talk about sleds, mittens, and snowballs, while children in warmer climates talk about the beach, crabs, and beachballs. The richer a child's experiences the more topics there are to talk about. Television, of course, has widened the knowledge that children have about the world in which they live. What they learn about the world also enlarges as they mature, and the topics for discussion increase and change accordingly. All of this knowledge about the child's world becomes the substance for coding meaning (semantics) into linguistic form.

FORM

Another major component of language is the form of the utterances that puts the content of knowledge children have about their world into words, phrases, and sentences. Form is the component of language that connects sounds with meaning and includes the categories of phonology, morphology, and syntax.

During the first years of life children are listening to the sounds in their environment and practicing the production of these sounds in a prelinguistic mode that is frequently referred to as babbling, echolalia, and jargon. This early period of listening to and practicing sounds and sound units, coupled with what children have learned about their environments, leads to the production of meaningful words. Most children begin to talk with single and two word utterances — no, bye-bye, mommy, more milk — when entering the second year of life. These single or two word utterances may mean different things when used in different contexts. In the often quoted example of the utterance "Mommy sock," Bloom (1970) demonstrated that within one day Kathryn used this telegraphic phrase on two occasions; each time it had a different meaning. One time she picked up her mother's sock and said, "Mommy sock" (Mommy's sock). The second time, "Mommy sock" was uttered while mother was putting Kathryn's sock on her foot (Mommy's putting my sock on my foot). Although "Mommy sock" had identical words and word order, the meaning changed with the situation. By the same token, multi-meaning words mean different things according to the context in which they are spoken. The child who knows a frog only as a critter will be mystified when he or she hears Mother say, "I have a frog in my throat this morning."

During the third year of life children have added many words to their lexicons and have discovered the semantic relationships among words which lead to the use of new phrase and sentence forms. As the content of their language increases, they learn new forms to express the ideas they already have. Between three and four years of age children have discovered the basic rules of the language they will speak, including phonologic, morphologic, and syntactic forms. From age three to first grade they will perfect their language form to come close to matching the adult form.

Phonology

Phonology, or the sound system, includes articulation, voice, rhythm, and stress. Articulation includes the perception and production of phonemes which are the sound segments (consonants and vowels). When appropriately sequenced, these voiced and voiceless sound segments are articulated into words. Phonology also includes patterns of intonation and stress. Intonation refers to the rise and fall of the pitch of the voice, and stress refers to the emphasis within a word that will make it meaningful: *el* 'ephant as opposed to ele*ph*ant; or the stress on a single word, *I* will not go to the movie in contrast with I will not go to the *movie*. It is apparent that intonation and stress add meaning to the message. Recent interest in research has been directed toward what are believed to be the antecedents or precursors to language development, often referred to as the prelinguistic stage of language development. Studies related to the prelinguistic features of language appear in the literature under the heading of speech perception and speech production.

SPEECH PERCEPTION

Speech perception, including sound awareness, sound localization, and sound discrimination, appears shortly after birth. Children respond to the sound of noisemakers within the first two months of life and can localize a sound source between four and six months. Even more incredible is the research demonstrating that one- and four-month-old infants can discriminate between the voiced and voiceless consonants /b/ and /p/. Eimas and others, (1971) measured the sucking rate of infants using a nonnutritive nipple while they listened to a series of sounds. The nipple was connected to instrumentation that made polygraph recordings of the sucking rate. A series of /pa/ /pa/ /pa/ sounds was presented until the sucking rate was stabilized. At a specified time, the sound /ba/ was presented, and there was an increase in the rate of sucking as compared to the baseline rate. The authors state that infants are able to sort acoustic variations of adult phonemes into categories with relatively limited exposure to speech, as well as with virtually no experience in producing these same sounds and certainly with little, if any, differential reinforcement for this form of behavior. The implication of these findings is that the means by which the categorical perception of speech, that is perception in a linguistic mode, is accomplished may well be part of the biological makeup of the organism and, moreover, that these means must be operative at an unexpectedly early age. (p. 92)

Similar studies demonstrate that infants also could discriminate between /ba/ and /ga/, a contrast between place of articulation (Eilers and Minifie 1975), and vowel contrasts of /a/ as in *father* and /i/ as in *it* (Trehub 1973). Although limited experimentation has been accomplished with the perception of stress and intonation, Spring (1975) found that infants discriminated between ba′ba (stress on first syllable) and ba ba′ (stress on second syllable). Morse (1972) reported that infants discriminated between /ba/ with a rising inflection and /ba/ with a falling inflection. Berg (1971) and Moffitt (1971) demonstrated that children between four and six months of age could discriminate pitch. Only a few publications are available regarding the infant's ability to discriminate between varying intensities and durations of sounds, and these have conflicting evidence. It is important to know that discrimination as assessed in these experiments is not the same as comprehension. However, these studies give generous evidence that the human auditory system is ready at birth or during the first twelve months of life to receive and process speech stimuli.

SPEECH PRODUCTION

With regard to speech production, investigators have observed that babies begin to vocalize early in life, usually starting with the birth cry. Bangs and Dodson (1979) found that over 80 percent of the infants in their study produced at least two identifiable vowel sounds by six months of age and at least two identifiable consonant sounds during the next six months. Between twelve and eighteen months the children could order consonant and vowel sounds in such a manner as to produce recognizable words. It is not clear how children extract certain perceptual features of sounds from the words that they hear, neither is it understood how they discover the phonological rules for producing these sounds to form words. Researchers do agree, however, that children discover the rules from the features of the consonant and vowel sounds that they perceive and the words they attempt to say.

Early studies of articulation by Roe and Milisen (1942), Irwin (1947), and Templin (1957) present evidence that the acquisition of articulation skills takes place in a somewhat orderly sequence. In general, children correctly produce the /p/, /m/, and /t/ sounds before the

/s/, /l/, and /r/. It is common knowledge that children misarticulate sounds — yamp for lamp, wing for ring — in the preschool years and even in first and second grades. However, there is a great variation of errors among children (Ferguson and Farwell 1975). Winitz (1969) states that it is not uncommon for a three-year-old to produce sounds placed at the seven year level on developmental articulation scales. Yet we know that some three-year-olds have so many misarticulations that much of their expressive language is unintelligible. By seven or eight years of age children's speech is expected to be free of errors in articulation.

Children also develop the prosodic features of language early in life by listening and experimenting with sound production. Lieberman (1967) and Ruder and Smith (1972) demonstrated through their research that around the age of one year, children imitate or spontaneously produce intonation, stress, and vocal pitch. Knowing this information, it may be interpreted that the early acquisition of these skills is basic to the development of normal voice production and its relationship to the semantic intent of the speaker. For the most part, the system related to prosody is not generally understood by young children. They soon discover, however, that a rising inflection usually indicates a question. They also discover later on that in words such as *blackboard* the stress is on *black*, but when black and board are spoken as two words, the stress is on *board*.

As the child's repertoire of sounds and combinations of sounds becomes longer and more complex and as prosodic features emerge, the listener interprets the child's speech as something that seems to be approaching meaningful language — babbling, jargon, and echolalia aspects of form in prelinguistic behavior. Babbling may be described as the sounds infants utter in short strings close to the sixth month of life. Between six and twelve months of age there are structural changes in the sound strings. The utterances become longer, and intonation and stress are present. This stage of speech production is often called jargon. Children are producing nonconventional sentences which, to their dismay, no one can understand. It is tempting, however, for parents to listen to the jargon, relate it to the context and come up with a made up sentence they believe the child uttered. Following along with jargon is the period of echolalia when children begin to match the sounds of others with their own. Between twelve to eighteen months of age a child will imitate such a string of syllables as *da-da-da*. In like manner, children may repeat a word or even two words that they have heard, yet they may not know the meaning of the words. This echoic stage, or echolalia, is classified as prelinguistic behavior. It is not uncommon, however, to find echolalia occurring at kindergarten or the first grade level when children upon request repeat, "I pledge allegiance to the flag of the United States of America . . ." long before they fully understand the broad concepts of pledge, allegiance, or United States of America. Echolalia, then, is present in the prelinguistic phase of language development and continues to be demonstrated after language is acquired.

Morphology

Morphology, one of the three categories of spoken form (see Bloom and Lahey 1978, p. 16) includes (1) units of words commonly referred to as vocabulary or the child's lexicon, and (2) inflections or grammatical morphemes. The child's lexicon is made up of substantive words and relational words. Substantive words include constant words (the child's name, street and street number), class words (hat, table, pencil), and category words (animal, people, clothing). Relational words modify or distinguish one object from another (big blue ball, little red ball). Inflected words are formed by attaching morphemes (s, est, ed) to nouns, verbs, and adjectives to modulate their meaning (cup–cups, pretty–prettiest, walk–walked).

LEXICON

As children increase their knowledge of persons, things, and events in their environment, so do they increase their vocabularies. Increase in word count includes various kinds of words that have generated considerable interest among linguists as well as among early childhood specialists who are concerned with programming for language deficient children. Before the 1970s the primary interest in assessing children's lexicons was to determine how many words they had in their heads for comparison with local or national norms. The trend during the seventies had been to determine what kinds of words children have in their heads, not how many. The following includes a discussion and a listing of the kinds of words that become the segments of sentence structure and provide meaning to linguistic utterances. Without knowledge and use of the varieties of words presented on the following pages, children will neither acquire adult language nor will they read for comprehension or perform mathematical skills of the "story problem" type.

Substantive words as defined by Bloom and Lahey (1978) are those that make reference to object concepts and are usually nouns in the adult model. Substantive words have certain properties such as roundness or certain functions such as wearable or eatable. They include constant words, class words, and category words.

Those words that make reference to a specific object, person, or place are *constant words*. One of the earliest words that children learn is their own name, a word that does not change unless shortened from Jean Marie to Jean or from Katherine to Kathy. Even with these alterations children close to the first year of life respond appropriately to their names. Even such objects as a child's special blanket may have the permanent name of "Blankie" and as teenagers they recall their very own "Blankie," but now refer to it as a "security blanket." Other words in a child's lexicon that generally remain constant include:

name of a city	name of parent
name of a state	name of sibling
name of a street	name of friend
a home address	names of letters
name of a pet	names of numbers

In addition to words that apply to a single object (child's name), there are words that name multiple objects, such as the word *car*. These are *class words*. When speaking of several cars, there are at least two common factors among them. They look alike because they have similar perceptual qualities, that is, shape, and they have similar functions, that is, transportation. Cars, then, form a class of objects and are labeled as cars. Although there are Buicks, Fords, and Cadillacs, some with two doors and some with four doors, and there are trucks, pickups, and station wagons, all have a common function and enough common perceptual attributes that children learn early on to classify them as cars. It is not surprising, however, to hear very young children using subclassifications such as *truck* and *jeep*. Class words increase rapidly from the time of the child's first word utterances through the second and third years of life.

Closely allied with class words are *category words*, such as food, clothing, and transportation. The category word *food* includes subcategories of vegetables, fruits, and meats. Within these subcategories we use the class words lettuce, orange, and pork chop. Category words appear in developmental sequence as evidenced in a study by Bangs (1980). Children were shown a page of pictures of an animal, person, vegetable, building, toy, fruit, and means of transportation. By the age of three 60 percent of the children correctly identified the animal and by three and one half years 90 percent did. Eighty percent identified the toy by four years, and 90 to 100 percent identified the person, vegetable, building, and fruit by four and one half years of age. Not until the end of kindergarten did greater than 80 percent comprehend the category word *transportation*. The study did not take into consideration the exposure these children had in the past with the category words. All children could identify the pictures of the objects.

Relational words describe an object in relation to itself or another object. All objects have attributes that make them distinctive: color, size, shape, temperature, texture, and beauty, to name but a few. These attributes are used to modify or distinguish one object from another. Although young children use adjectives such as dirty, funny, and nudie as attributes in single word utterances between sixteen and twenty-one months (Bloom 1973), these words occur in phrase and sentence form only when vocabulary and grammatical structure develop. These attributes are represented by relational words such as *big, his, under, fast,* and *pretty,* which give added information to substantive words. The attributes allow us to make statements about objects, such as *big spoon, his hat, under the box, fast runner* and *pretty lady.* An object may be described in relation to itself and include such features as (1) existence, nonexistence, recurrence, and disappearance, (2) its size, shape, color, (3) its function, and (4) its location. A relationship may also be described between one object and another from the same class. One ball may be soft and blue and another ball may be hard and white, yet they both belong to the same class — balls. Some words in our language do not have a stable reference because their use depends on the orientation of the speaker and listener and the content of the message. *Sister* to one child is not sister to a friend. Words such as *I–you, this–that, here–there, bring–take* have meaning only in the relationship between the speaker and listener and the content of the message.

> Bill, a four-year-old profoundly deaf child, had developed a fairly adequate vocabulary including substantive words and relational words of quality, quantity, position, and size, but he did not comprehend the meaning of pronouns. Bill was asked to respond to the following: "Give *me* a cup; *You* take a cup; *I* want a saucer; Point to *my* cup;" and the like. He failed every task measuring comprehension of pronouns. The teacher was aware that traditional methods of teaching deaf children often structure language for a child rather than help him discover the rules. Bill had been taught to answer "I do" several times a day when asked "Who wants a cookie? Who wants to be leader?" The pronoun *I* in Bill's vocabulary referred only to himself, not to another person. Mother had also been taught to emphasize the use of nouns and proper names in the home: "Go get Daddy's shoes" (never *his* shoes); "Where is Mommy's purse?" (never *my* purse). A change in teaching procedures allowed for rapid acquisition of pronouns.

Many relational words are contrast words or paired words: *big–little, happy–sad, soft–hard.* The literature includes varied terminology to discuss these terms. E. Clark (1973) discusses paired words in spatio-temporal terms *in-out, before-after* and dimensional terms *high-low, long-short.* Klatsky and others (1973) refer to these terms as "polar adjectives," and Bangs (1975) divides paired terms into the categories of quantity, quality, size, and position. Research conducted by these authors demonstrates that children acquire these words in a developmental sequence.

Just as children overextend the meaning of certain substantive words (all women are mommies), so do they extend the meaning of one word in the pair to cover both words. For example, Donaldson and Balfour (1968) found that in the word pair *less-more*, three-year-old children treated *less* as if it were synonymous with *more*, and *less* was given the meaning of *more*. When asked which of two trees (*pictures*) had *more* apples on it, and which tree had *less*, the subjects, aged three and five months to four and one month correctly identified the tree with *more* 91 percent of the time, but were correct only 27 percent of the time in identifying the tree with *less* apples. These results were replicated by Palermo (1973).

Research in the area of contrast words demonstrates that children at certain age levels respond overwhelmingly more correctly to one of the pair. This learning of one of the word pair before the other (overextension) has been explained by the concept of markedness (Lyons 1968 and H. Clarke 1969). Clarke classifies the paired terms marked and unmarked. Of the pair *tall-short* the unmarked member, *tall*, can be used nominally (the man is six feet tall) and contrastively (the man is tall). The marked term, *short*, however, may be used only contrastively (the man is short). H. Clarke (1969) calls the unmarked member of the pair the "positive" or more complex and the marked member of the pair "negative." Research reported in the literature shows that children usually learn the semantically positive terms before the negative terms. Bangs (1975), using objects instead of pictures for test materials, found the acquisition of certain words to be comprehended in a developmental sequence. Within each six month age group the words were documented as being comprehended when 80 percent of the children responded appropriately. With this criterion level, the positive member of the pair did not always precede the negative member of the pair. These specific pairs are marked with an asterik in the following examples.

Quality Words		Quantity Words	
heavy	(2-6 to 3-0)	*more	(3-6 to 4-0)
light	(3-6 to 4-0)	*less	(3-6 to 4-0)
*hard	(3-0 to 3-6)	*full	(3-6 to 4-0)
soft	(2-6 to 3-0)	empty	(3-0 to 3-6)

Position Words		Size Words	
top	(3-0 to 3-6)	big	(2-6 to 3-0)
bottom	(4-0 to 4-6)	little	(3-6 to 4-0)
*first	(5-0 to 5-6)	tall	(2-6 to 3-0)
*last	(5-0 to 5-6)	short	(4-0 to 4-6)

An interesting developmental stage in the acquisition of substantive words is that of overextended words. E. Clark (1973) defined extension as the addition of a word to a child's vocabulary and an overextension as the misuse of a word. Sometime around two years of age children may be heard to call all female adults *mama* (overextension), and it is common to hear children label a dog as a *dog*, yet horses and cows are also called *dogs*. One child called blankets, napkins, and dish towels night-night. Such overextensions may become extensions in a short period of time, or a child may continue to use the overextensions for several months. Clark also reported that these aspects of overextensions of category boundaries have been noted in the diaries kept by parents of children living in foreign countries, indicating that this stage of language development is universal. E. Clark (1973, p. 72) states:

> When the child begins to use identifiable words, he does not know their full adult meaning. He only has partial entries for them in his lexicon, such that these partial entries correspond in some way to some of the features or components of meaning that would be present in the entries for the same words in the adult's lexicon. Thus, the child will begin by identifying the meaning of a word with only one or two features rather than with the whole combination of meaning components or features (qua Postal) that are used criterially by the adult. The acquisition of semantic knowledge, then, will consist of adding more features of meaning to the lexical entry of the word until the child's combination of features in the entry for that word corresponds to the adult's. The hypothesis, therefore, assumes that the child's use and interpretation of words may differ considerably from the adult's in the early stages of the language acquisition process, but, over time, will come to correspond to the adult model.

Specifically, a child's lexicon includes a variety of relational words each of which must be understood if a child is going to reach adult language and read for comprehension (see Appendix 1, Developmental Behaviors). These words include:

position words	negative words
quality words	question words
quantity words	pronouns
size words	agent-action words
shape words	multi-meaning words
color words	social words
affective words	

Words that designate the location of an object or movement of an object toward a location — in–out, on–under, forward–backward, right–left, to the right–to the left — are *position words*. Children must have had experiences with the concepts of position, or they will not comprehend or use the words meaningfully. Activities of daily living, such as dumping sand out of a pail and pouring sand or water into a pail, walking into a room and out of a room, and taking clothes out of a drawer or putting clothes into a drawer, help children develop the concepts of in and out. By the same token, rolling a ball under a chair and putting a ball on a table, sitting on a chair, and seeing the cat under the chair provide concepts of on and under. In studies by Bangs (1975), where objects were used as test material, and Kraner (1976), where pictures were used, the results demonstrated clearly that words of position appear in a child's vocabulary (comprehension) in a distinctly developmental order. Children learn *in*, *on*, and *under* before they learn *in front of*, and *in back of;* later in kindergarten they learn *ahead of* and *behind.*

Relational words of quality — *quality words* — such as hard–soft, heavy–light and same–different, develop in a sequential order. Children learn *hard–soft* before they learn *same–different.* In a task assessing *same–different,* Mary is presented with a box containing buttons of three different sizes. The diagnostician selects one button and asks Mary to find one that is the *same* and then one that is different (two out of three trials). If Mary is unable to complete the task, the three different sized buttons are placed before her, and she is encouraged to sort the remaining buttons according to size. If correctly executed, the child can be said to have the basic concept of same–different for this particular task. If the child cannot sort or match, then an appropriate experiential program should be initiated. Children who do not have the concept of same–different or do not know the meaning of the words *same–different* will have difficulty in kindergarten when asked to "Draw a line under the one that is the *same* or draw a line under the one that is *different.*" Of course the question may be asked, "Does the child understand the meaning of the word *under?*" Knowing the level on which the child is functioning provides the teacher with baseline information used to develop teaching objectives.

All–none, full–empty, more–less, and each are words describing amount or *quantity.* Bangs (1975) found that by four years of age 80 percent of the children in her study could identify the box with *more* buttons and the box with *less* buttons, a concept related to numbers or numeration. It is important to recognize that in the English language, the words *more–less* represent a variety of concepts such as numeration, volume, and weight. Although children comprehend *more–less* relative to numeration at four years of age, we do not expect them to comprehend these words in relation to the concept of volume until they are six or seven years of age. For example, when two equal sized glasses are filled with water, and one is poured into a tall, thin beaker, children under six years most likely will point to the tall thin glass when asked, "Which one has *more*?" and to the other glass as having *less* water. This is the Piagetian concept of conservation. Words of quantity are basic to developing prearithmetic skills including, of course, the names of numbers for developing concepts — one, two, three, and so on, and the relationship of three chairs to three apples.

Of the *size words*, three-year-olds learn the word *big* before *little*. Why? Perhaps it is because children hear the word *big* more frequently: "You are a *big* boy"; "That's a *big* airplane"; or, "You want the *big* cookie?" Perhaps it is because they do not have the full concept of size as it relates to big–little. The question has not been answered. Tall–short and fat–thin are words of size that developmentally follow big–little.

Concepts of geometric forms, basic to the development of geometry and measurement, develop in a sequential order. Kraner (1976) found that 80 percent of the children in his study could point to the drawing of a circle and a triangle by four and one half years and to a square at age five. We can expect most children to match and to sort these shapes before they learn the *shape words*.

The majority of children begin to learn their *color words* during their third year, because they have been taught by parents and siblings. Perhaps it is thought to be a sign of intellectual prowess if a two-year-old can tell you the color of a ball or her dress; and parents do enjoy showing off their children. However, when one recalls the number of times during the day a child has a need to say red, green, or blue or to identify a color, one finds it is negligible. Teachers, therefore, have little need to stress color naming in the nursery level curriculum. Better that children, especially those with language delay, learn words for activities of daily living. As children pass through the three to five year age level, their utterances become longer and the sentence structure more complicated. Color words at this stage of language development do help children discover syntactic rules such as modifiers, *big*, *red* ball, and that the acceptable sequencing of the modifiers is "Give me the *big*, *red* ball" rather than "Give me the *red*, *big* ball." Bangs (1980) found that 90 to 100 percent of the children in nursery schools could identify and name colors red through purple plus black and white by four and one half years of age.

How well children deal with feelings about themselves and others is dependent in part on how well they can communicate their feelings with words. They need a vocabulary that will help them understand and express the cause-effect relationships in social interaction. Children must know the *affective words* that express how they feel or someone else feels: happy–sad, kind–mean, good–bad, love–hate, lonely, afraid, scared, and many others. A discussion of affective education and how these emotional words are used in group therapy is included in Chapter 3.

Negation, as it appears in phrases and sentences, is a complex system. Klima (1964) in an analysis of adult grammar includes approximately two dozen phrases, and an equal number of structural rules and transformational rules that relate to negation. Bloom (1970, p. 172) discusses three semantic categories of negation in Phase I of her study:

1. Nonexistence
   No pocket.

   Katherine not finding a pocket in Mommy's skirt, which had no pocket.

2. Rejection
   No dirty soap.

   Katherine pushing away a sliver of worn soap in the bathtub, wanting to be washed with new pink soap.

3. Denial
   No truck.

   Katherine, Mommy, and Lois looking for the truck. Where's the truck? Mommy picking up the car, giving it to Katherine. Here it is. There's the truck.

Bloom suggests that denial is last to occur because it entails holding two things in mind at the same time, the fact that Mommy was holding out a car instead of a truck and the false statement to be denied. As children become more facile with the rules of language, they drop the child model of negation and move into the adult model. Bangs (1980) found that 90 to 100 percent of children in nursery school at age three and one half years could point appropriately to pictures when asked, "Show me the doll *is* on the bed. Show me the ball *is not* on the table," with a score of two out of three correct trials for each *is* on and *is not* on pictures.

The acquisition of *questions* in child language is an important process because the use of questions can serve as a valuable means for children to gain information about their world. Questioning becomes a teach–test strategy between parent and child, each requesting that a constituent be specified and each providing answers.

The *Wh* questions, so called because all but one begins with Wh, include *who, whom, which, what, where, why, when, how.* These question forms seek information related to objects and persons, action, place, time, and process. Brown (1968) in a study of three children aged two to four, noted that they followed adult syntactic rules to form some of their questions — "*What* that?" "*Where* Daddy?" — and also formulated questions not derived from adult rules — "What his name is?" In general, the acquisition of the question form in child language follows the rule of simple to complex. Ervin-Tripp (1970) noted that normal children acquired the use of both *what* and *where* questions before *who* questions. We could expect that *when* and *how* questions would be the last to be generated, because the concept of time and defining do not appear in the majority of children until the end of their fourth year. Bangs (1980) found that 80 percent of the children in her study comprehended *when*, *who*, and *what* questions by five years of age (*When* does morning start? *Who* is on the bed? *What* is on the bed?), *why* questions at four and one half years (*Why* do we have eyes? Stores?), and *what* questions at four years (*What* do we live in? Ride in?).

Yes–no questions may be derived from a simple declarative sentence, "David hurt his finger" or by adding the word *did* and leaving the remainder of the sentence intact, "*Did* David hurt his finger?" There may also be a change in verb form from "David ran all the way home to "*Did* David run all the way home?" Requests of permission fall under *yes–no* questions as well, and we find again that they are derived from simple declarative sentences. "I may go too" becomes in question form "May I go too?" Tag questions, another *yes–no* form, are requests for confirmation that are appended to the declarative sentence, "David hurt his finger, didn't he?" or "I can go, all right?"

A *pronoun* is an example of a word whose meaning is dependent upon who is speaking the word and under what circumstances. This shifting is apparent with such pronouns as *you* and *I*, both of which may refer to yourself or to another person depending on who is speaking. Bangs (1975) found that by two years six months of age, 80 percent of the children in her study comprehended the meaning of the personal pronouns *I*, *my*, *mine*, *me*, and *your* when asked to perform such activities between the tester and the subjects as: "Show me *your* cup"; "*I* want a cup"; and "Which cup is *mine*?" By three years of age they comprehended *she*, *her*, *he*, *his*, and *him*. *You* followed at three years six months, and other pronouns appeared in sequential order. Developmentally it is clear that children learn the rules of relationship noted in pronouns at an early age and that the pronouns are acquired in sequential order beginning with the egocentric words *I*, *my*, *mine*, and *me*.

The *Action-Agent* test described by Gesell and others (1940) consists of a card with pictures of such objects as a bird, moon, and book. The child is asked to "Show me what flies. What shines in the sky at night. What we read." The purpose of the test is to measure the child's ability to identify an object by the word describing its function, thus demonstrating a knowledge of the relationship between an agent and its action. Bangs (1980), using a similar approach but asking the children to give an answer, found that 80 to 100 percent of the subjects could answer the following questions at the specified ages.

Age	Test Item
3-0 to 3-6	What flies?
	What sleeps?
3-6 to 4-0	What burns?
	What bounces?
4-0 to 4-6	What cuts?
	What stings?
4-6 to 5-0	What sails?
	What boils?

One could hypothesize that the developmental sequencing of correct responses is highly related to both experiences and frequency of hearing the words.

Because children can use a word in one context, does not mean they can use it in all contexts. *Multi-meaning words* are pronounced alike. Some are spelled alike, such as *bridge*, the game *bridge*, a *bridge* that spans the river, and a dental *bridge*. Other multi-meaning words are spelled differently but are pronounced alike, such as *sail* and *sale*. The semantic knowledge that children have is not always compatible with adult knowledge. Since words do not always mean the same thing, there may be faulty communication between the speaker and the listener.

On the cover of the book *The King Who Rained* (Gwynne, 1970) is a picture of a king flying through the air with rain falling from his body. Within the book is a picture with the caption, "Mommy says not to bother her when she's playing *bridge.*" The mother is stretched between two chairs, her head on one and feet on the other. The family pets, a cat and a dog, are walking from her feet to her head as if on a bridge.

Melanie was participating in a language reassessment. She was asked the question, "What sails?" Her reply, "Mrs. Lovenstein's garage." This appeared to be quite a bizarre answer unless one knew that Melanie's mother and neighbor had for the past week been collecting all their unwanted items of clothing and furniture for a neighborhood "sale" to be held in Mrs. Lovenstein's garage.

Hi, bye-bye, thank you, please, and other *social words* do not underlie later development of grammatical structure, and so, perhaps, do not belong in the category of relational words. However, these words do facilitate a child's interaction with other persons and are related to social development. Research has not demonstrated normative data that tell us the ages at which social words appear in a child's lexicon or the extent to which children of varying ages use social words. They are an important part of a child's vocabulary, however, and may be used as a teaching strategy for encouraging children to communicate with others.

INFLECTIONS

Inflections are grammatical morphemes (s, est, ed) that when attached to nouns, verbs, and adjectives modulate their meaning. The addition of the phoneme /s/, for example, will change singular to plural, cup–cups; indicate possession, daddy's car; and, when added to a verb, indicate present or regular action, walk–walks. Inflections may indicate number, time, or possession.

Plurals are examples of words that indicate more than one, by the addition of one of the plural allamorphs /s/ cats, /z/ dogs, and /uz/ glasses. It is interesting to note that children discover these rules on their own through listening and practicing. No one told them when they were learning language that they must add the unvoiced consonant /s/ to words that end in an unvoiced consonant to make it mean more than one (cups). Nor were they told that plurals were also formed by adding the voiced consonant /z/ when the word ends in a voiced consonant, (dogs) or a vowel (eyes), and the morpheme /uz/ when the word ends with the sound /s/ (glasses). Plurals are rule governed with the exception of irregular plurals: *mouse-mice, foot-feet, sheep-sheep.* When we hear children using *mouses* for *mice* or *foots* for *feet*, we know that they have discovered a rule, but have not learned that there are irregular plural forms.

Inflections also indicate one and more than one in a pronoun–verb relationship: she sits, they sit. Teachers listen carefully to what children say in order to determine whether or not they are using appropriate plural forms.

Verbs result from conceptual development and are a major determinant of grammatical structure. As with pronouns, their meaning changes when a grammatical morpheme is attached. The change is one of time and is brought about by the allamorphs /ed/ and /ing/: I walk to school, I walked to school, I am walking to school. Some verbs are rule bound, such as walk–walked, jump–jumped, and governed by a pronoun-verb relationship: he jumps, they jump. Irregular verbs are not rule bound such as run–ran and go–went. When a child makes the statement, "I ranned to the house" or "He goed home," it is evident that a rule has been learned. As with pronouns, children discover the rules of regular verbs and incidentally learn or are taught the irregular verb forms.

Possessive words express possession through noninflected words, such as *mine*, and inflected words, such as *sister's doll.* In the early stages of cognitive development children discover that certain objects belong to specific people. Two-year-olds come to believe that almost everything they hold in their hands belongs to them, and, when taken away from them, we frequently hear *"mine-mine-mine."* Concurrent with the "mine" stage is the child's ability to encode different information about objects: a boy's cookie may be round and good to eat, the cookie may belong to him (my cookie) or the cookie may belong to sister (sister's cookie). Through experience children recognize the specific object rights of others, and we hear "Mommy purse," then later "Mommy's purse," or "doggy bone," then later "doggy's bone." A child discovers that a certain chair is Daddy's chair, and other chairs are for anyone to sit on. Bang's (1980) found that 90 percent of the children in her study by four and one half years of age could identify correctly two out of three pictures when asked "Show me the baby's mother — the mother's baby. The daddy's boy — the boy's daddy. The mother cat's kitten and the kitten's mother." Younger children did not meet this criteria.

Syntax

Syntax refers to the appropriate ordering of words in connected discourse. The increase in a child's vocabulary is continuous with the development of syntactic structure. It is not the purpose of this section to discuss in detail the variety of ways in which words are ordered by young children or how they may be ordered to change the semantic relationships; the intent is to highlight some of the structures and their relevance to acquisition of child language. Between eighteen and twenty-four months of age children begin to put two words together — more milk, Daddy bye-bye. As the length of their utterances increases, they are discovering another set of rules that governs the appropriate sequencing of words in the full range of sentence types: declaratives, questions, negatives, and imperatives. As with the acquisition of phonological and morphologic features, the early stages of the child's syntactic forms are quite different from the adult form. We may hear reversals in children's early speech, *milk more*, but this violation of word order is not as prevalent as telegraphic speech where words are deleted leaving only the basic information needed, much as in a telegram, *Daddy go car.* Although syntactic structures have been studied separately from the semantic and morphologic features, the results have been less than satisfying, because these syntactic structures are never semantically empty. Syntax as a category of language form is closely allied with semantics. Sentences encode content. For example, the sentence

"The boy hit the girl" can be revised to "The girl hit the boy." One cannot, however, revise "The boy ate the candy" to "The candy ate the boy." The semantic power of word order in our language cannot be ignored.

It is apparent that sentences may be ordered in a variety of ways, some being more difficult for children to understand than others, even though the subject and predicate remain the same. For example, a sentence which is easy to comprehend might be, "The boy chased the dog." A more difficult form would be, "The dog was chased by the boy" or "Chasing the dog is what the boy was doing." The way in which sentences are presented to children is closely allied with the amount of information we may expect children to glean from the sentence.

Sentences may be formed by conjoining elements such as *and* and *but*. In the English language one may take any two or more sentences and link them together with a connector. As far back as 1914, Bohn (1914) found *and* to be the first connective form that children under three years of age use. Hood and others (1978) made the same observation. The sequence of connectors which have been reported to follow *and* in the development of children's sentences are *because, what, when, but, that, if,* and *so*. The relative frequency with which these connectors are used by children in the age range three to six years has been reported in the literature to reflect the order of development. The word *and* occurs more frequently than *when* and *so*. The connectors *so* and *if* are the two used least frequently.

The length of children's utterances is another aspect of syntax. The mean length of utterance (MLU) is the average number of words in a sampling of a child's sentences. Children show a progressive increase in sentence length up to four years of age (Nelson, 1973 and R. Brown, 1973). By twelve months of age children are using single words such as *mommy* and *bye-bye*. By twenty-four months of age they are expected to use two word phrases, such as *more milk* and *daddy bye-bye*. These two word statements soon expand into longer phrases or sentences, *Jenny more milk* and *My cookie all gone*. By three years of age children have expanded their utterances to an average length of three to four words. As the child's grammatical structures increase, so does sentence length. For example, sentence length increases as sophistication occurs in vocabulary development, the discovery of morphemic rules, the addition of question and negative forms, and the use of words to connect ideas. For research purposes the MLU up to a ceiling of four words has become a reasonable method for matching the language development of children with language deficiencies. The ceiling occurs during most children's third year, and although sentence length increases from then on, numerous sentences are only four to six words in length, and many are under four words. The averaging of a child's length of utterance after an MLU of four words is not a satisfactory matching procedure. As the MLU increases, varieties of sentences are generated and can be described according to sentence types: questions, modification, negation, conjoined elements, possessives, verb tense, and voice.

An in-depth study of syntactic structure would demonstrate that children do progress through fairly well-defined steps in the development of single word utterances to adult sentence forms. The ability to generate sentences occurs as the result of a child's linguistic deductions about words. The structure of language is dependent upon content and form. Although there are a finite number of words in an adult lexicon, there are infinite ways in which these words can be generated into phrases and sentences that convey what it is that the speaker wishes to say and how he will say it — the use of language.

USE

Children acquire skills in mastering the content and form of language and, at the same time, become increasingly aware of how to use it effectively in a pragmatic mode.

> Pragmatics is perhaps best defined as rules governing the use of language in context. As such, it does not define a separate kind of linguistic structure or "object." Rather, all of language is pragmatic to begin with. We choose our meaning to fit contexts and build our meanings onto those contexts in such a way that the two are inseparable, in the same way that "figure" is definable only in terms of "ground." (Bates, 1976a, p. 420)

Pragmatics is often referred to as affective language behavior or social competency in language, all of which probably means what Hymes (1971) calls communication competence. Pragmatics has traditionally been studied in relation to the linguistic stage of child and adult language, that is, how people select and use certain linguistic forms to get a listener to do, feel, or believe something, and how the listener interprets what is heard. More recently there have been studies related to prelinguistic pragmatics described as intentional–nonintentional communication.

Prelinguistic Use of Language

Sound perception and sound production, the phonological features of language, are linked closely with the form of language. Current studies reveal that these nonlinguistic sounds children make — crying, cooing, jargon, echolalia — are forms of intentional-nonconventional communication. Infants' sound productions may not be conventional, that is, they do not follow morphosyntactic rules. There is evidence, however, that these early sound productions are used to influence the behaviors of others.

Infants cry to communicate hunger or pain and laugh out loud when provided extra pleasurable stimulation such as playing airplane or bouncing on an adult's lap. It is also common knowledge that infants as young as three to four months respond with vocalizations when a person coos or talks to them. They may respond at the same time or in a listen–coo–listen–coo sequence. Stern and others (1975) elaborate on this form of infant communication to include simultaneous performance of gaze and vocalization and consider both to be an interpersonal reaction with emotional tone. Halliday (1975) discusses these vocalizations and states that they have no structure, yet are meaningful in their effects on other people. Children produce these acts with certain intents (*I want, Do as I tell you, Me-you interactions, Here I come, Tell me why,* and *Let's pretend*), and their vocal and gestural acts convey meaning to those who care for them. Delack (1976) and Lewis and Freedle (1973) present research to illustrate differences in the amount as well as the quality of infant vocalizations as a function of where the infant is located, for example, on a lap or on the floor. They also noted differences when someone was present or there was a familiar object close by, such as a bottle. This sensitivity to the environment is described as the genesis of the relation between sound and meaning. Current studies tend to support the notion that infants in the prelinguistic stage of language do indeed communicate.

Linguistic Use of Language

Children acquire skills in mastering the content and form of language, and, at the same time, they become increasingly aware of how to use them effectively. In the preschool years, they discover the three major aspects of how language is used (1) why people speak, (2) that people can choose among alternative forms of language structure in order to influence the listener, and (3) that people can understand indirect statements made to them. The use or pragmatics of language has traditionally been described in the grammatical mood of the sentence — declarative, interrogative, imperative, and exclamatory. These grammatical forms are used to describe an object or an event, to express feelings, to get the listener to act (do something, feel, believe) to solve problems, to entertain, or for various other reasons. By using appropriate grammatical form, speakers and listeners can communicate, but often communication breaks down because the intent of the utterance is misinterpreted.

> Father speaking to Dennis the Menace, "Remember, son, you only have *one* mother." To which Dennis replied, "How many should I have?"
>
> Mrs. Charters was presenting a lesson in writing. She gave each child a piece of paper, a pencil, and a ruler. In order to make straight lines on which to write, the teacher said, "Use your rulers to draw a straight line." Karen picked up her ruler and attempted to use it as a pencil.

What a speaker says may be quite different from what is implied. Young children and some older children with language deficiencies tend to be very literal in their interpretations. Therefore what is said by whom, where, when, and in what context becomes an important aspect of language use or the field of pragmatics.

SPEECH ACTS

One theory that has had great impact for researchers has been the speech acts theory introduced by Austin (1962) and the later work of Searle (1975), Dore (1974, 1975, 1976, 1977). The speech act describes the relation between the content and form of language and what is to be communicated. Searle (1969) emphasizes that children and adults select an appropriate speech form according to the situation at hand, that is, to make a statement, ask a question, refer, or predict. In the speech act theory, Searle analyzes four types of speech acts which represent what is going on when a speaker says something to a listener.

Utterance Act	This is the utterance of words and sentences.
Propositional Act	This is the production of meaningful sentences that say something about something.
Illocutionary Act	This is an intent of the speaker to have an effect on the situation. This may be to request, promise, demand, inform, or threaten.
Perlocutionary Act	This is how the listener interprets what is said and how the listener is affected, that is, persuaded, intimidated, impressed, or informed.

DIRECT-INDIRECT SENTENCE FORMS

Children, even in their preschool years, discover how to do things with words, and as they mature they become more adept at communication competency. They learn about direct and indirect forms of sentences and seem to have a large collection of these alternative utterance forms. They may utter a direct statement, *This is a good cookie*, or a direct request, *Give me a cookie*, or a direct question, *May I have a cookie?* Often, however, children as well as adults use indirect forms of request and seem to understand one another.

Heather, age five, was watching her grandmother prepare lunch which would not be ready for another ten minutes or so. Looking longingly at the cookie jar, Heather said, "Grandma, my mother lets me have cookies before lunch."

Parents may use one or the other of the following forms to request action:

Direct form: Pick up your toys.
Indirect form: Can you pick up your toys?

The latter is not an inquiry to test if the child can perform. It is a request to change the state of affairs. Children learn early how to interpret this kind of request. Other common forms of indirect requests are prefaced by Will you? Would/could you? Can't you? Why don't you? Must you?

Garvey (1975, p. 42) recorded the following conversation between two four-year-olds. A approached a large toy car that B has just been sitting on.

A: Pretend this was my car.
B: No!
A: Pretend this was our car.
B: All right.
A: Can I drive your car?
B: Yes, okay. (Smiles and moves away from car)
A: (Turns wheel and makes driving noises)

What a speaker says may be different from what is implied. Whether there is a developmental sequence in the acquisition of using and understanding speech acts is not clear. That children and adults comprehend and make use of these forms is well established.

RELATING NEW INFORMATION TO OLD

In addition to mastering the comprehension and use of direct and indirect forms, children discover some rules about how they must relate new information to what has gone on before. When Karen says, "I want one, too," the statement is meaningless unless the listener knows that Bill has just received an ice cream cone. When a mother was asked, "Why didn't your son go to the party?" the answer was "What party?"

The asker had wrongly presupposed that the mother knew there was a party. There are some instances ("Don't play with matches" or "Stay away from the deep water") in which prior information does not have to be given because there is previous knowledge to understand the statement. The importance of context for understanding messages is clear. The speaker must tie the new information in with old information that is relative.

PRESUPPOSITION

Children learn to speak one way in one situation and a different way in another, and they speak differently to different people (Katz and others 1976, Greenfield and Zukow 1978). Preschool children can adapt the content and form of their messages according to what they believe the listener knows and on what language level they function. Smith (1933a), in a study related to questions asked by young children ages eighteen to seventy-two months, found that they asked more questions when interacting with adults than when interacting with their peers. When adults were in the room with the children, more questions were asked of the adults than of the children. A study by Shatz and Gelman (1973) demonstrated that four-year-old children talked differently to two-year-olds than to four-year-olds or to adults. For example, they used more concrete verbs in the here and now with the two-year-olds. The four-year-olds talked with adults in much the same manner as with other four-year-olds. There even was evidence that the four-year-olds modified their messages in accordance with the maturity of the two- and three-year-olds, apparently based on their language development, their size, and the amount of attending they could do. Maratsos (1973) and Menig-Peterson (1975) found that three and four-year-old children modified both the form and content of their speech when speaking to a person who was presented to them as being blind. They were more explicit with their explanations to a blind person than to a sighted person.

METALINGUISTICS

Metalinguistics is concerned with a person's knowledge or interest in the rules of language. Not until the early school years do children have metalinguistic sophistication in knowing that a word is a word, that it is made up of certain sounds and can be defined and even written down. At the end of kindergarten some children can provide rhyming words when given a cue word such as *cat* ("What rhymes with *cat*?"). They are beginning to know that certain words start with sounds that are alike

("Name a word that starts like *ring*"). Not until the end of kindergarten do some children know the meaning of the word *sentence* and can they generate a sentence from one word ("Make a sentence with the word *fish*"). And not until well into or beyond first grade can they develop a sentence from two or three words ("Make a sentence with the words *boy-store*"; "Make a sentence with the words *father-dog-car*").

The ability to separate and integrate sounds and words into language is a metalinguistic task that is taught to children. However, some preschool children have a keen interest in language and its rules, as exemplified by the four year old son who said, "Hey mom, you know what? Free, four, and five all begin with the same sound."[1] Then there was Jim, a five year old, who demonstrated knowledge about language when asked, "How are a cow and a dog different?" He replied, "A cow has horns and a dog don't have horns. If a dog had horns, he would be called a *horn dog*." This boy could make up words.

There is a paucity of information about preschool children's knowledge and interest in language and about whether or not metalinguistic competency has any predictability for academic success in the basic subjects of oral language, reading, writing, spelling, and arithmetic.

SUMMARY

Child language development is a complex and not too well understood behavior, yet much has been learned from studies of sequential development of concepts, specific vocabulary words, morphosyntactic rules, and pragmatics. There is much more to be learned. Scientists interested in human communication and its disorders are progressing toward an understanding of language systems and the processes that generate them. A constant need is for better communication among the researchers in diverse scientific professions who currently are investigating bits and pieces of language. Even more urgent is the translation of scientific information into the language of the teacher and the clinician who are responsible for the training of children with language or learning deficiencies.

REFERENCES

Bates, E. *Language in Context.* New York: Academic Press, 1976b.

Bloom, L. and M. Lahey. *Language Development and Language Disorders.* New York: John Wiley and Sons, 1978.

[1]From a lecture by N. Reese in Houston, Texas, 1978.

Brown, R. *A First Language: The Early Stages.* Cambridge, Mass.: Harvard University Press, 1973.

Dale, P. S. *Language Development: Structure and Function* (2nd ed.), New York: Holt, Rinehart and Winston, 1976.

Dore, J. *The Development of the Speech Acts.* Hague: Mouton, 1977.

Halliday, M. A. K. *Learning How to Mean: Explorations in the Development of Language.* London: Edward Arnold, 1975.

3

preacademic and affective education

Oral language, reading, writing, arithmetic, and spelling are educational survival skills; the process of acquiring these skills is heavily entwined with the good feelings children have about themselves. Therefore, academic and affective education are never mutually exclusive categories, but rather they work in harmony to produce well-adjusted adults who can serve and relate to a society according to the benefits accrued from their academic environment and feelings of self-worth. Although this chapter has been divided into preacademic education (reading, writing, spelling, and arithmetic) and affective education (self-concept and interpersonal relationships), the intention is to show the relation of these skills to each other and to oral language. Oral language — its content, form, and use — (Chapter 2) is basic to all of the preacademic subjects as well as to socioemotional development, and all facets of preacademic learning are interrelated and must be taught as interrelated subject matter.

READING

In one of the comic strips of *FREDDY* by Rupe, Freddy is listening to a telephone conversation his mother is having. She says, "Dizzy Dooley's gonna go to a special class for his reading problems. . . . Yes, I've heard of it. It's a class for backward readers." With that piece of overheard information, Freddy calls his friend Dizzy Dooley and says, "I'll be your witness, Diz — You have a rough enough time readin' *frontwards!*"

Educators are a long way from knowing how children learn to read and what has gone wrong when they fail to learn to read. They do know that reading is related to vision and audition, maturation, and the school environment prior to first grade in which reading readiness and the teaching of reading takes place. There is agreement also that competence in written language draws on the knowledge of spoken language and assumes mastery of the content, form, and use of the features of language discussed in Chapter 2. Children must have knowledge of the concepts and events that are to be read (content) and a lexicon of substantive, relational, and inflected words (morphology), and they must apply rules that govern the ordering of these words (syntax). Competence in reading also involves the sound system (phonology). Children must be able to relate the acoustic to the graphic structures. When children have acquired these dimensions of language, they are ready to enter into a reading program, usually at the kindergarten level. After learning to read for comprehension, children will be able to interpret the goals and functions of what has been written and the context of the situation (use).

The literature abounds with studies concerning reading, primarily about reading disorders (dyslexia). Until recent years these reports have been descriptive analyses of what the teachers, reading specialists, and psychologists have observed in children who do not learn to read according to their grades in school. Partly as a result of this descriptive reporting, investigators have looked for a single cause of reading failure and a specific method that will enable all children to learn to read. No single cause has been found, and current speculation is that there is no unitary factor. Three names, Orton (1937) and Gillingham and Stillman (1960), stand out in the history of reading and reading disorders, but these specialists offer no panacea to the problem of reading failure. They, with their colleagues, however, have opened doors to enable research to continue in this area.

Perhaps one of the most outstanding contributions to the field of dyslexia was the organization of the Orton Society, a nonprofit scientific and educational society for the study of dyslexia. The membership is made up of specialists from diversified professions who continue to investigate the cause and treatment of reading failure. Until the solution to the problem is found, the obvious facts are still with us. There are children who learn to read through one method or another and children whose reading never becomes functional or is substandard according to academic standards.

The purpose of this section of Chapter 3 is to look at basic linguistic approaches to teaching reading to children who have not yet been labeled *reading failures* or *dyslexics;* these approaches are in keeping with the educational philosophy that appropriate teaching strategies in the preschool years may, to a large extent, prevent reading difficulties. If such is not the case, teachers early on can search for clues that may be interfering with learning processes (Chapter 3). The following approaches to teaching reading readiness skills are applicable to hearing-impaired, educable mentally retarded, language- and learning-disabled, and environmentally deprived children as well as to non-handicapped children.

Methods

Methods of teaching reading include the characteristic sets of instructional procedures and accompanying written materials. It is not the purpose of this section to review the numerous published methods of teaching reading, such as Gillingham and Stillman (1960), Spalding and Spalding (1972), Bloomfield and Barnhart (1961), Smith and others (1976), or others that describe still different characteristic sets in their instructional procedures and written materials. Rather, the author has chosen general linguistic approaches that are basic to teaching any child who is capable of learning to read and those approaches that may circumvent deficits in the learning processes of children who may become dyslexics.

Phonics (a word-attack skill). While there are only twenty-six letters in our language, these letters represent a little more than forty sounds. With these relatively few sounds we are able to speak all of the words we use. In order to read, it becomes necessary to learn what these sounds are and how they are represented in print. This skill may be accomplished through *phonics*, a method of teaching reading by applying phonemic sound values to letters and letter groups. Children learn to discriminate among words by what they look like and what they sound like. The words *pat* and *rat*, for example, have both auditory and visual differences appearing only in the first consonant of each word. The auditory differences are described in terms of the *phoneme* which is the smallest distinctive unit of a speech sound. The phoneme is usually placed between oblique lines /p/. The visual differences are described in terms of the *grapheme* which is the letter symbol or picture of the phoneme. A pair of letters representing a single speech sound, /ch/, /sh/, /ph/, is called a *digraph*. In the symbols of the International Phonetic Alphabet these digraphs appear as /tʃ/, /ʃ/, /f/. The phonetic alphabet is used primarily by speech-language pathologists, speech scientists, and linguists and generally is not incorporated into the teaching of reading.

There has been and still is controversy concerning phonics as a method of teaching children to read. Proponents of the phonics approach to teaching reading believe that children internalize a set of rules which map the printed words into their phonological system, and they use these rules to read novel or unfamiliar words. They believe that the discovery of the one-to-one correspondence between the phoneme and the grapheme provides a means by which readers can directly read single words that they have never seen before and that are not presented in context. Those who are skeptical about the phonics approach (Smith and others 1976) point out that phonics is rule bound, yet there are many exceptions to the rules. For example, each letter does not represent a specific sound — go, know, though, sew — and some letters represent different sounds — do, so, won, not. They feel all of this only serves to confuse children in the reading process. They suggest that phonics is neither a sure-fire method nor a complete method. There seems to be no disagreement among writers that reading is an extension of a child's natural language learning, including content, form, and use. There is also strong agreement among reading specialists that phonics has a place in the reading curriculum. The general approach to teaching children the phoneme-grapheme correspondence is accomplished by providing them with experiences in matching letters, matching sounds, and in matching letters to sounds; in discovering the process of making rhyming words; in identifying words whose initial sound is the same as the initial sound in a given cue word; and in the final step of being able to read words never seen before. The desired outcome of instruction in phonics as children move through the elementary grades is to develop in them the habit of using phonics as a means of unlocking words. In a phonics program children do not memorize rules for unlocking words, they discover the rules. The advantage of the phonics or word-attack method is being able to sound out and hence read unfamiliar words. Among the disadvantages, phonics has been described as a rigid approach to teaching reading, one that calls for much drill and difficulty in keeping children motivated. The creative teacher knows how to overcome these objections through activities that the children enjoy.

Look and Say Method. Utilizing this method, children memorize the printed word and in that way sight read. The teacher shows the word, says it, and the children repeat what they hear. With as many repetitions as necessary in a variety of teaching milieus and over whatever period of time is needed, they memorize the *picture* of the word and are able to read it. To check their reading comprehension, the teacher may use flash cards or words printed on the chalkboard. Although most teachers today do not use this program by itself, proponents of the method in the latter half of the 1800s and again in the 1930s used it exclusively. They believed that children were excited about being able to sight read a word and that their motivation was high to learn to read more and more words. Some children did learn to read through this approach. Many did not. The disadvantage of this approach is the concern that many children taught to read by this method do not discover the processes involved in attacking words they have not seen before. The experienced teacher will combine the *look and say* method with the phonics approach according to the individual needs of the children.

Experience stories involve a technique similar to the look and say method. After a field trip, for example, the children recall their experiences (language content and form), and the teacher prints their sentences on a large tablet or on the chalkboard (language form and use). Developing *experience stories* has the advantage, in keeping with linguistic knowledge, of using the children's patterns of sentence structure to facilitate the acquisition of reading skills. After writing the experience story, the teacher may prepare cards with printed words or sentence strips that match segments in the printed story, always using manuscript letters that approximate the typed form used in the readers. The children learn to match the word cards and sentence strips with the appropriate segments in the printed story. Another advantage of this method is that the vocabulary comes from the children, thereby motivating them to read because the content is in their line of interest. It is an informal method that holds the children's attention. A disadvantage is that there is no vocabulary control and no method of unlocking words that have never been seen. In addition, it takes an inordinate amount of time to construct the charts and the sentence strips, and there is always a chance that the children are not reading but are memorizing what they hear. However, the experienced teacher knows how to combine this method with the look and say and phonics approaches to enhance the early reading skills of the students.

Reading-Readiness Objectives

Readiness for reading is reached when children have learned most of the rules of the language they will speak and read and have a vocabulary level commensurate with the printed words. In the last several decades this readiness period has been assigned to the kindergarten level. Here children move through a sequenced reading-readiness curriculum that includes new printed vocabulary, sight word training, phonics as a word-attack skill, and the ultimate discovery of how to use these skills to read unfamiliar words. Perhaps it is important to note that children do have other word-attack skills in their repertoire. When they cannot read a word, they may look for a picture on the page that will provide a cue. They determine if this word fits into the context of the sentence or the story. Older children and adults also use context as a word-attack skill as well as prefixes and suffixes (inflections) to determine meaning. The following discussion, based on some of the previously mentioned pedagogical techniques for teaching reading, presents an eclectic and fundamental approach to objectives that are essential to getting ready to read. Emphasis is placed on new printed vocabulary, sight word training, and word-attack skills.

Vocabulary. To participate in a reading-readiness program children must know the meaning of words and phrases that the teacher uses in giving directions and that the children are required to use in giving answers. The following are samples of these words and phrases.

> Names of upper case letters: A, B, C, D
> Names of lower case letters: a, b, c, d
> letter
> word
> sentence
> sounds like
> starts like
> rhymes with
> sound of
> same as/different from

Sight Word Training. Going to school is for many children the anticipation of learning to read. In order to maintain the enthusiasm for this academic need, teachers often begin the reading-readiness program by teaching children to sight read several words. One of the first such words is probably the child's own name. In addition, picture cards with printed words under the picture are placed around the classroom to develop the concept that pictures as well as speech can be represented in written form. Teachers may prepare flash cards and use them as a stimulus for children to demonstrate their beginning reading knowledge. Once the children have learned to sight read a number of words, teachers begin to introduce them to phonics, which will help them unlock new words.

Word-Attack Skills (phonics). In general, word-attack skills involve a process of matching, a feat that children begin to master long before entry into kindergarten. Through early experiences they have training in both auditory and visual matching skills. They match the sound of the word with the name of the animal: *moo/cow, oink/pig, meow/kitty*. They learn to match objects to objects, pictures to pictures, and objects to pictures in categories as well as classes. As number concepts develop, children learn that two apples have the same numerical value as two chairs. They begin to write the numeral *2* in response to the word *two*. They develop concepts of relationships that provide the building blocks for learning to read. When they enter the reading-readiness program, they continue to develop their matching skills in the visual, auditory, and combined auditory–visual modalities.

Visual Matching Skills that children are exposed to or taught in kindergarten include at least the following:

Matching upper case letters: D–D
Matching lower case letters: d–d
Matching upper case to lower case letters: D–d
Matching single words
Matching phrases or short sentences
Selecting a picture that starts like a given letter
Selecting a picture that starts like another picture
Selecting from four pictures the three that start the same
Selecting from four pictures the one that starts differently from others
Pointing to the letter that is the beginning sound of the picture

Auditory Matching Skills that are introduced in kindergarten include at least the following:

Telling whether or not two words rhyme
Telling what rhymes with a given word
Knowing which words do not start like the key word (*ring*) when the words
   are spoken by the teacher: "Hold up your hand when I say a word that
   does not start like *ring*"
Recalling a word that starts like a given sound

Auditory and Visual Matching Skills. The combination of auditory and visual matching skills that are introduced in kindergarten include:

Identifying consonant sounds by pointing to the correct letters as the teacher
   produces the sounds
Producing consonant sounds when shown letters and asked, "What sound
   does this letter make?"
Producing consonant sounds when shown digraphs: "What do these letters
   say?"

As children progress through phonics training, they are introduced to long and short vowels in much the same way as they were to consonants. Phonics training with vowels, however, is usually a first grade activity. Children who have been through a reading-readiness program in kindergarten have developed basic skills for learning to read for information and for pleasure. Before entry into first grade we can anticipate that they will be able to meet the following objectives:

Recognize their own printed name from among ten other printed names

Point correctly to at least two of ten printed words presented randomly

Read ten printed words that are not spelled phonetically, words that were learned through the sight reading method

Read ten printed "words" spelled phonetically that are not real words; *Nis, bate, nav, riz*

HANDWRITING

A right-handed five-year-old child with no language or learning disabilities printed his name from right to left, a common error for kindergarten and some first grade children. The printed form shows firm strokes and neatness, qualities not common to many learning disabled children. Randy currently is entering college and has had no orthographic problems.

Writing is the process of transducing a linguistic message into a graphic form, often referred to as traditional orthography (T.O.). T.O. is a means of representing sounds of language with printed or written symbols in correct spelling form. Writing has its roots in oral language, reading-readiness skills, spelling, and the moto-kinesthetic ability to use writing tools for printing or cursive writing. The importance of making written information legible is not denied, yet all agree that it should not overshadow the merits of accuracy in spelling or in writing information. Elementary and secondary school teachers view these three aspects of written work in proportion to the purpose of an assignment. If the assignment is to present a composition on the concept of democracy and the student does so in a well-constructed theme, he has fulfilled the assignment despite having misspelled four words. Those errors should not lower his grade point, for the original assignment had nothing to do with spelling. Perhaps all of these considerations indicate a need for four merits: the ability to (1) write information, (2) structure appropriate sentences, (3) spell accurately, and (4) write legibly. The total writing process, namely, presenting information, structuring sentences, spelling accurately, and writing legibly, is perhaps the result of an integrated neurophysiological mechanism and environmental factors.

Handwriting Methods

Teachers are opinionated as to whether manuscript or cursive writing form should be taught first in order to produce free-flowing cursive writing. There is agreement, however, on the need for recognizing problems facing left-handed children and on how the problems can be reconciled. In all, teachers work toward improving (1) the quality of handwriting, its legibility and attractiveness, (2) quantity, the writing speed, and (3) correct spelling.

Whatever methods may be used to teach handwriting skills, society is made up of people who have superior, good, and poor penmanship. Legibility, of course, is a primary concern.

Prehandwriting Skills. Children before three years of age begin to develop skills basic to handwriting. The majority can make a crude copy of the examiner's drawing of a circle and a horizontal line. Between three years and first grade they perfect the drawing of vertical and horizontal lines, circles, crosses, and squares. Some nursery school programs introduce specific training designed to teach prewriting skills such as proper holding of chalk or pencil and left-right progression. In addition, these preschoolers practice making the counterclockwise circles and line movements common to both manuscript and cursive writing. In general, this kind of training begins at a chalkboard where gross motor movement can come into play. Motivation is easily obtained by making such things as faces with circles and wagons with circles and lines. With the acquisition of these skills, children may be better prepared to enter into a writing program, and writing, like reading, is something they truly want to learn to do.

Manuscript vs. Cursive Writing. Should manuscript or cursive writing be taught first? Proponents of manuscript writing say children should be taught to write letters like those that will be found in their readers. They also believe that drawing the letters is a less complex motor movement than writing script. Manuscript writing is currently the most popular method in kindergarten through first grade. Those who teach cursive writing from the start believe that, because it is the chosen form for future writing, it should be taught before the manuscript form. Proponents of cursive writing also state that it is mastered more easily if the child does not have to effect the change from manuscript to cursive. The issue is not settled. Teachers or school districts make their own choice.

A second question with no ready answer is also often asked. Should the writing be slanted in the time honored tradition or may it be vertical? Teachers are inclined to say writing is better if it slants. Is this a value judgment, or is there a functional reason as to why slanted writing is better? The issue, too, is not settled.

Arm Movement vs. Finger Movement. Teachers are aware that the movement for handwriting is a patterning process, requiring circular, up and down, and forward movements with constant pressure changes and horizontal, vertical, and spatial organizations. Children are taught, or develop on their own, a method that will produce the patterns necessary for written language. More than half a century ago children were taught the Palmer Method of writing, to keep fingers still and let their arm guide the pencil across the paper. Although their writing quality was often good during the training period, something happened when training ceased. Students reverted to total or partial finger movement. For some reason the Palmer Method was not retained, and the aesthetic qualities of the handwriting may or may not have changed. Although as adults we do not use the Palmer Method, there is a current trend to introduce the method to children who have neuromuscular disorders and difficulty controlling fine motor movements. The large muscle movements utilized in the Palmer Method may help these children produce more legible handwriting.

When a child is not shown a method for writing, he will usually use a tight and almost total finger movement. The side of the hand is set on one spot and the fingers move. At short intervals the hand is lifted and placed a bit further to the right. The disadvantages are apparent: cramping of the fingers over a period of time, poor formation of letters, and reduced speed. Currently a combination of the two methods is preferred. Children place their arms on the desk with hands tilted slightly to the outside, resting on the fourth and fifth fingers. As they write, their fingers guide the pencil, and the hand and arm slide across the paper. No matter what method, the act of writing entails neurological complexities, and practice is needed to perfect the product.

Handedness. Teachers follow certain basic rules in an attempt to help children write legibly. The paper is placed before the child parallel with the desk if manuscript is being taught and parallel to the writing arm when cursive is introduced. There is no need for texts on teaching writing to left-handed children if the following simple rules are observed:

1. If desk chairs are used, those with left-sided writing space are used for left-handed children.

2. If the paper is turned in such a direction that it parallels the child's left arm when doing cursive writing, then the child will see what he or she is doing and will not smudge the writing. Left-handed children who are taught to write with the paper arranged for right-handed children are forced to use an awkward back-hand position in order to view what they are writing.

Handwriting Objectives

Writing is a unified product closely allied with oral language, spelling, and movement. It becomes important to teach the movement skills early so that subsequently children will be able to think of what they are writing and not of how they are writing. The writing act must become an unconscious part of the process of getting information on paper. With appropriate writing tools and unlined paper, children by the end of kindergarten will have developed basic skills for manuscript writing and will be able to meet the following objectives: write upper case letters from dictation, write lower case letters from dictation, print and correctly spell their own name, and write numerals 1–10 from dictation.

Spelling

Children in the kindergarten class were being exposed to word-attack skills. They thought of words that began with the /d/ sound (*daddy, dog*) and the /l/ sound (*leaf, light*). As Elizabeth looked at some of her books at home one evening, she came across the word *doll.* She asked her mother, "What does daddy-o-leaf-leaf spell?"

Spelling, a process concerned with appropriate ordering of sounds or letters to form words, is an academic skill, yet its roots are in a reading-readiness program, so aptly demonstrated by "daddy-o-leaf-leaf." Research in the subject of spelling is mostly on a theoretical level with little information on how and when it should be taught. What has been written tends to indicate that the skills needed to spell words, either orally or in written form, are varied and may be independent of each other.

Prespelling Skills

Even before kindergarten children are learning how to match and to sequence, both prerequisites to spelling. They can line up their cars from smallest to largest, stack rings on a stick, and nest boxes according to their respective sizes. Then in kindergarten, while learning to match phoneme to grapheme as a skill for reading, children are also developing the concept of spelling and the skills for spelling. Two steps may be introduced at this level, in conjunction with the reading-readiness and handwriting programs: (1) the teacher dictates a word and the children spell it with letters that are printed on small squares, available in teacher supply stores, and (2) the children, from memory, choose their own words to print.

Spelling Objectives

We can expect that the majority of children, before entry into first grade, can print their own name from memory and spell it correctly, even though there may be letter reversals.

MATHEMATICS

> Gretchen, age four, was asked how many legs a dog has. Her reply was, "Let's see, he has two in front and two in back, and that makes three."

How old are you? When is your birthday? You may have one more cookie. What time is your TV program? It's on channel 8. These questions and statements reveal personal needs children have for number concepts, for number language, and number symbolism. Until recently preschool children have been exposed to number language incidentally, but with the advent of early childhood programs for both normal and handicapped children premathematic skills should be systematically planned and included in the curriculum.

Mathematics is a language of science that deals with properties and relations of quantity and measurement. As a language it must be concerned with the experiences and knowledge children have about quantity and measurement, the learning of substantive and relational words in the context of mathematics and the use of number facts: adding, subtracting, multiplying, and dividing. Questions related to size, shape, weight, volume, distance, and money are best answered through mathematical concepts. The foundation of mathematics — arithmetic — is the skill of computing with numbers and serves as the language for solving quantitative problems and communicating scientific facts. In general, arithmetic problems are presented in two forms, sentences and symbols. The verbal form is usually started in kindergarten: "If I have two cookies and you give me three more, how many will I have?" The answer is given in word form — five. Because it is easier to solve arithmetic problems with a set of symbols different from oral and written words, society has developed for computational purposes a language of numbers, symbols and signs, equations and geometric signs. Children in the primary and secondary grades learn that $2 \times 2 = 4$, and $a \times a = a^2$. It is apparent, then, that there is a one-to-one relationship between the words and the signs such as two/2, times/$\times$, and equals/=. This relationship is constant.

Methods of Teaching Arithmetic

The history of teaching arithmetic skills to young children has passed through three phases, drill theory, meaningful arithmetic, and active reform.

Drill Theory. Before the 1930s the emphasis was on drill with little attention paid to meaning or to functional use. This was an era of drill theory when children had to perform all of the operations without error. They memorized the multiplication tables and performed addition and subtraction by rote. They counted by fives and by tens, much as they had learned to count to ten before numbers had meaning. The teachers did not instruct children in the meaning of what it was they were memorizing. Brownell (1935, p. 2) a proponent of the drill theory wrote:

> Arithmetic consists of a vast host of unrelated facts and relatively independent skills. The pupil acquires the facts by repeating them over and over again until he is able to recall them immediately and correctly. He develops the skills by going through the processes in question until he can perform the required operations automatically and accurately. The teacher need give little time to instructing the pupil in the meaning of what he is learning.

Meaningful Arithmetic. The second phase, referred to as the era of meaningful arithmetic, started in the early 1930s and extended to the 1950s. It was believed that children should understand and see sense in what they learned, so using an activity method was introduced. Children brought their milk money to school and were responsible for correct change. Field trips were designed to provide real life situations for teaching number facts. It became an almost incidental type of learning. Reflecting this prevailing view was a statement by the National Council of Teachers of Mathematics made by Morton (1938, p. 269)

> Arithmetic is an important means of interpreting children's and adult's quantitative experience and of solving their quantitative problems. Consequently, the content should be determined largely on the basis of its social usefulness and should consist of those concepts and number relationships which may be effectively used.

Teachers were encouraged to be aware of individual differences and to provide individualized instruction when appropriate. Although the issues related to the *drill theory* vs. the *meaningful approach* were not resolved, much progress toward finding an approach was made. The roots to an active approach to teaching number concepts and quantitative language to preschool children started to take hold in the 1950s. In addition, a structure was established upon which future teachers could add new approaches to continuing issues.

Active Reform. The third or active-reform period took place between 1955 and the mid-1960s and carried a strong impact on the teaching of arithmetic. This reform probably reflected the nation's scientific and technological needs, so strong in the 1960s. Although the meaning era preceding the active-reform period did make arithmetic more meaningful, it was mostly through methodology; the subject was taught in a different setting, but the content was not changed. In the active-reform period the curriculum was woven around a mathematical theme often referred to as "modern mathematics." The theme demonstrated that we have a number system with a base of ten and a place value. For example, the numbers one through nine take one number and hold one place. The number ten requires two numbers with zero as a place holder. Teachers employed such devices as the abacus, chart slots, flannel boards, or coins to teach number concepts. Children learn, for example, that the number 432 is represented by four beads on the left of the abacus (four one hundreds), three beads in the middle (three tens), and two beads on the right (two ones). Although there has been controversy over the issues of "modern mathematics," much good has probably come from it.

Currently, elementary school teachers are making inroads into combining all approaches to teaching mathematics. They find that drill makes the use of facts automatic. Methods using activities enable the child to solve everyday problems. Teaching the meaning behind our number system gives promise of opening the door to algebra, geometry, and higher mathematics — areas that many students do not aspire to because of poor mathematical background or lack of motivation, or both. Most important is the recognition for teaching number concepts and quantitative vocabulary to children in their preacademic years in order that they may enter first grade with a foundation for learning to solve quantitative problems.

Mathematics Objectives

The very beginning of a mathematics program takes place in the preschool years and is based on three general principles that lead to the formation of objectives: (1) learning the quantifiable classification and attribution of objects and events, (2) learning quantitative vocabulary, and (3) developing number skills.

Quantifiable Attributes. Both objects and events have measurable quantifiable attributes that relate to the field of mathematics. Objects include such attributes as size, capacity and volume, temperature, weight, height, length, and shape. Events include such attributes as time. Through their sensory mechanisms children see, hear, feel, taste, and smell the different attributes of objects. Through their perceptual-motor systems they experiment with what is in their environment. They come to know that objects come in different sizes or that sounds can be loud and soft, yet they cannot measure the size of an object or quantify in decibels the loudness of a sound. In the preschool years they are learning to compare, classify, and order. They discover that objects have more than one attribute; one ball may be big and red and belong to Tom, yet another ball may be little and blue and belong to Katie. These attributes develop from experience, and as children mature they are able to order objects according to specific characteristics: littlest to biggest ball, shortest to longest sticks. Parents purchase such toys as stacking rings and nesting boxes that will give children experiences with ordering. Teachers use a variety of materials like Cuisenaire rods, color chips in varying shades, and objects of varying weights. Ordering objects precedes and builds ability for comparing.

Closely allied with the quantifiable attributes of objects and events is the basic concept of measurement. In essence, measurement is a process by which numbers are assigned to attributes of objects or events. If one object has more of one attribute than a second object, then the first object will be assigned a higher number. Of four strings the longest string will have the highest number and the shortest string the lowest number. Measurement is accomplished primarily by: (1) counting, (2) reading a scale on a calibrated instrument, such as a thermometer, audiometer, and ruler, (3) computation including addition, subtraction, multiplication, and division and (4) combinations of the above. The following are descriptions of measurable attributes of size, capacity and volume, temperature, weight, height, length, shape, and time.

The attribute of *size* is perceived at an early age. Before three years children reach for the big cookie in preference to the little one, and by age four the majority comprehend the meaning of the words big and little. They also can see that a nickel is bigger than a dime and sometimes are "tricked" by an older sibling who trades his nickel for his young brother's dime. Big brother knows more attributes and/or measurement of coins than does his younger brother. Children learn that some toys are too big for some boxes and that some shoes are too small for some feet.

The attribute of *capacity and volume* is a developmental concept of the perception of occupied space. Although capacity and volume are related properties, a young child can visibly discriminate between capacities but does not perceive volume, that is, the space occupied. At the beach children find that it takes many scoops of sand to fill a pail or several cups of water to fill a pail. As children mature they begin to speculate as to which of two containers will hold more water or less water. Teachers of preschool children provide opportunities to pour liquids and other pourables, such as sand and rice, into different sized containers so that the child may be introduced to the concept of capacity and volume.

The attributes of *temperature* are probably perceived first by touch. Children can feel hot water from one faucet and cold water from another and compare the differences. Later on they learn to look at a thermometer that has been in ice water and then placed in hot water. Before their very eyes they see the liquid in the thermometer change as a result of temperature change. It moves from the bottom to the top, or the teacher says it gets higher. It is not necessary at this time to learn about mercury or degrees of temperature, only that there is a comparison to be made and language to be learned.

The attribute of *weight* is perceived by young children. They learn very early that there are some things they can lift and some they cannot lift. By four years of age the majority of children can distinguish between a heavy and a light block when asked to "Give me the heavy block, the light block." Older children can experiment with a two pan balance scale which will verify their own "feel" of weight.

The attribute of *height* is observed early by little children when they say, "Daddy is bigger than me," meaning taller. They often are confused about height because they tend to look at the tops of things. A boy standing on a chair may, therefore, consider himself taller than his daddy. Teachers check a student's concept of height by asking, "Which is taller, the table or the clock on the wall?"

The attribute of *length* is closely allied to height. The difference between length and height is chiefly one of orientation. Height is on a vertical plane and length a horizontal plane. Children discover that an object is as tall as it is long and the relationship may be proved by drawing around a stack of blocks that are placed in front of a paper, then placing these same blocks in a horizontal position on the piece of paper placed on the floor. The comparison is easily made.

The attribute of *shape* is a concept of geometry and measurement. Young children learn to sort and to match circles, squares, and stars and to match pieces of puzzles to the appropriate recessed areas. These are preacademic activities beginning as early as eighteen to twenty-four months of age.

The attribute of *time* cannot be developed without appropriate instruments, such as calendars and clocks. Although children are not mature enough for time concepts until late kindergarten and the primary grades, preschool teachers employ basic techniques for teaching time concepts. The children are taught that when the timer rings the activity will stop.

Perceiving the attributes of objects and events becomes basic to developing a vocabulary that is related to mathematics.

Quantitative Vocabulary

Although children with limited oral language can be taught arithmetic computation with numerals only, the advantage of having knowledge and use of the semantic and morphosyntactic features of language cannot be denied. Vocabulary and sentence structure, then, are important facets for learning mathematical skills. Kraner (1976), using drawings, developed a Preschool Math Inventory which includes substantive and relational words that bear a direct relationship to arithmetic and mathematics. Using an age span of three to six years, he categorized the words under the headings of quantity, sequence, position, direction, and geometry/measurement. The words are examples of the labels that are comprehended only when the concepts have developed. Standardization of his criterion-referenced test with a mastery level of 80 percent revealed that the concepts and labels develop in a sequential age order. For example, he found that his subjects could point to the first object in a series of pictures by four years six months of age, but not until five years six months of age could they point to the last object. Knowing the approximate age levels when mathematical concepts and words emerge is helpful in planning programs for children whose conceptual or vocabulary development, or both, is deficient.

Specific vocabulary related to mathematics includes cardinal number words and words of quantity, sequence, position, direction, and geometry/measurement. Words for *cardinal numbers* begin with *one*, or *zero*, if you consider the latter a number, and continue in a sequence of *two*, *three*, *four*, and so on to infinity. Although learning to count by rote gives a number a name, children do not gain a number sense through this task. It is simply a task of memorization.

Words of quantity assist in answering questions like "Which number is larger? Smaller?" Children can also follow directions if they know the quantity words, "Arrange the numbers from smallest to largest. Show me all of your pennies. Point to each one."

Words of sequence are related to such directions as "Show me who is first in line. In the middle of the line. Ahead of the rabbit."

Words of position are related to such directions as "Show me the one on the left. On the right. Which ball is in the box? Out of the box?"

Words of direction are related to the following: "If you have three pennies and I take two *away* from you, how many will you have?" "Draw a circle *around* the flower." "Show me the arrow that tells you to go to the right. To the left."

Words of geometry/measurement are related to such directions as

"Show me the triangle, rectangle, square." "Show me the tall tree, short tree." "Which one has three sides? Four sides?"

The perceptive teacher will be certain that her preschool children are exposed to or taught the concepts and words that relate to one of the basic skills of academic achievement, namely, mathematics.

Number Skills. Number concepts, counting, and number facts have been and continue to be a major portion of the kindergarten and primary level curriculums. Children, however, become aware of numbers at a much earlier age. Most children have the concept of oneness before three years of age, know the meaning of the words more–less by four years of age when asked, "Which box has more buttons? Less buttons?" and call a circle by its name before age five. Perceptive teachers preparing preschool children for number skills are well aware of the need to follow the gradual developmental processes of concept building and language acquisition that have been presented in the preceding portions of this section on mathematics. These abilities to compare and order objects according to a specific attribute, together with the knowledge of words that label the specific attributes, form the building blocks for dealing with numbers and their counterpart— numerals. Number skills include number concepts, counting, and number facts.

Before children can assign a number word to a set of objects they must have number concepts — the concept of conservation and one-to-one correspondence. When children can sort objects from various classes into specific attributes, such as color, size, or shape, they are said to have the concept of conservation. Without this concept children are not ready to work with numbers. Teachers provide experiences with one-to-one correspondence by giving a boy nine pencils to distribute to himself and the other seven members of the class. When the boy discovers that there is not a child for the ninth pencil, the teacher uses the phrase "more than needed." She does not count the children and then count the pencils, for this is more closely allied with number facts, that is, "If there are eight children in a class, and we have nine pencils, how many will be left over?" The game of musical chairs is another form of a one-to-one correspondence experience. The first time children participate in this activity they find that there is one less chair than children. The teacher asks "Who was left over?"

Just as children learn to associate the word *chair* with the object chair, so must they learn to recognize the word *two* and associate it with sets of two. When children know that two chairs are not the same objects as two oranges but that these groupings or sets have a common factor of "twoness," they are said to have number concepts. When the children have the imagery and language for twoness, the numeral 2 can be introduced. Not until they have the concept of two should children be introduced to threeness and the numeral 3. Certainly they should not be expected to write the numerals until prewriting skills have developed. Some teachers prefer to teach concepts of two and three before introducing one. They believe that children will comprehend the meaning of sets of objects more readily if first introduced to more than one object in a set rather than a set of one.

The concept of one-to-one correspondence requires that other features of the objects be excluded. Children have difficulty with this concept because they are distracted by irrelevant information, attributes other than what are being looked at. For example, when items in each of two sets are arranged in the same position, the child can say that the sets are the *same*, but when the objects in one of the sets are spaced further apart, the child may become confused and say that the sets are *not the same*. Children have developed concepts of both conservation and one-to-one correspondence when two sets of equal numbers are said to have the *same amount* irrespective of the size, class, position, or any other attribute of the objects within the sets.

Fractions which are a part of something, as distinguished from a whole something, provide a higher level concept of one-to-one correspondence and conservation. Before children can develop the concept of fractions, that is, two halves of an apple correspond to a whole, they must know the meaning of a unit or of a whole apple. When the apple has been cut, there are three questions to be asked: (1) What was the unit? (2) How many pieces of apple are cut from the unit? and (3) Are the pieces the same size? These are basic questions underlying the concept of fractions. Very young children will see an apple cut into pieces and believe there is more apple after cutting it than before. They do not have conservation for fractions. Most children before entering first grade, point correctly when asked to "Show me the whole apple, half apple." However, they cannot select half an apple when the pictures include one-fourth an apple and three-fourths an apple. Half is anything less than whole. The concept of fractions is an academic level task and is taught only incidentally in a preacademic curriculum.

Counting by rote is the mere repetition of number words with no meaning attached. Although parents are proud of the youngster who can recite one, two, three . . . and teachers often emphasize counting by rote early in the preacademic curriculum, it is not the most basic element in number skill development. Learning to count by rote before discovering number concepts is probably an unnecessary exercise, yet it most likely will appear in conjunction with the acquisition of number skills. Counting through ten is accomplished early in kindergarten and the task of learning to count to one hundred is a late kindergarten or early first grade accomplishment; counting to thirty is basic to learning the sequence of numbers up to 100, which is a rule-based skill. It is not uncommon to hear a child break a rule when reaching twenty-nine and reciting the next number as twenty-ten. Counting by rote usually needs to be taught only through thirty, at which point a rule has been learned and the forties and fifties follow in a logical sequence.

Rational counting which follows counting by rote is based on the rule that the next item in the sequence is given the next higher number. If a set has twelve cars, the child may touch a car and give it the number one. The next car is two, the next three, and on to twelve. The last number counted is, of course, the number in the set. During kindergarten children learn to rational count to at least twenty.

Some teachers believe that preacademic mathematics should emphasize number concepts before rational counting. The basis for this judgment is exemplified in the following sequence.

> Karen was asked to "Put three blocks in the box." Because she had been taught to rational count, she pointed to the first block and said one, to the second block and said two, and the third block and said three. Then she dropped the block with the label three into the box. This indicated that number names were associated with only one object.

Perhaps the last step in the acquisition of preacademic number skills is the area of *number facts*, which is concerned with the ability to see the relationships among numbers and the similarities of the processes involved in adding and subtracting and in multiplying and dividing. Not until kindergarten are the majority of children ready to be introduced to addition and subtraction and only then with sets of no more than five. Children in specific activities are exposed to or taught the concepts of adding and subtracting and proving their answers.

> After the class has roasted peanuts, the teacher holds three peanuts in her hand then closes it so that the children cannot see. She asks Bill to give her two more and tell how many the teacher will have. He answers five, and she asks him to prove it by placing all the peanuts on the table. John has three peanuts in one hand the teacher asks him how many he will have left if she takes two. His answer is two, and he proves himself wrong when asked to "prove it."

Relating mathematics to the real world requires a knowledge of classes of objects and events, attributes of objects and events, a quantitative vocabulary, concepts of conservation and one-to-one correspondence, and relationships among numbers in the process of adding and subtracting and multiplying and dividing. Mathematics is a language-based science that is an important tool for academic achievement. The foundation for mathematics is developed during the preacademic years.

Dennis the Menace for punishment is sitting in his rocking chair facing the corner of the room. He is holding his cat in his arms, and his dog lies on the floor beside him. "Why are cats and dogs so EASY to unnerstand . . . and people so hard?"

Developing preacademic skills in the areas of oral language, reading, writing, spelling, and arithmetic is an important ingredient in a child's preparation for formal education. Equally important is a child's affective education, which is designed to answer such questions as: Who am I? How do I feel about myself? How do I feel about others? What is my value system? Although it does not appear to be a formidable task to create an interaction between preacademic education and affective or emotional education, few pragmatic attempts appear in the literature. The underlying reasons may be related directly to the belief of many educators and parents that a child's training in the affective and moral domain should be parent centered and not a concern of the classroom teacher. Furthermore, only when children exhibit emotional disorders or become incorrigible should the teacher take such action as to call in the parents for a conference or refer them to the school counselor. Surely there is a better way of helping children with emotional growth than to wait until after the fact. Although there are few published curriculums in affective education, teachers are finding means by which to integrate academic and affective education into the classroom or resource rooms. The emphasis is upon prevention of emotional disorders that result primarily from poor self-concepts and prevention of a value system not acceptable to society, both resulting in poor interpersonal relationships.

A child's self-concept and interpersonal relationships are important aspects of growing up and meeting the social and moral values of our society. The term self-concept refers to how people view themselves, their knowledge of their good and bad points, and how they deal with their feelings and belief in themselves. All of this must be nurtured in early years, and, if properly done, children have a better chance of developing ego strength that helps them deal effectively with their environment. A poor self-concept, reflected in such phrases as "I cannot learn to read" "I cannot finish my work on time" or "I am not liked by my friends," usually leads to anxiety and frustration and often to unacceptable behavior. A child's self-concept affects learning, and learning affects self-concept. As children develop good feelings about themselves, they become acceptable persons and know what to expect from themselves and their environment. Often what is learned academically does not help children as persons.

Getting along with people, being accepted as an "all right person," or establishing acceptable interpersonal relationships is closely allied with one's self-concept and feelings of self-worth, "I am a person who knows how to react favorably with other people." Establishing acceptable interpersonal relationships requires skill, and there are complicated rules children must discover in order to develop value systems and become socially acceptable. How well a child uses the rules from his repertoire of social acts determines his acceptance or rejection from peers as well as adults. There is not always a consensus regarding a right way or a wrong way with moral issues, for much of the decision making by parents is dependent upon cultural mores, religious beliefs, or what values they learned during their own nurturing and maturing years. Furthermore, character traits have different values at different levels; for example, children under three years of age are not expected to share, yet by four to five years of age children do and are expected to share at least part of the time. Yet, there certainly are basic rules that make sense in terms of everyday human relations. These rules relate to many affective categories including honesty, empathy, sharing, manners, respect for authority and tactful use of language, to name but a few. Early on parents with their own value systems attempt to teach their children what they consider to be right from wrong; some are successful others are not. Even teachers without an affective educational plan indirectly provide experiences for social growth: taking turns sharing, helping in the classroom, respecting property rights; some children discover the rules, some do not. Teachers apparently feel a need to include training in the development of acceptable social acts within the preacademic or academic programs. What probably has been lacking is the impetus to develop affective curriculums that will provide a closer tie with basic subjects.

Method

Bessell and Palomares (1967) have emphasized in parent counseling sessions the importance of applying preventive mental health techniques rather than trying to patch up the problems of the full blown emotionally disturbed child. They have identified three specific problems that they believe contribute to a child's poor self-concept and unacceptable interpersonal relationships: inadequate understanding of the cause-effect relationships in social interaction, insufficient understanding of the motives underlying human behavior, and low self-esteem.

In order to prevent emotional problems or help to alleviate already existing problems, teachers are beginning to give systematic attention to affective education. Although most of the methods employed are designed for primary and elementary school levels, some of the basic principles have been translated to the preschool or preacademic level in the form of communication skill training. Language, including content, form, and use, is an important tool to implement, control, and modify social interaction. Children must have knowledge of their own feelings and feelings of others, must develop a vocabulary to express feelings, and must gain insight into pragmatic rules that teach them how to use language effectively.

Acquiring a Vocabulary of Affective Words. The concepts and their word symbols related to children's feelings about self and others form the foundation for communicating on the affective level. Teachers listen to the emotionally loaded words children use, such as love, hate, mean, nice, naughty. The children are asked to define these words operationally and to give examples. The teachers develop classroom activities that introduce new words to increase the child's vocabulary of affective words. These words help children express and deal with their feelings as well as the feelings of others.

Effective Use of Affective Linguistic Skills. In the preschool years children discover that people talk to gain information, to influence decisions, to make statements, to express feelings, and for other reasons. They learn that they can choose alternative linguistic forms to influence the listener, and at a surprisingly early age they learn to discriminate between indirect and direct statements. In addition they learn how to add new information to old to broaden concepts, and probably unconsciously they know that they should talk differently to different people depending upon the person, time, and place. All of these skills related to the use of language have been discussed in Chapter 2.

One of the few published curricular materials and guidelines for introducing affective education into the schools is the Magic Circle (Bessell and Palomares 1967, Bessell and Ball 1972), which has also been translated into both Spanish and French for use abroad. This program takes place outside the classroom for a daily twenty-minute period. Eight to ten children and the teacher sit in an inner circle with the remaining children seated in an outer circle. The inner circle of children is the active group, while the outer circle members observe. The objectives are to help children develop a vocabulary for expressing their feelings, to build good self-concepts, and to understand cause and effect in interpersonal relationships and the motives underlying human behavior. Certain ground rules are established in the beginning, such as no child shall say anything unkind about a peer or laugh at a peer's mistakes. Up to six weeks are devoted to discussions of one theme. For the older children leadership responsibilities are shifted from the teacher to the children. There has been great enthusiasm for this program and many testimonials commending its worth. Unfortunately no longitudinal research has been documented to demonstrate its validity.

In a program similar to the Magic Circle to help children develop good feelings about themselves, one teacher spent time each week in a circle with the children. The teacher would say something nice to the boy on her right, "I like the clean, shiny shoes you have on today." That child would make a positive statement to the girl on his right, "I like your long, black hair." On some days to the tune of "The Wheels on the Bus Go Round and Round," they all sang, "We like Mary's long black hair, long black hair . . . all day long."

Other approaches are used to help children communicate their feelings. Once a week a teacher may utilize a twenty-minute period for asking children to complete open-ended questions such as:

I like children who _____.
I am afraid when _____.
I like myself when I _____.
I like grown ups to _____.

Then they might ask the children, "What might you do if a child shoves you?" Comparing answers of children from different developmental age levels may be a revealing way of studying emotional needs of children at various age levels. Furthermore, the astute teacher will listen carefully to each child's answers and gain insights into his or her fears and misunderstandings. To supplement this information, teachers will plan ways during the school day to reinforce the acceptable and extinguish the unacceptable behaviors.

Specific behavior modification programs in a classroom activity may prove to be a successful technique in teaching rules about interpersonal relationships as well as modifying the unwanted behaviors of some of the children who are disruptive to the point of interfering with the progress of their peers. One teacher laid out a six-week behavior modification program that was a part of the daily preacademic instruction. A follow-through study demonstrated the success of the program (see Appendix 6, Behavior Modification Program for Kindergarten Class).

Objectives. The concept of helping children develop good feelings about themselves and becoming future well-adjusted citizens is not new. Affective education is being introduced gradually into the preacademic and academic curriculums. More attention to these concepts should be included in teacher training programs and should be field tested in research studies to determine the validity of affective education as a preventive and remedial process for dealing with socio-emotional development. Teachers must begin to write such measurable objectives related to self-concept and interpersonal relationships as: before entry into first grade the children will be able to (1) define 80 percent of the affective words that have been presented during the year as measured by a teacher-made test and (2) before entry into first grade children will be able to tell five positive things about themselves as measured by a teacher-made test.

Most preacademic and academic curriculums have centered on the nonsocial world. There has been a movement, however, in the past decade to add affective education to the public school curriculums. Shantz (1975) believes

> The study of social development is important on two counts. First, it provides a more complete picture of the child's cognitive development indicating what types of concepts and processes are evident in both the nonsocial and social domains at particular age periods. Second, the way in which children conceptualize others presumably has an important effect on their social behavior with others. (p. 258)

SUMMARY

Oral language, reading, writing, spelling, and mathematics are considered the basics of education in academic settings. This chapter has delineated some of the skills that precede these basics and recommended that preacademic readiness programs begin as soon as feasible with children who have language or learning disorders, or both. Furthermore, the field of affective education has been discussed with the trend for including in the curriculum semistructured programs that relate to the development of acceptable interpersonal relationships. The combination and interrelation of preacademic and affective educational programs may prevent future emotional problems.

REFERENCES

Bangs, Tina E. *Birth to Three: Developmental Learning and the Handicapped Child*, Chapter 5. Boston, Mass.: Teaching Resources, 1979.

Bessell, H., and G. Ball. *Human Development Program: Preschool and Kindergarten Activity Guide*. Human Development Training Institute, Inc., 1727 Fifth Avenue, San Diego, Calif., 1972.

Bessell, H., and U. Palomares. *Methods in Human Development*. Human Development Training Institute, Inc., 7574 University Avenue, La Mesa, Calif. 92041, 1967.

Bryan, J. H. "Children's Cooperation and Helping Behaviors," in *Review of Child Development Research*, ed. E. M. Hetherington, pp. 127-181. Chicago: University of Chicago Press, 1975.

Copeland, R. W. *How Children Learn Mathematics*. New York: Macmillan, 1979.

Evans, E. D. *Contemporary Influences in Early Childhood Education*. New York: Holt, Rinehart and Winston, 1975.

Gordon, T. *P.E.T. Parent Effectiveness Training*. New York: Bantam Books Inc., 1978.

Schaefer, E. S. "Family Relationships," in *The Application of Child Development Research to Exceptional Children*, ed. J. J. Gallagher. Reston, Va.: The Council for Exceptional Children, 1975.

Shantz, D. U. "The Development of Social Cognition," in *Review of Child Development Research*, ed. E. M. Hetherington, pp. 257-323. Chicago: University of Chicago Press, 1975.

4

learning
requirements

INTRODUCTION

Learning is the process of developing a skill or acquiring information and is measured by the change between pre- and posttesting. What cognitive skills must children have to learn to talk, read, write, spell, develop competence in mathematics, and perform acceptably in their interpersonal relationships? How does learning take place? Is the infant born with an organized neurologic structure which develops independently of experience, or is this logical structure not present at birth but emerges as a result of a balance between the organism and its environment? Are some skills acquired and others learned? Theories in response to these questions have been developed and researched over the centuries, and numerous texts have been written on the theories of learning. Perhaps the most significant thing about the theories is the wide disagreement which prevails among the theorists. It is not the purpose of this section to discuss theories of learning or to relate these theories to the neural correlates of sensation, attention, perception, motivation, and memory-retrieval (Berry 1980). The purpose is to review the behavioral research in cognition that relates to the acquisition of preacademic skills: oral language, reading, writing, spelling, arithmetic, and work habits.

Children develop a sensory awareness of what is in their environment. They hear, see, feel, and use all of their sensory modalities to become aware of what is around them (sensation). They attend to the stimulus (attention) and perceive its attributes (perception), and, if appropriately motivated (motivation), they will remember what they experienced (memory) and retrieve information when needed (retrieval). These sensory-neural correlates do not function as independent factors but rather as a group of interactive mechanisms that contribute to the learning process (integration). The inefficient intra- or interperformance of these cognitive mechanisms may be the underlying cause of failure to learn what it is that parents and teachers want children to learn or that children themselves want to learn. The following discussion concerns primarily the sensory modalities of audition and vision. The writer recognizes the importance of tactile, olfactory, and gustatory senses in cognitive and language development, but, due to the constraints of book length, these sensory influences are not discussed.

Sensation

Sensation is dependent upon a stimulus that acts upon appropriate receptors. If the receptors are intact, sensation, which may be thought of as the immediate physiological correlate of the stimulus, is created. The child becomes aware of the stimulus. The two avenues most closely allied with the acquisition of oral and written language are, of course, audition and vision.

The question is asked, "Did you hear it?" If the answer is "No," then a reason for the negative answer must be sought. With regard to vision the question is asked, "Did you see it?" Again, if the answer is "No," then a reason for the negative answer must be sought.

Attention

Attention may be defined as the length of time a subject maintains an orientation to the stimulus. We may describe children as having short attention spans when they skip rapidly from one set of stimuli to another with little if any information gleaned from the experience. We refer to children as being inattentive when they are not attending as we would like, but, in reality, they may be attending very well to stimuli of more importance. Finally, we have those children whom we label as good attenders.

Attention may be voluntary or involuntary. It is voluntary when a person attends to a task such as reading a book and becomes involuntary when there is an outside intrusion such as the telephone ringing. Some children have difficulty in shifting away from the outside intrusion back to the task at hand, as exemplified in the following situation.

> The diagnostician was administering a battery of tests to John. The telephone in the adjoining room rang three times and ceased. This was a rule instigated to avoid numerous rings while testing was in progress. John fixated on the fact that no one answered the phone. He could not shift to another test item until the examiner went to the phone and pretended to talk with someone.

What factors influence the child's attention to specific stimuli? Most studies of selectivity in attending are environmentally related with little research reported on how one's own behavior affects attention. We observe and report attending behaviors of infants and young children and attempt to find ways of helping children as they mature to attend to relevant material. We observe that infants attend to visual and auditory stimuli shortly after birth. Within the first months they visually track an object in a horizontal, vertical, and circular motion. They engage in hand watching very early and by six months of age have discovered and attend to their feet. Shortly after birth the infant gives reflexive responses to loud sounds and within a few months attends to the human voice and is quieted by it. The more experience infants and children have and the more frequently adults accentuate relevant features by pointing to them or discussing them, the more likely will the children's attention be drawn to the likenesses and differences of stimuli, concepts basic to learning.

Children may have poor attending habits for one or more of the following reasons:

> They do not attend to the significant features of the task at hand, and therefore do not comprehend the objective of the task.
>
> They do not attend long enough to the significant features of the task for comprehension to occur.
>
> They cannot shift their attention from one set of stimuli to another.
>
> Their inability to attend appropriately may be a result of fatigue, stress, anxiety, or other similar factors.
>
> There may be sensory deficits that interfere with attention. It is difficult to attend to a visual or auditory task if vision or hearing, or both, are impaired and only partial information is viewed or heard.

Parents and teachers develop strategies that are designed to attract and maintain children's attention to tasks that are to be learned. These strategies may be started shortly after birth and continue through the preacademic and academic years.

> What have been called "cradle gyms" are stretched across the baby's crib to attract attention. Patterned bumpers on the inside of the crib are

thought by some to hold the interest of the infant. Rattles and musical toys are also attention getters.

When introducing picture books to children, parents point to the objects and name them. In fact, picture books for the beginner usually contain one simple picture per page.

When telling stories from picture books, parents point to each object, person, or activity as the story unfolds.

Parents and teachers call the name of a child to secure his or her attention.

Teachers may place a square of colored paper on a child's desk with the activity centered on the square. This technique rivets the child's attention to the specific task at hand.

In a classroom a teacher may use the words "boys and girls" to gain group attention.

It is evident that attention facilitates perception and is conjoined with motivation and memory in a learning situation.

Perception

Perception is the process of attaching structure to sensation. In order for a stimulus to be perceived as it was received, there must be intact sensory-neural mechanisms, awareness of the sensory excitation, and attention to the stimulus. When the activity of listening becomes integrated with the sensation of hearing, auditory perception takes place. What do we hear when we listen? If the auditory image or perception in the child's brain does not match the auditory stimulus, he or she is said to have an auditory perceptual disorder; the stimulus was not structured appropriately. By the same token, when the activity of looking becomes integrated with the sensation of seeing, visual perception takes place. What do we see when we look? If the visual image or perception in the child's brain does not match the visual stimulus, the child is said to have a visual perceptual disorder.

Perception is studied in terms of the many aspects of seeing and hearing, namely, distance, direction, form, size, color, motion, and figure ground as well as perception of self. All of this patterned information is basic to concept formation and language development. Babies are not born with knowledge of distance and direction; they see the moon and reach for it. Only through maturation and hundreds of trials and errors does distance become meaningful to them. Closely associated with distance is space, and apparently there is a general type of developmental sequence related to the acquisition of spatial concepts and their word symbols. We know that children, for example, learn the meaning of the words *in*, *on*, and *under* before they differentiate between the words *right* and *left*. Spatial perception in the auditory modality is evidenced between four and six months of age when children begin to localize a sound source. With regard to form perception Fantz (1961) found evidence of form discrimination in young infants by observing their fixed preferences for different patterns. As more infants are studied, the more their visual abilities appear to resemble those of adults, although they may be primitive in the newborn (Bond 1972).

Just as infants can perceive differences in form through the visual modality, so can they discriminate between sets of sounds that impinge on the eardrum. Children as young as one month perceive differences between syllables *pa* and *ba* (Eimas and others 1971 and Moffitt 1971), and by six months of age they can discriminate changes in frequency and pitch (Berg 1971 and Moffit 1971). With regard to perception of color, Peeples and Teller (1975) reported that by two months of age infants discriminate a colored light from a white light. The speed at which objects move is perceived by young children, but not until they develop sophisticated concepts of time are they able to predict the rate at which an object is moving. The identification of words in the presence of noise or the identification of an embedded figure in a cluttered or ambiguous picture is usually referred to as figure ground perception. The ability to select the figure from the ground is dependent, of course, on the amount of clutter or the completeness of the figure in the visual task and by the ratio of the signal to the noise in the auditory task.

Although auditory and visual perception play major roles in learning about our environment, we cannot overlook the development of self-perception or body image in infants and young children. The prick of a diaper pin, the warmth of the bath water, the feel of their bodies in an upright position, the grasp of an object, their learning to walk upstairs, the localizing of a human voice, and the hundreds of other sensations received by babies as they mature all help to develop an awareness of the physical self, commonly referred to as body image. The study of body image often is tied in with self-concept or how I perceive myself as a person in the environments in which I must function. Good feelings about self are basic to the development of appropriate interpersonal relationships.

Failure to perceive the intended pattern organization may be the result of conditions surrounding the event, for example, (1) past experience, (2) previous set, (3) nature of the sensory-motor pathways, and (4) developmental levels. Textbooks in psychology present demonstrations with adults illustrating that perception changes because of past experiences and previous sets. One has only to visit a nursery or kindergarten program to find evidence of the same behavior in children.

As Louise left the classroom to run an errand, Johnny noticed that she had something in her pocket which made it bulge. He immediately identified it as a box of matches and called the teacher's attention to it. "Ms. Mauzy," he said, "Louise has a box of matches in her pocket, and she is going to burn something!" "Do you think so? Let's not worry about it. Let's wait and see." Louise returned and was asked, "Do you have a box of matches in your pocket?" to which she replied, "No." She reached into her pocket and retrieved a piece of heavy folded paper. "You have learned a lesson, children," said Mrs. Mauzy. "Sometimes your eyes play tricks on you." Had Johnny previously been scolded by his parents for carrying matches in his pocket?

Not only are past experiences and previous sets related to what is perceived, but the condition of the sensory mechanisms is also. Varying degrees of impairment of the visual system may affect discriminatory processes. The child with limited or no peripheral vision may fail to match large pictures because she does not see the outer portions of the picture where the differences may appear. By the same token we know that children with certain types of sensory hearing impairment experience a reduction or a distortion of the speech signal; they do not perceive sound as it is presented. It is not unusual, then, for a child with sensory hearing impairment to give an inappropriate response to a statement which was slightly unintelligible. The classic example is the hearing-impaired boy who excels in all subjects except spelling. If he does not have time to watch the teacher as she dictates the spelling words, he must rely on his faulty listening mechanism. Therefore he misspells because he mishears. The sensory mechanisms may be intact, but children may exhibit perceptual errors due to their level of developmental patterning. Some research has demonstrated that gross segregation of figure from background is present at birth, but perception of form requires a fairly extensive period of learning. Children may be expected, therefore, to discriminate between an oval and an angular object before they can make a finer discrimination between circles and ovals. Some children in kindergarten as well as first grade have greater difficulty with discrimination of mirror images than with upside-down figures. In reading-readiness tests they will recognize the one which is different if it is upside down but may fail the task if the figure is facing to the left when all others face to the right.

How we perceive objects and events is dependent upon a variety of outside influences as well as on the internal coding processes. Deciding which interferences cause inappropriate responses is not always possible.

Karen, age nine, can look at a drawing of a diamond and call it by name. She is unable to copy it accurately. Does she draw it as she perceives it? Or, does she have an accurate visual image yet lack the ability to convert the image into a motor skill?

What might affect the accuracy with which children use perceptual features for classifying or matching things? Heider (1971) found that brightness and saturation affect the accuracy with which three-year-olds can match colors. Nursery school children can match three-dimensional objects more accurately than two-dimensional items, possibly because there are more features available in three-dimensional objects (Kraynak and Raskin 1971). Familiarity with features was found by Frith (1971) to improve the accuracy of young children's matching. Familiarity of materials, method of presentation, and use of instructions are strategies teachers use to facilitate a child's recognition of an object's attributes; for example, a specific ball is round and blue, made of rubber, can bounce, can roll, and is not edible. As children get older, they develop their own efficient strategies of search and exploration to improve their ability to identify specific features of objects, persons, and events.

There is an abundance of literature related to visual perception, and within the last decade there has been research related to auditory perception. Because there are no definitive theories broad enough to explain the visual and auditory perceptual problems that teachers claim to observe in the classroom, teaching strategies have become educated guesses. Diagnosticians and teachers have little available to them that will assist in discovering the cause of visual and auditory perceptual problems in children and little if any evidence to prove that perceptual deficits can be treated with remedial help. The primary reason for this dilemma is the difficulty in trying to separate perception from such other neurological substrata of learning as sensation, attention, motivation, memory, and retrieval. It becomes apparent that if one defines perception as the process of attaching structure to sensation, one would need either a cerebroscope to view the structures of the brain related to visual perception or an internal auditory recording device to discern the accuracy of the auditory image the child received. Psychologists, audiologists, and neurophysiologists continue to research theoretical concepts and develop tests that attempt to define perceptual properties of vision and audition. They are continually hampered by the relation of the specifics of learning, including structure, function, and behavior.

Motivation

Performance occurs because of a drive, a need, or an inducement, and this prompting to action is termed motivation. The purpose of motivation in a learning situation is to arouse or to cause the child to attend more closely to his or her environment or to the specific task at hand. There probably are primary drives for motivation that are genetic, that is, built-in forces that vary with the neurophysiological makeup of each individual. Secondary drives are more related to the reward or punishment one receives for a job well done or a job poorly done. The environment and people within the environment provide powerful secondary drives in children's learning. In general, we attempt to reinforce good behavior and to inhibit unwanted behavior through punishment or by ignoring the situation. These reinforcement and extinguishing techniques have been discussed frequently in the literature of the 1970s under the rubric of Behavior Modification, which uses rewards or positive reinforcement to teach new behaviors. We usually attempt to reinforce good behavior with extrinsic or tangible rewards, such as a smile, a gold star, or a piece of candy. The ultimate goal is to assist children in developing a system of intrinsic rewards of self-satisfaction from a job well done.

Extrinsic Rewards

Adults are motivated to work for direct rewards in life: a pay check, vacation, new car, or praise. We assume that children also want something tangible for their efforts: their names on the chalkboard, a flower seal on their written work, or oral praise.

Ms. Mauzy found that motivation was heightened when quick rewards were given. During activities which required oral responses, she would have the children sit on the floor when they answered correctly, and stay in their seats if they failed to answer correctly.

It is not unusual to find children who are apparently motivated just by the presence of the teacher. What are the penalties if the teacher is the primary source of extrinsic reinforcement? The children may become so dependent upon him or her that future independent study skills will be acquired with difficulty. Furthermore, with some children, responses to such specific motivational techniques as praise or a gold star quickly become extinct. Because of the dilemma, teachers often spend too many hours searching for new rewards instead of trying to help children have good feelings about themselves through intrinsic rewards.

Intrinsic Rewards

To succeed in independent study, children must become intrinsically motivated. This is accomplished through a method of self-discovery which leads to satisfaction and an inducement to try the next step.

James places the horse in the appropriate place in the form board and looks to the teacher for some extrinsic reward. With each successive trial he asks for approbation. Jill, with the same form board, selects an animal and after the third error succeeds in correct placement. She smiles, picks it up, looks it over, and replaces it. Another animal is selected. This time Jill looks for a cue to help her make the correct response. When the board is complete, she asks the teacher for another one.

Jill is gaining intrinsic recompense from learning the basic principles underlying the problem to be solved. She is preparing herself for independent study. James is still immature in his motivational needs, but, with the help of the teacher and parents, his inner satisfactions will develop. One teacher approaches the task by minimizing external rewards.

Ms. Sunkle assigns seat work to her class of seven and announces that no discussion will take place until each child has finished the assignment. She walks by every desk and stops by Karen who is making an error. She points out the clue to the correct response, but no more is said. Karen sees the relationship, smiles, and moves on to the next problem.

What techniques can be employed to help children obtain satisfaction from their own discovery?

Motivation will spring from the satisfaction of learning. Children often provide their own continuing motivation and reinforcement.

Motivation is improved if an unknown task is linked with a known task.

Motivation is heightened if some kind of reinforcement is provided by an outside agent.

Motivation is more apt to occur if frustrations and fear are eliminated.

Motivation is higher when a child is doing something that is liked rather than disliked.

Motivation from within is built upon sequential success. If children are motivated, they will attend, and, if they attend with positive intentions, they will have a better chance of storing information in their memory banks.

MEMORY RETRIEVAL

Memory, another facet of learning, is the ability of sensory-storage systems to hold perceived events. These memories, whether in planarian, rats, or humans, are stored and retrieved through a neurophysiological-chemical process that is not too readily understood. Whatever the process, memory is not thought of as an independent faculty. Rather, it is an integral part of sensation, attention, perception, and motivation and cannot function independently. Within the category of memory itself there are numerous component processes and possibly a variety of structures that interact in complicated ways for short-term and long-term storage of information as well as for recall or retrieval of information. How all of this transpires is not clearly understood, but useful information can be obtained by studying the behavior of children and adults through tasks that purport to measure some of the facets of memory. Ornstein (1978) and Kail and Hagen (1977) have given an excellent review of research related to memory development in adults and children and should be of interest to early childhood specialists.

Short-Term Memory

Short-term and long-term memory as well as memory recall are hypothetical constructs that are responsible for the storage and retrieval of information. Short-term memory may be operationally defined as a temporary holding reservoir for incoming information. It has a limited capacity for the number of discrete units that it can hold at any one time and represents information on a temporary basis. Classical tests for measuring short-term memory such as Digit Span (Wechsler 1974 and Terman and Merrill 1973) assess the number of digits that can be remembered when produced at one-second intervals. Other short-term memory tests may require the subject to hold information for thirty seconds or five or ten minutes, and these are still classified as short-term memory. Because short-term memory represents information on a temporary basis, the information may be dropped or it may be added to long-term storage. Children exercise short-term memory as a transitory skill when they add a column of figures: 2 plus 5 is 7 plus 4 is *11* plus 9 is *20.* They hold for a brief period of time the numbers 7, 11, and 20 in order to report the answer. Information is stored and retrieved in a short-time interval, and it is discarded or forgotten under certain circumstances. For example, forgetting may occur when there is interference. If you ask a person to remember a series of digits such as 2, 4, 9, 4, 8, and, before the numbers are repeated back, the subject is to count backwards from ten, the original series will have a good chance of being forgotten. A cough, a telephone bell, a person entering the room may also cause forgetting to take place during a short-term memory task.

Long-Term Memory

Long-term memory represents information on a permanent basis. Through an unknown process, information from short-term memory may be transferred into long-term memory, allowing the short-term memory system to begin to process the next set of data. What is stored is not a replica of the experience of stimuli received, but rather it is believed to be what is perceived after the processing has taken place. If there are deficiencies in the perceptual storing processes, we can assume that what is stored is not a good representation of what was intended to be stored. Therefore, children in classrooms may give incorrect answers because they stored inappropriate information. This leads to the question of how people recall or retrieve memorable events. One school of thought says we do a memory search and when the information is retrieved, we ask ourselves if it is acceptable. Sometimes we know, and sometimes we do not know. Recall, then, is the active process of searching through memory stores and is facilitated by mnemonic devices, such as rehearsing, categorizing, and cuing.

Strategies in Memory-Mnemonic Devices

As children mature they acquire creative and often complex ways or strategies to remember and to retrieve information. Researchers are generally in agreement that we do not improve memory per se, but we improve our strategies for remembering and recall. Also there is the viewpoint that use of strategies to facilitate memory is a developmental aspect of learning (Hagen and others 1975). Studies with very young children demonstrate that they are nonstrategic in storing and retrieving information. They show little evidence of planning how they will remember, and they do not give any indication that they use specific strategies for recall. Yet, they do remember. There is much anecdotal data as well as a few studies to demonstrate that very young children retain memory for a spatial location (Acredelo and others 1975). Two-year-olds remember after one visit where the toy drawer is located at the grandparents' home, and they need few experiences to remember the spot in the cupboard where the cookies are stored. Their memories are even better if parents remind them that they are to *remember* where they put their coats or their toys. How this is accomplished is not clear. Not until school age do children begin to discover mnemonic devices to store or retrieve information. What are the strategies that are available to assist in storing and retrieving information when needed? Among the strategies employed are cuing, rehearsal, categorizing, making associations, note taking, and outlining.

Cuing may be defined as the association by which one thing recalls another. Very young children remember better when shown an object and told to find one like it. For example, when Joe loses a shoe, Mother holds up its mate and asks Joe to find the other one. Although he may not understand the language "Find the other one" the shoe as a cue will assist his recall. Kindergarten teachers use cue cards in the phonics lesson. The cue card may have a picture of a ring, and the children are asked to name something that starts like *ring*.

Rehearsal techniques are used to teach preschool children to count by rote, to learn their A B C's and to memorize nursery rhymes. The children rehearse what they hear after each presentation by parent or teacher. The task is made easier by grouping, such as the musical recording of the alphabet song. Young children rehearse by picking up the appropriate object and saying, "This is the big one. This is the little one." It is believed that young children do not have strategies for memory, just the mechanical procedures described. As they mature, however, they rehearse on their own and develop sophisticated mnemonic devices for remembering and recalling. They find it easier to remember 357-214-987 than an unbroken string of 357214987.

Categorizing. Perhaps the clearest form of the hierarchical strategies of memory and retrieval are those of categorizing and making associations. When asked to recall words from a long list of words, only some of which fall into category groups, older children may sort out the categories, hence retrieving more information than had they not categorized. Kobasigawa and Orr (1973) asked kindergarten children to recall drawings of various animals, vegetables, furniture, and vehicles. When the members of a category were presented together, more drawings were recalled than when the drawings were presented in an unsystematic arrangement. In like manner, when given a long list of words, such as *fish, chimney, hat, lake, boy, house,* the mnemonic device of remembering associated items may be used: *fish-lake, chimney-house, hat-boy.* There seems to be little disagreement that organization facilitates the amount of material that can be stored and the amount that can be retrieved.

Soviet researchers suggest that developmental changes in comprehension, social activities, and motivation are basic to the acquisition or discovery of mnemonic devices for remembering (Smirnov and Zinchenko 1969) and that the awareness of the memory system is probably not well developed in young children. They do not have metamemorial knowledge and therefore cannot plan strategies for remembering or retrieving as can an older child or adult who knows about such mnemonic memory devices as categorizing, making associations, writing notes to remember, rereading a chapter for detailed information, or retracing one's activities if a book is lost. Both metamemorial knowledge and skill in using the knowledge are an outcome of cognitive growth and learning experiences. Older children plan and use their strategies in an intelligent and informed manner. Much of the interest in metamemory has stemmed from the work of Flavell (1971, 1977) and Maynahan (1973) who believe that knowledge of memory and recall are important aspects of memory storage and retrieval.

Structural vs. Functional Development of Memory

Do everyday experiences involved in learning influence the early stages of memory development, or is this stage primarily dependent on structural features that change with age? Morrison and others (1974) suggest that there are minimal, if any, developmental changes in terms of the structural features of the memory system. Their findings, supported by others, delineate between hard-wired aspects of the memory system, which they believe may not change substantially with age, and the strategies and processes used to store and retrieve information. They suggest that the hardware is there and the person or someone on the outside must program the hardware. Furthermore, they believe that increasingly efficient cognitive development can be observed and described with little changes occurring in the computer hardware itself. What is certain is that reciprocal effects of structure and function are related to memory, and children remember because of meaningful interaction with their environment.

Educational Implications

Translating cognitive research into classroom instruction is not always an easy task. With reference to a child's remembering and retrieving, teachers need to evaluate and analyze the instructional tasks in terms of the demands they place on short-term memory, long-term memory, and recall. Teachers should be aware also of the variety of methods used to help children store certain kinds of information to be used in the acquisition of language, preacademic subjects, affective education as well as in general activities of daily living. The following questions reflect the variety of ways that a task may be presented.

Through which sensory avenue were the stimuli received, auditory or visual? That is, was the subject asked to remember a series of digits that were read to him or her, or were those digits flashed on the screen? How did the subject respond to what was remembered? Did the subject recall the numbers orally, write them on paper, or select the correct ones from another series of numbers?

Was the subject asked to remember meaningful or nonmeaningful material? For example, were the auditory stimuli nonsense syllables or meaningful sentences? Were the visual tasks related to unidentifiable shapes, shapes with names, or to printed words? Or, was the task a visual-motor memory skill, such as paper folding or block tapping?

How many practice periods were allowed? Does the subject do better with each successive trial, and at what point does the subject level off?

With regard to temporal factors, at what rate were the stimuli presented?

For how many minutes, hours, or days after presentation is the subject asked to recall the material? In other words, how does the investigator differentiate between short-term and long-term memory?

Is the subject given credit for the number of correct responses, or is the factor of sequence important? In a test of memory for numbers, can a child repeat all the digits but not in sequential order?

Was the material presented to the individual child or to children in a group? Do children remember better with individual instructions or with group instruction, or does it not matter with some children?

How much noise interference was present? Does a child remember better in quiet surroundings?

How loud was the investigator's voice when presenting the material? Are messages that are hard to hear hard to remember?

Were the visual stimuli in manuscript or cursive form, in color or black and white, on an uncluttered or cluttered page?

In a test of short-term auditory memory for sentences, do children fail to remember the sentence because they have not mastered certain sentence types or because of the length of the sentence? For example, a child may be able to repeat, "The boy climbed the tree," but not the more complex sentence, "It was Daddy who ate the cookie that was on the plate."

Do children from three years to first grade develop strategies for remembering and retrieving, or is this a skill of school-age children and adults? Research points to the latter.

Parents and teachers must continue to devise teaching strategies that will help children remember in order to develop the skills and concepts that are needed for the acquisition of oral language, reading, writing, arithmetic, and affective education. What are some of these teaching techniques?

Young children like goal-directed activities and, in general, do not like to engage in activities that serve no purpose. Give children a need to remember.

Telling children to look at something is not the same as asking them to remember what they are looking at. Teachers use the word *remember* frequently.

Giving children cues may help elicit responses. Photos are taken while visiting the pet store and used later as cues for recalling the events of the visit.

Children are asked to rehearse to-be-remembered things. They may repeat individually, or the teacher may choose to have the children rehearse as a group.

Early and repeated instruction in categorizing objects, such as toys and food, as well as teaching associations, such as shoe–foot and hat–head, may be the beginning stage of developing sophisticated mnemonic devices for remembering.

In contrast to the technique of repetitive drilling of, for example, digits or sentences of varying lengths to improve memory, it seems more logical for the teacher to develop teaching strategies and to arrange the environment in such a manner that children will discover ways in which they can improve their own memory skills. This early training may be basic to the development and the use of mnemonic devices common to children in upper elementary and secondary school levels. The present conceptualization of pedagogical techniques probably raises more questions than have been or can be answered.

Integration: Central Processing

The task of sorting memory from other cognitive functions in research designs or in the classroom appears to be impossible. Recent studies continue to point in the direction of the interrelation of mental processes. The crux of the problem may lie in an integrative mechanism of the brain, which, theoretically, sorts and puts together incoming or stored information. The following vignette of Alice is an example of possibly poor integrative skills.

> When teaching the concepts of on top and underneath, Mr. Foster gave the children a piece of paper with a picture on the top of the paper and one underneath. After coloring the pictures, they were asked to hold the papers parallel to the desk (demonstrated by the teacher) and to point to the one on *top* and the one *underneath*. He further added that the pictures were not to be taken home. Alice raised her hand and said, "But Mr. Foster, can't I take this one home [pointing to the top picture] and leave this one at school [pointing to the underneath picture]?"

Central processing is no doubt responsible for another learning requirement — work habits. Preschool children are not known for their excellent work habits. Perhaps their inability to structure their environment to meet adult standards is due to lack of experience rather than to perversity. The payoffs for keeping toys in a toy box, crayons in their containers, paste off the desk area, and books on the shelf are only some of the classroom rules learned through experience. Teachers in preacademic programs begin early to teach organization, planning, cooperation, completion of work, and other aspects of school routine that come under the heading of work habits. Work habits, which include the ways in which children perform seat work and other classroom activities, are dependent upon the integration of sensation, attention, perception, motivation, and memory skills. Children must be aware of, perceive, and attend to the acceptable ways to structure their environments; be motivated to conform to what is acceptable; and remember how it is that they conform. Teachers in their daily lesson planning provide experiences that help children integrate their cognitive skills with a goal of developing constructive work habits which are basic to academic achievement. Teachers can help to instill good work habits in children in the following ways:

> Practice in following group instructions is an everyday activity. Children must attend to what the teacher wants them to do and the sequence in which it is to be performed. "Children, take your chairs to the table, put your library books on the shelf, and come to the door when I call your name."

Participating and cooperating in group activities is stressed in ways that will develop good interpersonal relationships.

Learning to work independently is a skill that can be taught in a preacademic program. Motivation through intrinsic reward is the key to successful independent study.

Organizing materials in the immediate environment may be learned through the appointment or election of a weekly monitor whose task is to give the classroom an orderly appearance. The teacher may provide instructions to the monitor at the beginning of the week, and the classmates perceive and remember what is to be expected of them when their turn occurs.

Completing work within a reasonable time limit is a goal for all children. Because of the individual differences in the children's rate of production, teachers must monitor what can be expected of each child.

Learning to be neat in seat work activities is developed by them through the teacher's demonstration of, for example, putting only a few items at a time on the desk or table space, pasting effectively, folding a piece of paper so the corners meet, and throwing unwanted material into the trash basket.

SUMMARY

In the classroom and out of the classroom the child's brain is not waiting in a vacuum for the next statement, question or visual cue. On the contrary, the brain is busily occupied with either past memories, the present scene, or future plans drawn from stored information. This information is made possible only through intact sensory-motor avenues that include awareness, attention, perception, motivation, and memory. Furthermore, integrated neuronal activity in the brain, often referred to as *central processing*, is responsible for organizing the incoming sensory data into some form for immediate or future use. The integration or central processing of all incoming data is crucial to learning.

In reality, we are all in the field of learning. We are trying to modify behavior, to keep it moving appropriately, or to get it going when it is not going well. Numerous texts have been written on the theories of learning, and perhaps the most significant thing about the theories is the wide disagreement which prevails among the researchers. As diagnosticians and teachers, however, we cannot wait until scientists agree on theories. We must base our own teaching techniques upon the knowledge at hand. We must recognize the importance of cognitive skills in the development of oral language, reading, writing, arithmetic, and affective education, discussed in the preceding chapters, and, as new information in the cognitive area is presented, we must adapt it appropriately.

REFERENCES

Bourne, L. E., R. L. Dominowski, and E. F. Loftus. *Cognitive Processes.* Englewood Cliffs, N.J.: Prentice-Hall, 1979.

Kail, Jr., R. V. and J. W. Hagen (eds.). *Perspectives on the Development of Memory and Cognition.* Hillsdale, N.J.: Lawrence Erlbaum Assoc., 1977.

Ornstein, P. A. (ed.). *Memory Development in Children.* Hillsdale, N.J.: Lawrence Erlbaum Assoc., 1978.

5

testing

INTRODUCTION

Testing, for purposes of this chapter, is an organized system of observing and recording different types of behavior with a goal of utilizing the information to structure the teaching process for language- and learning-handicapped children in the developmental age range three years to first grade. Emphasis is placed on what Tobin (1978) calls the "disordered function approach" rather than the "disordered systems approach." That is, there will be more concern about the evaluation of behaviors children demonstrate rather than about the etiology or neuroanatomical processes that may be involved in language learning. This chapter is concerned primarily with the kinds of behavior involved with language and learning and discusses the purpose of testing, what is to be tested, test selection, scoring and interpretation as well as reporting.

A language and learning assessment may be all that is needed for some children, yet it may be necessary to provide a complete audit for other children in order to rule out medical or psychosocial, or both, problems. Furthermore, multiple-handicapped children often require extensive evaluations. Obtaining a complete audit of a child's assets and deficits may involve three models, namely, medical, psychosocial, and psycholinguistic. The medical model under the direction of the physician is concerned with the diagnosis and treatment of all health problems, including sensory, neurological, and motor. Other professionals, such as the audiologist, physical therapist, radiologist, and electroencephalographer, assist the physician in obtaining a medical diagnosis. Under the psychosocial model we find the psychiatrist, psychologist, and social worker, each concerned with the entire network of relationships among father, mother, child, siblings, peer group, teacher, and all other persons who may influence the child's self-concept, feelings of self-worth, and interpersonal relationships. The psycholinguistic model, under the direction of the speech-language pathologist and educational diagnostician, includes the areas of acquisition of child language to its adult form, the developmental steps related to preacademic subjects, and the development of cognitive behaviors. These specialists, who will be referred to as examiners, incorporate their findings into the total audit of each child.

PURPOSE OF TESTING

The goals of testing are early identification, assessment, and evaluation of children with language or learning deficiencies, or both, in order that early intervention programs may get under way. The time to make an appointment for a language and learning assessment is when a parent, physician, relative, or friend suspects the child has a problem. True, some children talk before others, and those who lag behind initially catch up with their peer group. Notwithstanding the validity of the developmental lag concept, there is more often than not a tendency to wait too long for this "catching up." During this time the child with something more than a maturational delay may unwittingly be neglected, sometimes beyond remedial help. If early identification is not accomplished, children may find myriads of ways to protect themselves from their inadequacies. They may gain attention by disturbing others (hitting, pinching, pushing), by withdrawing from their peer group and becoming engrossed with specific toys, or by becoming disobedient when requests are asked of them (sassing or refusing to comply). To cut through these compensatory mechanisms when the child is five or six years old is a much more difficult assessment and training task than it would have been at an earlier age. Parents are often the ones who are keenly aware of problems, and the specialists should listen to them. They are insightful regarding their concern with developmental milestones. Their uneasy states of mind are real and should not be dismissed with a "Be patient, your son will be all right" or such excuses as the following:

Karen isn't talking as well as other children in the neighborhood, yet her Aunt Louise was late in talking and is now a college graduate. Don't worry.

Bill can't color and cut like his older brother could, yet my friends say give him time.

I told my physician that I was worried about George, my two-year-old, because he was not talking. I didn't think my son could hear. I was afraid to say this to my doctor, but I did. His advice was to wait until George was three and then bring him back for another check up.

Children should be referred for appropriate testing whenever parents express anxiety over what they feel is a problem. To be told early that the child is in difficulty enhances the chances for success in a training program. To be advised that a problem does not exist releases parents' tension. Too many parents of children with handicaps are suffering from feelings of guilt because they did not follow their hunches or were willing to accept the developmental lag concept. Parents' observations of their children should not be ignored.

Testing, as an organized system of observing behaviors, serves at least three purposes: identification, assessment, and evaluation.

Identification

To predict through screening tests which children will be future academic failures is a more tenable concept than to wait until the problem becomes apparent. This point of view is taken by many professionals who are searching for predictive or screening tests that will identify, in supposedly normal populations of children, those who are a high risk for academic achievement and thus may profit from early training. The fact that the latent abilities in very young children are difficult to measure accurately does not preclude trying. Identification of children with handicapping conditions is usually accomplished through the screening of large populations. The screening procedure requires a short period of time, and the results are used only to refer for additional testing. The results are not used to label, formulate objectives for training, or predict future outcomes. Although there are screening instruments on the market, the majority sample only one behavior, such as language or motor development. Two examples of individual screening tests that sample a variety of behavior in the age range birth to three years are the Bayley Scales of Infant Development (Bayley 1969) and the Birth to Three Developmental Scale (Bangs and Dodson 1979), both of which sample types of behavior in the areas of language, problem solving, social, personal, and motor development. One of the few scales that include the birth to six year age span is the Denver

Developmental Screening Test (Frankenburg and others 1970) which screens in the language, social and personal, and motor behavioral areas and serves the purpose of identifying high-risk children.

In light of Public Law 94–142, there is a need for techniques to screen large groups of children for early identification of language and learning problems and to follow through with appropriate in-depth assessment. One such method uses a form letter that is sent home with children in regular kindergarten through third grade classes. Upon receipt of requests for children to be evaluated, the secretary makes appointments and the examiner administers appropriate tests designed to predict future academic failure.

Dear Parents:

The Pasadena Independent School District currently has preschool classes for children who have language or speech problems or who have difficulty in learning. We believe that pre-school training will accelerate progress of these children giving them greater opportunity for academic success from first grade on. In order to locate the youngsters who will benefit from a preschool training program, staff from the school district will be available to assess your child sometime during the month of March. You will be advised shortly after that time whether or not preschool training is indicated.

If you are interested in having one or more of your children between birth and the kindergarten level tested, please read the following questions. If your answer is "Yes" to one or more, call now the person listed below for further details regarding an appointment.

1. Do you have a child who has a language problem, that is, uses poor sentences or has limited vocabulary?
2. Do you have a child who has a speech problem so severe that you and others have trouble understanding what he or she says, that is, poor articulation, poor voice quality?
3. Do you have a child who does not seem to be able to follow your instructions or does not remember what you ask him or her to do?
4. Do you think your child may have a hearing loss?

Very truly yours,

Call Ms. Bernier
524-3136

_____

Program Director

Children in most states are eligible for enrollment in preschool special education classes by three years of age. Some states lower eligibility to birth. Early identification through screening tests, therefore, is imperative if early intervention is to take place.

Assessment

The assessment validates data obtained from the screening instruments and provides some in-depth knowledge of the problem. Because no assessment tool can cover the total range of a child's repertoire of behaviors, an assessment may range from a battery of tests that looks closely at a variety of behavior to a single test that relates a child's vocabulary comprehension level to a norm-referenced population, such as the Peabody Picture Vocabulary Test (Dunn 1959, 1965). The specific purposes of an assessment are: (1) to obtain baseline data that provide an audit of the kinds of behavior a child has and of those yet to be acquired, (2) to use these data for writing an individual educational plan (IEP) of goals and objectives, which is now a requirement of Public Law 94–142 (see Chapter 1), (3) to assist the teacher in grouping the children, and (4) to provide behavioral data for program instruction. The test items must provide something that can be used, and there must be a relationship between what the test measures and the curriculum. The author knows of no single standardized test that measures all the language and preacademic behavior of children in the developmental range three years to first grade. References at the end of this chapter provide the examiner with a selection of standardized and nonstandardized tests, which may be helpful in identifying the kinds of behavior children have and those yet to be learned.

Evaluation

Evaluation is an ongoing systematic procedure that samples behavior over a specified period of time and involves pretesting, interim testing, and posttesting specified types of behavior. The purpose of evaluation is to obtain information on the learning rate of each child and to serve as an accountability measure: did the children learn what was purported for them to learn as written in the objectives, and have the expected changes really occurred? Only through evaluation or reassessments can decisions be made as to whether a child should continue part or full time in special education classes.

WHAT TO TEST

Before selecting a test, examiners must have a clear understanding of what it is they wish to measure. If the objective is to obtain an Intelligence Quotient (I.Q.) score, then the Stanford-Binet Intelligence Scale (Terman and Merrill 1960, 1973) may be the choice. If the need is to measure a child's use of linguistic rules in a peer group relationship, the choice may be to record language samples and then to do a linguistic analysis of each sample. For purposes of this text, what will be tested is what is to be included in the preacademic curriculum: (1) the content, form, and use of language, (2) the avenues of learning or cognitive skills that bring together a language-learning framework, (3) social personal relationships, and (4) motor skills (see Appendix 1 for Developmental Behaviors).

Oral Language

In the area of language the examiner is concerned with the children's understanding and use of the symbol system that reflects their knowledge of the environment in which they have lived. The symbol system includes a lexicon and a system for ordering words into appropriate morphosyntactic relationships.

When assessing language, it seems expedient to include language comprehension items (how well does a child understand what is said when no verbal response is required), and expressive items (how well does a child respond orally to the stimuli presented). Such an approach allows for an assessment of children whose speech is unintelligible or who are reluctant to speak in a test situation.

Lexicon. In Chapter 2 it was stressed that a child's ability to comprehend and generate sentences is directly related to knowing the meaning of words singly or in relation to one another. The author discussed in some detail the variety of words that represent the nature of the child's lexicon, including content words, relational words, and inflectional words. It is important to know what kinds of words children have in their lexicons.

Syntax. The assessment and curriculum in this text do not focus heavily on syntactic form but rather on the semantic relationships of words. It is hypothesized that children with language or learning deficiencies will discover the rules of syntactic form, as do children who develop language in a normal pattern. The difference will lie in the lateness of discovering the rules and in the greater length of time needed to apply them. They will use the same rules, although they may be less complex. The analysis of language samples presented later in this chapter and the references at the end of this chapter will assist the examiner in knowing which syntactic structures a child has and which ones are deficient or missing.

Use. There is current interest in studying the pragmatic aspects of children's language — the reason why children speak, the alternative linguistic structures from which they can choose to influence the listener, and their ability to understand both direct and indirect statements (see Chapter 2). The research in the use of language has been primarily descriptive; little has been accomplished in formalizing tests for measuring this dimension of language. Measurement becomes an important issue, however, when children use language in such a way as to affect their peers or others negatively. Such children may be said to have "pragmatic deficiencies." The use of language should not be overlooked when considering what is to be tested.

Arithmetic

Arithmetic is a symbol-based subject using word symbols and mathematical symbols, the latter being acquired in kindergarten and in the elementary and secondary school grades. In preacademic programs it is important to assess the child's lexicon of constant, relational, and inflectional words that code arithmetic concepts, like number words, five, whole, more–less. Furthermore, there is a need to assess concepts and skills related to counting by rote, to rational counting, number concepts, adding and subtracting as well as to the one-to-one correspondence between the numeral and the word, 2–two.

Handwriting

The examiner is interested in assessing handwriting skills that are practiced very early by children as they make marks on paper with crayons or pencils. Later they draw lines and circles both of which are basic movements for writing letters and numbers.

Reading

Because reading is a counterpart of oral language, children must develop a vocabulary and sentence structure that will match the language of the books they will read in first grade. The child's lexicon, syntax, and use of language must be assessed. The examiner will measure also the child's progress in phonics, reading specific words, and any other reading skills which are taught in the kindergarten class.

Social and Personal

It is important to know how children feel about themselves and what their feelings are about other people. Observing their interpersonal relationships in structured as well as unstructured environments often gives clues as to why some children develop appropriate self-concepts and others fail. There needs to be greater emphasis than currently exists in assessing the social and personal skills of children in their preschool years.

Motor

The assessment of motor skills is usually assigned to the physical therapist who is trained to observe and record the gross and fine motor development of handicapped children. With this information the teacher can provide alternate classroom procedures for meeting the special needs of these children.

Avenues of Learning

Perception, attention, memory, retrieval, and central processing are all basic cognitive skills which are the substrata of language learning and are needed for preacademic subjects namely, reading, arithmetic, writing, and affective education. Although these avenues of learning are difficult to assess as separate entities, the examiner should attempt to pinpoint deficiencies in these areas in order to assist the teacher in developing instructional strategies that will alleviate or circumvent the problems.

TEST SELECTION

In general, tests fall into two categories: formal tests that are standardized according to norm-referenced or criterion-referenced data and informal tests that are not standardized. It is important that both categories meet the criteria of validity, reliability, practicability, and reportability. Validity is simply asking if the test measures what it purports to measure. Reliability demonstrates comparable results between test and re-test data within a short time frame. Practicability is concerned with selecting a test that will provide useful information and will not involve an unreasonable amount of time for administration. Reportability refers to test data that can be reported in the language of the person receiving the results. (This may be more a function of the examiner's ability to translate professional language into lay language than a function of the test per se.) Within the various specialty fields serving handicapped children, both standardized and non-standardized tests are used.

Standardized Tests

Tests may be standardized on national, state, or local populations and should attempt to meet the following criteria:

1. Samplings from a wide area
2. A percentile cutoff point which tells the diagnostician what percent of

the children in the study passed the item. In general, the higher the cutoff point the more diagnostic the test item
3. An equal number of males and females
4. An adequate number of subjects, statistically based by the person standardizing the test
5. A representative sampling of ethnic populations and socioeconomic groups
6. An interrater reliability of .90 or better
7. Test-retest reliability greater than .75

These standardized tests may be norm referenced or criterion referenced. A norm-referenced test (NRT) is designed to interpret the performance of a person in relation to a reference group, whereas a criterion-referenced test designates the performance of the person in terms of mastery of specific concepts and skills within a curriculum.

Norm-Referenced Tests. In an educational setting, norm-referenced tests provide an individual score which relates the child's standing in a specific reference group. The Intelligence Quotient (I.Q.) was one of the earliest scores used to determine whether or not a child was normal. The first and most widely used norm-referenced test that yielded an I.Q. score was the Stanford-Binet (Terman and Merrill 1937, 1960, 1973). In general, the child's I.Q. score designates intellectual performance in the normal, above normal, or below normal range, and the score gives no information as to the specific assets or deficits in the areas of language and cognitive skills. Following the I.Q. tests were those that provided a Developmental Age, a Language Age, or a Learning Age, each representing a single number that rates the child against the reference group; again, the score provides no data that would assist the teacher in developing objectives and lesson plans. Another form of the norm-referenced test is the achievement test. Scores obtained from achievement tests usually provide a percentile or grade equivalent score in such academic areas as reading and arithmetic. For example, a child may be performing at the eightieth percentile in a third grade reading class or at the 2.5 grade level in arithmetic. Again, there is no information that tells the teacher which concepts and skills are missing if a child is functioning below the expected achievement level. Although I.Q. and achievement tests have their place in research, they are quickly giving way to curriculum-based tests which come under the category of criterion-referenced tests. (See the end of the chapter for a list of norm-referenced tests.)

Criterion-Referenced Tests. Unlike norm-referenced tests, criterion-referenced tests are designed to reflect comprehensively the content of a particular curriculum. Information from a criterion-referenced test is used to prepare the teaching objectives and lesson plans that will meet the needs of the children. For example, the Vocabulary Comprehension Scale (Bangs 1975) assesses the child's comprehension of pronouns. The results of the test will reveal which pronouns a child knows and which are not known. Because the vocabulary is developmentally sequenced, a teacher can select the pronouns the children need to learn and include them in his or her performance objectives and daily lesson plans. In actuality, the instructor teaches to the test and measures each child's gains by the number of words learned. A criterion-referenced test keeps the teacher apprised of which forms of behavior the children have mastered and which have not been mastered and allows for writing objectives for the appropriate scope and sequencing of behaviors. There is less "over-teaching," that is, time spent on what the child knows, and less teaching that is too many steps beyond the child's language and cognitive level. The criticisms of criterion-referenced tests center around the adage found in psychology texts, "Do not teach to the test" or around the belief that parents still want a number, an I.Q. score or a grade level. It is hoped that this preoccupation with numbers is waning and that there will be a universal acceptance of the philosophy underlying criterion-referenced tests (see the end of this chapter for references on criterion-referenced tests).

Nonstandardized Tests and Additional Data

While researchers continue developing standardized tests to measure the semantic and morphosyntactic features of language and the cognitive skills necessary to communicate orally and to read, write, and perform mathematical skills, examiners as well as teachers make use of nonstandardized tests and other instruments to determine a child's needs. These methods include: case histories, diaries, observations, check-lists, language samples, and teacher-made tests.

Case Histories. In general, two types of case history questionnaires have been designed to serve somewhat different functions. One is a form to be filled in by parents, and the other is a summary of pertinent case history data that is prepared by the examiner. The questionnaire to be filled in by the parents (see Appendix 2, Case History Form A: For Parents) provides the examiner with statements of the child's problem and of those factors the parents feel may have brought on the problem. The general case history form (see Appendix 3, General Case History Form B) is to be used by the examiner as a means of clarifying what the parents have written or to obtain additional data. It includes, under general headings, key words which serve as a guide during the interview. Appropriate recording of symbols before each key word clearly delineates significant and nonsignificant information as well as areas in which information is lacking. The final case history report is usually written in essay form but with well-delineated statements of the child's assets and deficits.

Much time may be consumed interviewing parents, summarizing, and recording pertinent data. In order to make this time profitable, the examiner must ask the question, "Why do I want this information?" The following offers some specific reasons for obtaining case history data, which include birth history, motor development, medical history, language and speech development, interpersonal relationships, and family and school data.

Birth history data:

1. are important to proper diagnosis. Parents often request an appointment for their child at a speech, language and hearing center before obtaining a medical examination. Any information the diagnostician can obtain that will assist the physicians should be recorded and forwarded to them.

Certain pre- and postnatal conditions of the infant are known to correlate highly with language and learning disorders. Illness of the mother during her first trimester of pregnancy, alcoholism, and excessive smoking may adversely affect fetal development. Medical scientists continue to report a high incidence of central nervous system dysfunction in children whose records show abnormality in one or more of the following: gestation period, length of labor, and birth weight. Furthermore, cyanosis, jaundice, and convulsions are known to be related to problems in newborns.

2. indicate areas of parent anxieties. Parents of children with handicaps often suffer from many anxieties. The birth history may reveal that a child was the only living one of four pregnancies; parents may become overly solicitous for fear of what could happen to their only child. A mother may report that her son had several seizures during his first year of life; the question "Will he have more?" continues to haunt her. Appropriate parental counseling by the physician is indicated when the diagnostician finds medical information which is causing parents anxiety.

3. assist the teacher. Teachers will have better rapport with parents if there is a mutual understanding of past events which cause current anxiety.

4. are important to clinical research. Scientists in the professions of speech-language pathology, audiology, and psychology are interested in correlating certain types of behavior with medical and developmental data.

Motor development data:

1. are important to proper diagnosis. Has the patient always been delayed in gross motor development? If true, and this information correlates with slowness to acquire language, speech, and social maturity, a diagnosis of general retardation may be hypothesized.

Some children who are late in acquiring adequate speech reveal a history of eating problems such as, difficulty with sucking and chewing solid foods and persistent drooling. This information may indicate fine motor incoordination of the articulatory mechanism, possibly associated with articulatory disorders. Such a diagnosis is helpful in planning a training program for this child.

2. indicate areas of parents' anxieties. The fact that children do not walk when their peers walk or are still wetting their beds long after others have stopped gives parents good cause for anxiety. However, attempts to bring about walking skills and bladder control before a child is ready may contribute to poor parent-child relationships and further anxiety. No one should be blamed. Parents' problems must be understood and alleviated by appropriate counseling.

3. assist the teacher. Knowing that a child's deviant gait is the result of an orthopedic problem will indicate to the teacher a need for working closely with the orthopedic surgeon or physical therapist, or both. Much that is done in the classroom may be directed toward improving the orthopedic problem.

4. are important to clinical research. Many questions concerning motor development remain unanswered. Specifically, the speech clinician is still in need of an answer to the question, "Will maturation take care of Joe's articulation disorder, or does he have a permanently faulty articulatory mechanism?"

Medical history data:

1. are important to proper diagnosis. Careful questioning of parents may point up pertinent diagnostic information.

Two-year-old Melissa was being assessed because she was not talking. The examiner asked her mother, "Does she understand anything you say?" "Oh yes, " she replied, "but only when she wants to understand. I know she hears because when her back is turned to me she understands *bye-bye* and can point to her nose and eyes on request. But some days she will not do this."

The examiner has a clue that this may be a child with hearing impairment. The words that have been said loudly enough and close enough are recognized but only when spoken at this same distance and loudness level. Audiological and otological studies would be indicated to determine the presence or absence of hearing impairment.

2. indicate areas of parents' anxieties. Parents often retain feelings of guilt if they were responsible for the car accident which caused their son's head injury or if they were not at home when he suffered a severe convulsion. A father may have a difficult time accepting his son because of his dysplastic features such as, malformed ear, misshapen head, club feet.

3. assist the teacher. It is important for the teacher to be apprised of a child's propensity for seizures and how they should be handled in the classroom. If a child is on medication or the medication is changed,

the teacher should observe the student for any behavioral differences. The qualified teacher keeps records which will assist the physician in the program of drug therapy.

Which children have allergies and to what? Pets? Foods? Flowers? Teachers can control the classroom environment for children with allergies but must have access to the medical histories to do so.

4. are important to clinical research. Currently there is no valid way of predicting which drug will continue to produce acceptable behavior in children. There is every reason to believe that teachers' and parents' observations of children under drug therapy may give clues to investigators who are searching for answers. Teachers play an important role with a research team.

Language history data:

1. are important to proper diagnosis. Parents may report that their child performs on age level in all modalities of learning yet uses mostly gestures and jargon to communicate. Sensory hearing impairment may be postulated.

When a child's language development is late, although hearing is normal and opportunity has been plentiful, central nervous system dysfunction will be considered.

2. indicate areas of parents' anxieties. If a child is cerebral palsied, blind, or a polio victim, the handicap is visible. Not so with all language delayed children. Parents often are subjected to and become disturbed by such questions as "Does the cat have your tongue, son?" "Why don't you deny him his food or toys if he refuses to ask for them?" A child who does not communicate adequately is a frustrating problem to parents.

3. assist the teacher. The teacher will want to know if the parents have punished a child for not talking or have overrewarded him when he did say something. Such information suggests discussion topics for group parent conferences. Knowledge of previous methods used in training is helpful. Conversations with former teachers are often enlightening.

4. are important to clinical research. Pertinent language information as recorded from case histories may be of subsequent value in research studies.

Speech history data:

1. are important to proper diagnosis. Some children can be understood only by their siblings who often are used as interpreters. This information leads the diagnostician to believe that the child has at least some functional language, but it is masked by severe articulatory problems.

2. indicate areas of parents' anxieties. Stuttering, high pitched voices, or unintelligible speech cause great parental concern. Friends

and relatives are quick to offer suggestions and "cures," none of which seems to alleviate the problem. The result is extreme anxiety in both parents.

3. assist the teacher. New students who stutter are often embarrassed by their nonfluencies. A teacher may either avoid asking such a student to perform orally before the class until the child appears ready, or prepare the class appropriately for acceptance of the deviant speech.

4. are important to clinical research. Nonfluencies and severe articulatory disorders are usually described in research literature. Investigations which discover causation will be welcomed by clinicians who are seeking a rationale for training.

Interpersonal relationship data:

1. are important to proper diagnosis. Aggressiveness, hyperactivity, distractability, and perseveration are characteristics of some children with language and learning problems. This descriptive behavior is meaningless by itself, but studied with the total case history it may become an important part of the differential diagnosis.

2. indicate areas of parents' anxieties. When children are subjected to undue stress, primitive activity may come into being. If they have many failures during the day, they tend to build defenses against further failure. These may take the form of tears, daydreaming, tantrums, or extreme affection. Parents cannot accept such deviant behavior, yet they have no answers as to how it may be controlled.

3 assist the teacher. A teacher can avoid many classroom casualties if she knows the child's fears, play habits with peers, and general disposition. Anticipating behavioral problems in the classroom and circumventing them may mean the difference between an adequate and inadequate learning milieu.

4. are important to clinical research. There is some research evidence to indicate that unacceptable behavior in children—inability to cope with an unstructured environment, inadequate peer group relationships, poor social perception, and tempers which can be turned off as quickly as they are turned on—is organically based. Such children may demonstrate convulsive equivalents with no known cause, such as stomach aches, leg cramps, headaches, and fever. If these kinds of behavior are scientifically verified to be organic disorders and appropriate treatment is discovered, parents and teachers will have solved many child-rearing problems.

Family data:

1. are important to proper diagnosis. There is evidence in the literature to indicate that some of the problems of children are hereditary, such as hearing impairment, general retardation, reading disabilities. Inquiry into familial problems may be the only clue to etiology.

2. indicate areas of parents' anxieties. What parents would not be

filled with anxiety if they had an invalid grandparent and five children in the home, an income which could not adequately care for the family, and were faced with bringing one daughter to special classes each day? The diagnostician records such pertinent data and often refers the family to a social worker who can study the home situation and provide solutions to the problems.

3. assist the teacher. It is often a slow process to teach a child with learning disabilities the skills needed for oral and written language. Teaching problems are multiplied if the parents are bilingual and speak mostly their native language at home.

If the parents work, or if the child lives part time with the father and part time with the mother because of marital separation, responsibility for the home training must be decided upon.

4. are important to clinical research. Is a disturbed parent-child relationship caused by parents, or is it a byproduct of the child's deviant behavior? This is a moot question, which needs to be researched further.

School data:

1. are important to proper diagnosis. A child who has attended a nursery or play school will have demonstrated many of his language and learning skills to the teacher. Relating current abilities to previous behavior helps determine learning rates.

2. indicate areas of parents' anxieties. Parents want their children to succeed with their peers. To be told that a daughter can no longer stay in a play school because she is too undisciplined is a family tragedy. Parents unwittingly tend to blame themselves, and by so doing become extremely anxious over disciplinary procedures.

3. assist the teacher. Teachers will be grateful for any previous information about a child in a play school, preacademic or academic program. The subject matter he was exposed to, what he learned, from whom and where, and at what time are all important pieces of information.

4. are important to clinical research. As of mid-1980, no scientific research has demonstrated that children with specific learning disabilities do better in academic subjects if they have had preacademic training. The clinical judgments of many teachers favor preacademic training. Research is forthcoming.

Diaries. Parents may have kept developmental data in their child's baby book that could add significant information to the case history. In addition, teachers often ask parents to keep diaries of selected developmental areas that can be compared with the child's performance at school and that also provide the parents with evidence that the child has made gains over time.

Observations. Diaries are based upon a chronology of observations that have been recorded over time. Other observations are not recorded over time. Both parents and teachers are alert to a child's performance when alone and with a group and use these observations to modify behaviors. The examiner, if time permits, may find it profitable to watch the child in a play situation, either alone, with peers, or with the parent, and to record pertinent information that would help to make sense out of case history data that may be difficult to interpret.

Checklists. Checklists contain sequenced behaviors in a variety of categories that are used by teachers and parents to identify the kinds of behavior children have and those they have not acquired. Starting with those that are present, the teacher selects subsequent kinds of behavior on the list and these become the objectives to be met. The behaviors on the checklist are usually taken from documented sources or from educated guesses as to what children can do sequentially at different age levels. There are numerous assessment packages and checklists that have become available in the last decade. One of these, the *Portage Guide to Early Education* (Bluma and others 1976) contains within its curriculum a checklist that is used to identify the kinds of behavior children can perform and those they cannot. Each type of behavior on the checklist has a number that corresponds to a curriculum card which lists activities for developing the behavior. This guide is an example of a nonstandardized criterion-referenced test used by teachers to develop objectives and lesson plans. The checklist in this text (see Appendix 1, Developmental Behaviors) is used for writing curriculum objectives in the areas of oral language, reading, handwriting, arithmetic, and social and personal relationships.

Language Samples. Language samples consist of a set of fifty or more children's utterances in specified contexts that have been video taped or recorded and handwritten and then analyzed according to specific methods (Bloom and Lahey 1978; Crystal and others 1976, Lee 1974; Longhurst and Schrandt 1973; Muma 1973; and Tyack and Gottsleben 1974). Obtaining and studying language samples in a "normal" population have provided developmental data related to the mean length of children's utterances; content, form, and use of language; and productivity or the amount a child says in a given period of time. These developmental data, then, are used as criteria for identifying language deficiencies in children with language and learning disorders. The state of the art of obtaining and analyzing language samples is still in the realm of the researcher. The time and expertise involved in attempting to obtain valid information is too consuming a task for the average examiner or classroom teacher. However, a simplified approach, which may be of some value to the teacher, is either to ask parents to keep a record of what their child says or to have the classroom aide record samples of the child's speech during the school hours. Certain basic rules must be followed, however, such as reporting whether the sample was taken while the child was talking informally with peers or others or whether the samples were elicited through simple questions or by asking the child to relate or describe an event. The art of questioning, of course is to avoid yes-no answers or other one word answers. "Are you a boy?" or "Do you live in Texas?" will elicit obvious yes-no answers. By the same token, only one word answers will be given to such questions as "What color is your shirt?" or "How many peanuts do you have?" The astute examiner, teacher, or parent uses the following: "Tell me about. . ." or "Describe. . . ." Lynch (1978, p. 354) has stated that "Even if formal systems of analysis are not employed, the language sample provides valuable information." She presents a form for making handwritten notes which could be used by persons who are appropriately trained to be accurate observers and recorders (see Appendix 4 Figure 5-1, Form for Recording Language Samples). The data obtained are of value only if the teacher is knowledgeable about the acquisition of child language to its adult form and can develop techniques for improving the child's content, form, and use of language.

Teacher-Made Tests. Teacher-made tests, like checklists, are non-standardized criterion-referenced tests that pre- and posttest the performance objectives that have been developed for the children. Bangs (1979) presented an in-depth discussion of accountability and evaluation design in education, and includes the following five elements in a performance objective: (1) *who* is the person for whom the objective is written, (2) *what* is the person expected to learn, (3) what *measuring* tool will be used to determine whether or not an individual meets the stated objective, (4) how much *time* should be allowed to meet the objective, and (5) what *degree* of proficiency is expected of the learner.

By (4) October 15 the children (1) will identify by function (2) as measured by a teacher-made test (3), eight out of nine (5) of the following pictures (2): house, cat, needle and thread, clock, scissors, piece of clothing, cow, toy, fish. (See Appendix 5, Teacher-Made Test.)

Sociograms. Another form of a teacher-made test is a sociogram, which is neither a scale nor a checklist but a peer-nominating technique which allows for contributions by peers into a child's behavioral profile. One of the simplest forms for obtaining information about peer relationships is to ask the children to name their best friend. Another technique is utilized when it is time for dismissal. The teacher asks the leader for the day to stand by the door and ask her best friend to stand behind her. The best friend then selects a best friend, and the procedure continues until all are standing in line. To record the information the teacher has the names of the children on her clipboard with the leader's name at the top. The first child chosen receives a score of one, and subsequently chosen children receive the next higher number. Over time the teacher can average these scores and plot the range for each child.

The higher scores may designate those children who have poor self-concepts or unacceptable interpersonal relationships. The teacher develops strategies for helping children with their social and personal problems.

Diagnostic Teaching. Informal testing by the teacher or an aide is not a new concept, but it has become, with the advent of Public Law 94-142, a tool for making the teacher accountable for what it is that she says she will teach the children. Teachers, therefore, have an on-going testing-training program often referred to as diagnostic teaching. They attempt to discover how children learn and how they make use of what they have learned. Because norm-referenced tests are not used for writing learner objectives, teachers must take a heuristic approach to their diagnostic teaching programs. Many language and preacademic behaviors can be assessed to a better advantage in a classroom milieu than in a standard test environment. This involves the use of pre and posttesting with teacher-made tests. It also involves taking language samples and observing social and personal behaviors. The interpersonal relationships of children are described more readily by the teacher who has observed the children with their peers, parents, strangers as well as with himself or herself. That teacher is quick to find the child who is insensitive to the kind of behavior to which other people are sensitive or the child with fears, jealousies, and shyness. Even though diagnostic teaching is in progress each day, the teacher should be aware that the success of a skill in one context may be measured as a failure in a different context. The teacher should always be aware that a child's retention of a specific skill in a specific task may be transient and not generalize. In order to measure the stability of a learning situation, or transfer of learning to a new situation, the teacher has to have an on-going diagnostic teaching program and keep a record of what the children have learned and what they have not learned. The teacher should be practicing accountability in education.

TEST ENVIRONMENT

Every child becomes a new challenge to the examiner who manipulates the test environment in such a way as to obtain the most valid information possible from a child.

Physical Aspects of the Room

The appearance of the assessment room for formal testing is such that the child will find the immediate test materials the most interesting objects in view. This means a fairly sterile room. All materials not in use must be out of sight and far enough away that the subject cannot reach them. The examiner has to be thoroughly familiar with all the test items and their location so that selection can be immediate. Time is often an important factor when children are being tested. In addition, when assessing an active, mobile child, the examiner will find it advisable to sit between the subject and the exit!

Rapport

Knowing that no two children are alike, examiners adapt their materials and techniques to each child's needs. Although it is customary to sit across a table from the examiner, some children will not conform. One child may prefer to participate in the examination while standing. Another may sit by the table but only on his or her parent's lap. It is not the examiner's responsibility to modify this behavior, only to observe and record it. Children should not be reprimanded for unacceptable behavior so frequently that the assessment becomes a lesson in discipline. Inflexibility in assessment techniques is a primary cause of incomplete testing or failure to obtain usable results.

Children often associate persons in white coats with painful experiences, like getting immunization shots or dental care. Examiners should avoid this kind of apparel to lessen the chance of frightening a child. By the same token, those who hold Ph.D. degrees seldom introduce themselves as "doctor" in the presence of the child.

Rapport with mothers and fathers is also essential. Parents who bring their children for an assessment of their problems have many concerns. "Will Ted talk for the examiner? Will he cry? Will he have a temper tantrum? Will I have to talk about my marital problems? Will I be blamed for the many things I have done wrong in rearing my children? How much will the assessment cost? What will the examiner recommend? If I have to go to the school for parent training, who will take care of my other preschool children while I am away?" The examiner's attitude and conversation during the first five minutes with the parents and child can help to alleviate the tensions that are known to exist. A warm greeting, sitting for a minute or two with them in the reception room, or providing an opportunity for questions may circumvent what might have been a stressful relationship.

Should Parents Observe the Assessment?

There is no rule as to whether parents should or should not observe the assessment. The examiner will know which is advisable through previously obtained reports and clinical judgment at the time the parents are greeted. In general, the flexible and experienced examiner will find many advantages in having parents observe testing procedures.

Parents should be permitted to observe their child in the test room under the following conditions:

If the child appears immature and fearful. If she clutches mother, hides her head in her lap, or begins to cry, the chances are she needs her parent. Children may fear the unknown. Taking them away from mother to an unfamiliar room may be a traumatic experience. Is it any wonder that tears and tantrums prevail? To avoid a rebellious scene, one or both parents may be invited to accompany the child to the test room. Usually the parents sit quietly and the child becomes so engrossed in the "games" that she ignores all but the examiner and the materials.

If the examiner wishes to demonstrate the child's performance to the parent. Such a demonstration may become the basis for a successful conference on the results of the assessment. For example, a father may be surprised to see that his child does not point to the picture *chair* when the stimulus word *furniture* is said but may quickly point to it when the stimulus word *chair* is given. "Did you notice, Mr. King, that David knows many words such as *chair*, but not the category word to which it belongs, *furniture*?" The father replied, "Yes, and I was not aware of it." Assessments are made to help parents and teachers obtain a better understanding of their children, their assets and deficits. Knowing some details of the problems leads directly to remedial action. If parents have observed the assessment, home training suggestions become meaningful and often benefit the entire family.

If the child's speech is unintelligible. Parents often understand what their child says when an examiner cannot. For this reason the parent, who is the best interpreter, will be needed in the test room. When a parent or any observer comes to the test room, he or she should be asked to sit somewhat behind the child and be instructed to make no comments or corrections. If mother or father attempts to rephrase the question, answer for the child, or hint at the answer, the examiner might say laughingly, "Be careful, or I'll be obtaining a test on you!"

Parents should not be permitted to continue to observe their child in the test room if when there, it becomes apparent that the child would perform better alone. Parents are usually the first to sense such a situation and are not reluctant to leave.

Creativity

When the examiner first confronts a child for purposes of a language and learning assessment, quick decisions must be made. Can testing begin immediately, or is there a need for a short play period? Which toys should be given to the child? Which test should be introduced first? Hypotheses are formulated and tested as the assessment progresses. Wrong guesses are made, and new ones continue to be created. Within a relatively short period of time a skilled examiner observes and records what has been heard and seen. These quantitative and qualitative judgments will form the audit of the child's assets and deficits.

Listen to Parents and Child

With few exceptions parents are good reporters. They desire to present an honest chronology of their child's behavior in an effort to secure the counsel and advice of the persons who are assessing. Parents can furnish needed information if examiners will listen.

Four-year-old Kay did poorly on all test items related to hand skills. Mother later reported that she had never allowed her daughter to paint, cut with scissors, or color because the two-year-old would use the materials and cause problems. Home training suggestions were offered and carried out. Within a short period of time Kay developed hand-eye-motor skills commensurate with her age. Mother's comment was "Kay was not low in hand skills, she was low in 'mothering skills.'"

Time Allotment

It is unrealistic for an examiner to expect the majority of young children to maintain a high level of attention over a long period of time. The examiner must be so familiar with the materials and the manner of testing that the assessment can be administered in less than an hour with preschool children. If a child does not respond in a formal testing situation, the examiner can select a room in which the child may move about freely. Pictures and toys should be presented in a variety of ways, and responses should be recorded. This kind of an observation program works well with children originally not testable. They generally begin to relate well to the examiner after a few days in a one-hour observation class. Formalized testing may be possible on the second or third day. A few youngsters will not be ready for an assessment with standardized tests for several months. Under no circumstances should they be kept for this length of time in an observation class. A subjective report of the child's performance should be presented at the appropriate admissions committee meeting so that the child can be placed in a class where diagnostic teaching can transpire.

Order of Item Presentation

For children who are shy or aware of their language difficulties, the examiner in a formal test will present nonverbal tasks first, such as block building or paper folding. Such an approach may make the child more comfortable in the test situation and subsequently willing to respond to verbal test items. Informal testing usually accomplished while observing children in natural environments has become the popular mode for assessing behavioral skills. The order in which behaviors are observed is not nearly as important as is operationally defining the behaviors and developing teacher-made tests for observing and recording the behaviors.

SCORING

Some children, because of their charming manner or attractiveness, immediately appear more capable than they are; others, because of grotesque facial features or their generally "dull" appearance, may elicit a false hypothesis of severe intellectual retardation. Examiners are aware of these false hypotheses and others. Throughout the testing the examiner must never assume that because children perform poorly on one section of the test battery, they will continue to score poorly. Few children demonstrate flat profiles of their language and learning skills.

Quantitative Interpretation

The purpose of testing is to determine which kinds of behavior children have learned and which they have not learned, and, therefore, pass-fail scores are assigned to the child's performance on each test item. Examiners, however, do not approach the test situation as a technician. They apply decision-making skills to help determine whether a child is failing the item due to external factors or because the behavior truly has not been acquired. Some children, for example, perceive their own errors and are disturbed by their failures. When the examiner senses this, the child is told that this "game" is a hard one but to go ahead and try; during a series of failures, a task that will bring success is introduced. The examiner endeavors to praise the child's efforts, not the correct response. At times a child's response may be ambiguous and impossible to score. The examiner may say, "Tell me what you mean. Tell me more about it." Some directions for administering specific tests, however, may be quite rigid. The examiner notes in the manual how many times a question may be repeated. If questioning beyond the requirement is needed, the item is marked a failure. If the child scores correctly with additional cues, a qualitative note should be entered beside the test item.

Qualitative Interpretation

Skilled examiners, knowing that tests do not always measure what they purport to measure, look for qualitative aspects of a child's performance which may give insight as to why the item was failed. Sometimes the reason is not revealed. In such instances the teacher may be able to seek the answer while diagnosing and teaching in the classroom. In addition to the qualitative interpretation, the examiner is interested in knowing at what level below the failed item the child was able to perform. These observations may give entry-level information into the curriculum. The following examples are the kinds of subjective impressions the examiner may make while assessing a child.

Recognition of Objects by Function. When asked, "Which one do we drink out of?" the boy correctly points to the cup. When asked, "Which one do we cut with?" he points again to the cup. Did *cut* and *cup* sound alike to him? Or, is it that he does not know the word *cut* or the word *knife*? If given a knife, would he pretend to cut?

A girl cannot point to "Which one do we cook on?" Is it because the toy stove or the picture does not look like the built-in hot plates and oven that she has seen in her and in her friends' kitchens?

Identifies Objects by Category. A girl cannot point to the appropriate picture when asked to "Point to the toy." The examiner asks her to point to something she plays with. The answer may be correct. A notation is made on the margin of the score sheet.

Names Objects by Function. The action-agent test items may reveal useful information about the child's language development and communication skills. Does the child give answers by gesturing only? If this has been true in other parts of the test, the case history may reveal an emotional block when oral communication is required.

Sometimes children give strange answers to questions, for example, a "sounds alike" answer. There are children who always like to make some kind of a response, so when asked "What melts?" they may answer "milk." When asked "What aches?" they may answer "eggs." One can hypothesize that they do not know the meaning of the words.

A child may give answers which describe function rather than name the thing that represents the function. When asked, "What scratches?" they may answer, "Scratch my hand"; "What swims?" they answer, "In the swimming pool"; "What flies?" answer, "Fly in the air." The examiner will make note of the fact that this child names by function. Perhaps he or she has a retrieval problem and cannot recall names.

Defining. When a child is defining words, describing a picture, or volunteering information, direct quotations of what is said are written on the test form. These language samples are valuable in making a cursory analysis of the child's sentence structure.

When asked, "What is a ball?" does the child repeat the question rather than answer it? Echolalia may indicate that the question had no meaning to the child.

Relational Words. A boy is asked to point to the *long* one and then to the *short* one but fails the item. The examiner or the teacher will give the boy a set of long and short sticks to determine if he can sort them. If so, he has perceived the attributes of length regarding these sticks but does not have the linguistic labels, *long-short.*

Numbers. Does a girl correctly hand the examiner two cookies but not two blocks? Perhaps she has not generalized the concept of twoness because mother has worked only with cookies at home.

Repetition of Sentences. Were the children unable to remember the sentence because they were distracted by something? Was it an attention deficit rather than a memory deficit?

Paper Folding. One boy scored on age level, but his work habits were poor and his finished product was "sloppy." Did he demonstrate problems of fine motor coordination?

Copy Designs with Pencil and Paper. A girl has difficulty copying the forms presented to her. Has she had experience with pencil and paper tasks?

Another girl refused to pick up the pencil and draw. The parents had spent many hours trying to teach her to print her name. She never experienced success because her parents always insisted she could do better. Now she rejects pencil and paper tasks.

Block Patterns. Only those items that require placing one block behind another were failed. Is this a problem of depth perception or is it maturational lag?

One girl did not score on some of the designs because she did not use the correct number of blocks, yet the design was well formed. The examiner checked other portions of the test to determine if she performed poorly with numbers.

The experienced examiner not only gives a plus or minus score but searches for reasons why the child failed the item. Furthermore, the examiner determines at what level the child can function appropriately. These kinds of information help the teacher develop objectives for the instructional program.

REPORTING

The results of an assessment may or may not be given orally but always must be in written form and filed in the client's record file. Included in the file is a release of information statement signed by the guardian allowing him or her to control dissemination of the test results. Before writing the report, the examiner should ask the question, "For whom is the report intended, the parents, school personnel, physician, insurance agent?" Knowing for whom the report is intended allows the examiner to vary terminology and the emphasis of detail. After the report has been written, the examiner should ask a second question, "Am I reporting anything that will attach a stigma to the child, a mark that may influence professional persons to make inappropriate choices in future treatment or training?" A terminal diagnosis is always to be avoided. Reporting is an art and can be accomplished only by qualified examiners who are competent in reporting pertinent information to appropriate referral sources and who understand the feelings of parents who must receive the information.

Reporting Results of the Assessment to Parents

Examiners often use the following techniques in reporting to parents their child's level of functioning or gains over a specified period of time.

Report to Both Parents. Parents are anxious to receive the findings of their child's assessment. Often, because of anxiety, they hear only the desirable aspects; sometimes they hear only the less desirable; and other times they leave the session in utter confusion. A mother may come alone and leave with a clear understanding of the report but be unable to find words to translate the information to her husband. It is not always possible for a parent to leave work to attend a conference, but usually special appointment hours can be made. Both parents need an explanation of their respective roles in helping their child. In most cases both fathers and mothers want to be a part of the team and do function very well with the team.

Establish Rapport. In general, parents expect that a conference will reveal the defect they hoped did not exist. With this psychological set, they are apt to hear few of the opening remarks. To help them become socially comfortable and focus on the important facts, the examiner may open with trivia. "I had a pencil a moment ago. Oh, here it is. One day my desk drawer has ten or fifteen pencils, then suddenly it seems to have only one or two. Guess I'm careless about leaving them elsewhere." Parents become better listeners if the scene is relaxed and also if they hear good things first.

I was pleased with Helen's responses. Even though she sat on your lap, she did try to do all the things I asked her to do. Her shyness didn't affect the test results. Weren't you pleased at her efforts to correct her own errors? She was a joy to assess.

Use Lay Terminology. Too often the important factors of a report are ensconced in professional language which is not meaningful to parents, for example:

The psycholinguistic battery of tests which I administered revealed behavior that is common to children diagnosed as having minimal brain damage. The assessment of her avenues of learning is not indicative of mental retardation. She demonstrated auditory perceptual problems which will interfere with learning if not corrected early in her life. Much of her current behavior is due to the minimal brain dysfunction which was reported to you by your neurologist. We will enroll her in our linguistically based program next week.

Minimal brain dysfunction, auditory perceptual problems, not retarded — is this good news? Initially the parents believe it is. Then a relative asks for an interpretation and receives a confused answer. Parents, while their children are in class, begin to discuss the terms in the waiting room or over coffee. They feel someone in the group will clarify these mysterious labels. Confusion mounts. One parent hears of another training program which is different and promises a rewarding future for the child. Inquiries are made and some children are transferred. Parents are still not satisfied. They become distraught and feel a need to do something other than what they consider is being done; so they organize a parent group. Other uninformed, confused parents with no basic understanding of their children's problems join together and begin a crusade for better medical attention and better training programs. They raise money to bring in speakers who, they hope, will provide an answer to their dilemma. Professional people either add to the confusion by failing to define the terms adequately or fraudulent lecturers propose a "new technique," and cults develop almost overnight.

Why do parent pressure groups form? There are several reasons, but in general the answer is directly related to poor communication among the parents, examiners, and teachers. When parents are satisfied with their understanding of the problem, can verbalize it to others, and are given something constructive to do about it, they do not need to join parent pressure groups designed to seek quick or sure "cures." The skilled examiner is one who can interpret for parents professional terminology into language they can understand.

Summarize the Results. Drawing a profile of a child's assets and deficits is one way of simplifying the professional jargon that often serves only to confuse parents. The names of the specific tests are labeled in functional terms across the abscissa as noted in Figure 5-1. A line representing the child's age is placed halfway down the ordinate. All assets are plotted above the age line, and all deficits appear below the line. Specific mental ages are seldom provided because parents tend to retain a number, often out of context.

Ms. Bartell, let's take a look at what is meant by all the "games" Richard and I played. I think it will be clear to you if I draw a profile of the things he does well and those things which he does not do so well. Across this line I am going to write the different abilities which I tested. These are the abilities related to Richard's future success in school. In the middle of the profile, I will draw a heavy line which will represent his age. Today he is three years and eleven months. Now we are ready to take a look at his test scores. In this first slot I will write "Understands what is said to him." As you already know and have reported to me, he probably understands only short phrases such as "Pick it up." "Go get your ____." "Where's Daddy?" So, I will place a dot far below the heavy line. Next I will write "Talking." If a child does not understand much of what is said, we do not expect him to do much talking. He does say "Bye-Bye." "No." and "Daddy car." That's a good start, but we will have to place another dot here. Now we will look at "How well does he remember what he hears?"

Figure 5-1 Language and Learning Assessment Profile as Presented to Parents

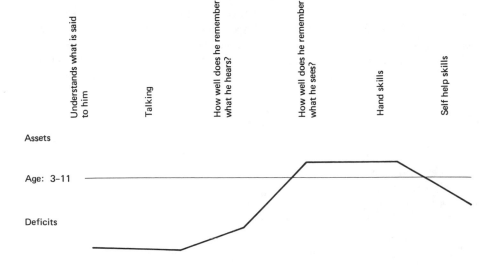

He could repeat only single words or at best a two-word phrase. Here we place another dot. In contrast to how well he remembers what he hears, we now look at "How well does he remember what he sees." On all of these test items he scored above his age level which is a plus and goes above the line. He also scored above age level on what we call *hand-eye-motor skills*. Remember how well he could copy the designs with the blocks and how well he performed on the pencil and paper tasks? This is another plus. The last item refers to *Self-Help Skills*. Richard was close to age level but certainly could be better. You said that you and your husband do much for Richard that you feel he could do for himself. Now, do you believe that this represents the levels at which your son is functioning? Do you have any questions? When he is enrolled in the language development class, he will be given tasks to do in the areas above the line that will make him feel successful. The teacher will find the lowest level at which he can perform in these deficient areas, again making him feel successful. Then she will begin to move him toward the solid line. Do you have any questions? You may have this profile to take with you. At the end of the school year we will reassess Richard and add his new profile to this one.

Not knowing the cause of a child's language and learning deficiencies, parents may assume the blame and develop feelings of guilt and remorse. When summarizing an assessment for parents, the examiner is careful not to blame them for the child's problem.

Blaming yourself, Ms. Bartell, for Richard's problem is ridiculous. He does not talk as well as other children his age, and that means he needs some help. The fact that you brought him in early for an assessment was the best thing you could have done. Let's not worry about placing the blame, let's get to the business of helping Richard. Your physician and our staff are eager to get started.

Not only does the examiner refrain from placing blame but also from making predictions.

You asked me, Ms. Bartell, if your boy would ever be ready for college. I can't answer that question any better than you could answer it for other parents. I have made too many mistakes predicting, so I have learned the hard way to observe progress as it comes along and to plan for the future in small steps. I believe you will be more comfortable if you try to think of Richard in the present, not the future.

In summary then, Mrs. Bartell, let's look at Richard this way. He is a little boy who is more like other little boys his age than he is different. He can hear and see, has arms and legs, can think, and has many more similarities. The way in which he is different is in his inability to understand what people say to him and in making people understand him. This is why you brought him to us. This, you knew. He will be enrolled in a program which is designed to develop oral language and the skills which will be needed for reading, writing, spelling, and arithmetic. In addition, you and your husband will be provided with many suggestions which will help you in a home training program.

The final summary of the total assessment should leave the parents with a clear understanding of at least the basic problem, an ability to explain the problems to others, and the promise of the best training program available.

Reporting Results of the Assessment to Others

The Admission, Review, and Dismissal Committee (ARD). Public Law 94–142 requires that the test results of all handicapped children be presented to the ARD committee of the school district to determine eligibility for admission into a special education program, for review of progress, or for dismissal if indicated. Each school district has its own format for what is to be reported and the form for reporting. In general, the information requested is related to the curriculum and presented in sufficient detail that goals and long-range objectives can be written.

The Physician. A report to a physician is based on two general procedures: the report is brief but communicates its intent, and the report invites the physician to request detailed information if desired. On occasion a child may reside in a distant community where the referring physician will be responsible for redefining and reinforcing the impressions and recommendations of the language and learning assessment. In some instances the physician may be the one who locates the appropriate training program. Under such circumstances reports must give a detailed account of quantitative and qualitative judgments which ensued from the assessment.

Special Requests. Reports for insurance companies, court trials, social workers, or family relatives are often requested. No matter from whom the request comes, the examiner must have a signed parental consent form before a report can be sent.

SUMMARY

There is always a reason for an assessment. It may be to determine how the child functions intellectually or academically as compared with a norm-referenced group. Or, the purpose may be to assess the concepts and skills a child has that relate to the curriculum. Tests may be standardized, a technique that provides a fairly valid means of determining the developmental sequencing of behaviors in a normal population, or a test may be nonstandardized, such as a teacher-made test which pre- and posttests the behaviors that the teacher has written into her objectives. The selection of tests and test items as well as the reporting of the data are currently moving toward curriculum-based tests and away from I.Q. testing. The trend is toward a close relationship between assessment and curricular content.

NORM-REFERENCED TESTS

General Ability

Bayley, N. *Bayley Scales of Infant Development.* New York: New York Psychological Corporation, 1969.

Frankenberg, W. K., J. B. Dodds, and A. W. Fandall. *Denver Developmental Screening Test* (rev. ed.). Denver, Colo.: Denver Ladoca Project and Publishing Foundation, 1970.

Hiskey, M. S. *Hiskey-Nebraska Test of Learning Aptitude.* Lincoln, Nebraska, Union College Press, 1966.

Kirk, S., J. McCarthy, and W. Kirk. *The Illinois Test of Psycholinguistic Abilities* (rev. ed.). Urbana, Ill.: University of Illinois Press, 1968.

Leiter, R. G. *Examiner's Manual for the Leiter International Performance Scale.* Chicago, Ill.: Stolting Co., 1969.

Terman, L. M. and M. A. Merrill. *Stanford-Binet Intelligence Scale.* Boston, Mass.: Houghton Mifflin, 1960.

Wechsler, D. *Manual for the Wechsler Intelligence Scale for Children.* New York: Psychological Corporation, 1974.

Wechsler, D. *Manual for the Wechsler Preschool and Primary Scale of Intelligence.* New York: Psychological Corporation, 1967.

Vocabulary Comprehension

Ammons, R. and H. Ammons. *Full Range Picture Vocabulary Test.* Missoula, Mont.: Psychological Test Specialists, 1948.

Dunn, L. *Peabody Picture Vocabulary Test.* Circle Pines, Minn.: American Guidance Service, 1959.

Dunn, L. *Expanded Manual Peabody Picture Vocabulary Test.* Circle Pines, Minn.: American Guidance Service, 1965.

Morpho-Syntax

Carrow, E. *Carrow Elicited Language Inventory.* Boston, Mass.: Teaching Resources, 1974.

Carrow, E. *Test for Auditory Comprehension of Language.* Boston, Mass.: Teaching Resources, 1973.

Foster, R., J. J. Gidden, and J. Stark. *Assessment of Children's Language Comprehension.* Palo Alto, Calif.: Consulting Psychologists Press, 1972.

Lee, L. L. *Northwestern Syntax Screening Test.* Evanston, Ill.: Northwestern University Press, 1971.

Lee, L. L. *Developmental Sentence Analysis.* Evanston, Ill.: Northwestern University Press, 1974.

Social-Personal

Doll, E. *Vineland Social Maturity Scale.* Minneapolis, Minn.: American Guidance Service, 1965.

CRITERION-REFERENCED TESTS

Bangs, T. E. *Vocabulary Comprehension Scale.* Boston, Mass.: Teaching Resources, 1975.

Bangs, T. E. *Language and Learning Assessment: For Training,* Experimental Copy. 7532 Chevy Chase, Houston, Tex. 77063, 1980.

Bangs, T. E. and S. Dodson. *Birth to Three Developmental Scale.* Boston, Mass.: Teaching Resources, 1979.

Kraner, R. E. *Preschool Math Inventory.* Boston, Mass.: Teaching Resources, 1976.

6

program
design

The first hazard in organizing a preacademic program for children with language and learning disorders is of paying insufficient attention to details. A stable program needs both a system and flexibility, a system for teaching the children and flexibility within it to provide for individual differences. Such a notion implies that instructional programmers should establish a basic educational philosophy, develop a curriculum guide, and a scheme for program organization.

EDUCATIONAL PHILOSOPHY

Educators function under a system of principles which underlie the educational guidance of their students. These principles become the educational philosophy that is essential to program development and implementation. At least three doctrines are encompassed in the instructional programming as presented in this text: (1) early identification, assessment, and training, (2) a generic approach to teaching children with language and learning deficiencies, and (3) accountability.

Early Training

The need for early training of preschool handicapped children was first recognized in the mid-1960s by the U.S. Office of Education, and, by 1968, monies were available through grants from the Bureau of Education for the Handicapped to develop model programs in the range birth through third grade. The end result of field testing these models and disseminating the information was the passing in 1975 of Public Law 94-142, the Education for All Handicapped Children Act. This legislation provides free and appropriate public school education for all handicapped children, in most instances between ages three to twenty-two (See Chapter 1). Some states have already lowered the age to birth, and it is conceivable that such will be legislated nationally. Although there has been a national commitment to early intervention, the question still is being asked, "Will early intervention in a preacademic program enhance the chances for academic success?" The early childhood specialists believe it will, and their fundamental beliefs are directed toward preschool education of the handicapped. The rationale for their beliefs, however, is more through reasoning than through factual demonstration. The reasoning is based on educated judgments of teachers who are involved in the training of preschool language- and learning-handicapped children. Gains the children make are measured through such devices as pre- and posttests, parents' diaries, and clinical observations. The children do get better. What is not known is how these children perform over long periods of time, for there is essentially little, if any, well-designed, long-range, published research to prove that early intervention with this category of children does pay off.

Hall and Tomblin (1978) conducted a follow-up study of children with normal intelligence who had either language disorders or articulation disorders. Eighteen in each group were studied with respect to communication skills and education performance thirteen to twenty years after their initial contact with a speech and hearing clinic. In the initial contact, the children were identified by specialized tests and placed in the articulation or language category. In the follow-up study, parents reported that nine language-impaired subjects continued to exhibit communication problems as adults, compared to only one of the articulation-impaired subjects. Standardized educational testing during the elementary and secondary school years indicated that the language-impaired group consistently achieved at a lower level than the articulation-impaired group, particularly in reading. This is not a surprising finding in that acquisition of oral language skills is basic to reading. No mention was made of language-intervention techniques in the preacademic or academic years. The authors stated that the extent and persistence of these difficulties into adolescence and adult life have not been well documented. DeAjuriaguerra and others (1976),

Weiner (1974) and Garvey and Gordon (1973) conducted follow-through studies, and all concluded that the child with a language problem will most likely be confronted with difficulties in academic performance. In their study Evans and Bangs (1972) reviewed the later academic achievement of a group of preschool children who had been defined as language and learning disabled, some of whom were enrolled in a preacademic program. The experimental design included subjects from the same locality and similar socioeconomic status, all with normal hearing and comparable intelligence scores. Four groups of children were selected from the total number of children assessed: (1) the normals who were predicted to have no academic problems and were not enrolled in the preacademic program; (2) the language and learning disabled children who received no preacademic training; (3) the language and learning disabled dropouts who, for one reason or another, did not stay full term in the program; and (4) the language and learning disabled graduates who stayed with the program until the age of six to seven years.

Of the three, four, and five-year-old children in the 1963-66 study 75 percent were located in 1969, and their school records were studied with relation to grade level in reading and arithmetic. (See Table 6-1.)

The disadvantages of this study are obvious: (1) small numbers of students were studied and (2) the children enrolled at ages three to four years were only seven to eight years of age when the academic data were collected, and the five- to six-year-olds were approximately ten to eleven years. Yet, the data are impressive for this short-range study.

Table 6-1 Follow-Up Study of Language and Learning-Disabled Children. Numbers and Percentages of Subjects Achieving on or Below Grade Level, by Groups.

	Reading Total		*Arithmetic Total*	
	On Or Above Grade Level	Below Grade Level	On Or Above Grade Level	Below Grade Level
Controls — Normal	9	3	8	4
N = 12	(75%)	(25%)	(67%)	(33%)
Controls — Learning Disabilities	2	9	1	10
N = 11	(18%)	(82%)	(9%)	(91%)
Experimental Dropouts	2	6	4	4
N = 8	(25%)	(75%)	(50%)	(50%)
Experimental Graduates	16	7	15	8
N = 23	(70%)	(30%)	(66%)	(34%)

*Science Research Associates Achievement Tests
(Evans and Bangs 1972)

Early intervention in training children with language and learning disorders is still in the realm of an educational philosophy. Researchers continue to design and implement longitudinal studies which eventually should reveal factual statements regarding the advisability of early pre-academic training. Until research contraindicates the need for preschool (birth to first grade) education of children with language and learning disabilities, early childhood specialists will continue to develop and implement programs for all handicapped children as soon as the deficiencies are identified.

Generic Programs

A generic approach to certifying special education teachers embraces the theory that all language- and learning-disordered children who qualify for preacademic instruction can profit from the same sequenced curriculum that includes acquisition of oral language and the basic readiness skills for reading, writing, spelling, arithmetic, and affective education.

Generic Teachers. Teachers who are knowledgeable in the scope and sequencing of normal behaviors in language and learning should, with additional techniques for training the hearing impaired and multiple handicapped, be qualified to provide instruction to children labeled normal, hearing impaired, mentally retarded, language and learning disordered, and environmentally deprived. They should also be able to instruct children with combinations of these handicapping conditions and those who have visual impairment. This philosophy has been studied only recently from the viewpoint of the differences, if any, in the way handicapped children develop language and learning skills. Investigators Moorhead and Ingram (1973), Leonard and others (1976), Lackner (1976), Ryan (1975) concluded from their research that the differences among these categories of children relate primarily to the lateness of onset of language development and the slower rate of development. Some investigators also noted that during the language acquisition period certain sentence types were used more or less frequently by the various groups, but the sentences were not necessarily bizarre. If these data are valid, then teacher-training programs should decrease emphasis on the handicapping conditions and increase emphasis on the preacademic and academic needs of the children.

It is interesting to note that in a report of a Delphi Survey (Reynolds 1973), which involved approximately 1,100 professional persons in different areas of education from all parts of the nation, respondents predicted there would be a decline over the following decade in the number of different kinds of special education certificates offered by state Departments of Education. When analyses were made of predictions from such subgroups as college faculty in special education, the results showed that there would be only three or four certificates by 1983, and these would probably include special certificates in the areas of deaf education, education of the blind, and speech correction, with a general certificate for other special education areas. There has been much discussion following the Delphi Survey regarding the current narrow preparation of special education teachers as well as the need to issue certificates to persons who are prepared to teach a wide range of handicapped children. Noncategorical certificates in special education should be provided to those personnel who develop generic competencies to perform effectively with children who have various handicapping conditions, and categorical certificates should go to those persons who develop highly specialized competencies to work with some exceptional children. These exceptional children may include the trainable retarded and the trainable multiple handicapped, both groups falling short of ever reaching the preacademic level of learning. Irrespective of the handicapping condition, children who are potential language learners will develop concepts through environment experiences, and, according to their potential, they will make use of cognitive skills to develop the vocabulary, grammar, and use of the language they will speak and read.

Generic Curriculums. The labeling of children — deaf, perceptually handicapped, cerebral palsied, mentally retarded, brain damaged — is a common practice. Various curriculum guides have been developed to meet the needs of children in these specific groups. Publications abound with such titles as *Arithmetic for the Deaf, Speech for the Deaf, Language for the Deaf, Basic Mathematics for the Retarded Child, Readiness and Reading for the Retarded Child,* and *Teaching the Retarded Child to Talk.*

The implication? That the education of one category of children with handicaps is quite different from the training of youngsters in some other category. This is false reasoning. The goal for all children is to have them reach full potential so that they may function as contributing members of society. The education of the educable retarded or hearing-impaired child is not significantly different from the education of any other child, although the quality and quantity of what is learned will vary within and among categories.

The great need is for one basic preacademic curriculum guide designed to assist the teachers in their efforts to help each child reach his or her potential in the areas of oral language, reading, writing, arithmetic, and affective education. The birth to first grade skills required to meet these academic goals become the core of the preacademic curriculum guide for all preschool language- and learning-disabled children regardless of their handicapping conditions.

Accountability

Accountability in education is a systematic approach for determining a learner's needs and the effectiveness of the teaching program. Accountability in education is just recently making inroads and has been long overdue. Children have remained in remedial reading programs year after year with no clear-cut measurement of their progress. Others have been promoted from one grade level to the other without an in-depth evaluation of their skills. With the advent of Public Law 94-142, more stringent rules have been placed on the educational process, namely the writing of performance (behavioral) objectives (see Chapter 5). With regard to accountability, Bangs (1979) believes

> it is not enough to state that a newly developed technique "appears" to be worthwhile. It must bear some measure of proof that it is accomplishing what it purports to accomplish. Educators, therefore, are not being accountable for their teaching programs if they select untested techniques and utilize them without measuring their effectiveness in terms of the child's achievement of program objectives. Furthermore, accountable programs cannot tolerate such value judgments as, "The children in the class are doing better." The children are doing better than who? Better in which skills and by what measuring tool? Joe is not talking very well. Is his speech intelligible? Is his vocabulary on age level? What grammatical structures are missing? Is his language acquisition level commensurate with his mental age, and by what measuring tool? Value judgments are risky in an educational program that aims for accountability for what teachers teach and students learn. (p. 145)

Accountability as well as early intervention and generic programs comprise a set of at least three philosophical principles under which educators practice their profession.

CURRICULUM GUIDE

A curriculum guide is a master plan that includes the content of what is to be taught and in what sequence. It states the objectives to be met at predetermined levels and the orderly progression from where the children are to where they are going. The goal of the curriculum guide is to exert some kind of control on the environmental factors in order to keep children moving according to their rate and style of learning. The ultimate responsibility for effectively implementing the curriculum guide is given to the teachers who use their training, experience, and creativity to motivate children to learn. With a curriculum guide teachers can determine the appropriate educational placement of children and can organize and implement the instruction. The curriculum guide also provides a master plan for a systematic approach to orienting new teachers. Different curriculum guides use different models for meeting the preacademic or academic needs of children with language and learning disorders. The three models discussed most frequently in the literature are the linguistic model, the perceptual-motor model, and the specific disabilities model. The linguistic model, which forms the structure for the curriculum guide in this text, concentrates on teaching language through its content, form, and use. The perceptual-motor model attempts to improve cognitive skills through a variety of gross and fine motor activities. The specific disabilities model trains specific elements of cognitive abilities.

Perceptual-Motor Model

The perceptual-motor program, which has to do with improving cognitive skills (Ayers 1975; Barsch 1967; Cruickshank and others 1961; and Kephart 1960), is not clearly understood, and there is wide disagreement as to its relationship to the acquisition of oral language and academic subjects. Von Haden and King (1974) define perceptual-motor learning as "the process of developing improved efficiency in body movement through a carefully organized program of learning activities. It is based upon the principle that people develop their native potential through many experiences, one of which is perceptual-motor learning. There are those who believe that body control, body image, self-concept, social adjustment, academic learning, emotional stability, and general personality can be improved through perceptual motor training" (p. 288).

The instructional program is designed to enhance body image, awareness of time, spatial judgment, and movement control. Laterality, reaction time, balance, manual dexterity, locomotion, agility, visual fixation, and auditory skills are among the functions included in the program. The learning activities include crawling, walking lines or balance beams, metronomic pacing, relaxation exercises, hopping into squares or circles, drawing, and writing. The work is done in classrooms, gymnasiums, and clinics. How significant this program is in relation to academic achievement has not been determined. No one would deny that improving the motor skills of any child provides more opportunities to participate in gross motor games and increases feelings of self-worth and the sense of a good self-concept; but the author was unable to find any research in the literature to prove that perceptual-motor training significantly improves language, academic, or cognitive skills. However, motor activities do serve as motivational activities to teach oral and written preacademic skills.

Specific Disabilities Model

The specific disabilities approach has been popularized by the Illinois Test of Psycholinguistic Abilities (ITPA) through the work of Kirk and others (1968) who stated that the objective of the ITPA is to "delineate specific abilities and disabilities in children in order that remediation may be undertaken when needed" (p. 5). Specific disability training is based on the assumption that training the specific elements of cognitive abilities — sound blending, phoneme synthesizing, auditory memory for sequential information, grammatical closure, and auditory discrimination — will improve a child's language skills. Hammill and Larsen (1974) reviewed the results of thirty-eight studies that trained children in these skill areas using the ITPA as the criterion of improvement. They concluded that the effectiveness of such training has not been conclusively demonstrated and that the increased use of specific disability training programs seems unwarranted. Bortner (1971) in a study related to learning disabilities concluded that there is no body of evidence to support the current practice of remediation of specific abilities. Bloom and Lahey (1978, p. 547) state,

> We are not aware of any studies that have found improvement in general language development after the remediation of specific abilities - perhaps because few have looked for such transfer of improvement in language use. Without evidence that such abilities are necessary for the development and use of oral language, it is questionable that the remediation of specific abilities should dominate a remedial program for children who are learning language slowly and with difficulty.

Continued research with perceptual-motor and specific disabilities models perhaps is warranted, but until there is evidence that they are valid approaches, Bangs and Mauzy (see Chapters 7 and 8 on instructional programming) are more comfortable with the linguistic model which teaches the content, form, and use of language and their application to the preacademic subjects.

Linguistic Model

The linguistic model, which by its title is a language-based program, includes three elements that are incorporated into the curriculum: (1) instructional content areas, which include acquisition of oral and written language on a preacademic level, (2) sequenced forms of behavior that are used for writing performance objectives, and (3) teaching instructional content areas as interrelated units.

Although the cognitive areas discussed in Chapter 4 are basic to language learning, they are not used as objectives in the child's educational plan. Current studies reported in the literature (see Chapter 4) give no research data to prove that teaching geared to a cognitive skill will alter neuro-anatomical-physiological structures hence making them more functional. However, the teacher, through assessment data, is apprised of the specific cognitive abilities and disabilities of each child. From these data she develops teaching strategies that will eliminate the environmental causes of the deficits, or she will find ways to circumvent the deficits. For example, the children are not drilled in such an activity as repetition of digits with the objective of being able to repeat longer strings of digits, for there is no evidence that this activity generalizes to other memory tasks. On the contrary, the teacher finds appropriate motivational techniques to hold the child's attention in order that his or her memory skills are used to full potential. In addition, mnemonic devices which will help children remember may be taught, or the teacher can provide information in small bits so that it can be remembered. These are teaching strategies that help children utilize their cognitive skills in language learning.

Instructional Content. In the society in which we live, great emphasis is placed upon academic achievement, as evidence by compulsory education laws. We want our children to graduate with a high school diploma or to receive vocational training that allows them to become partially or fully self-supporting citizens. What is the basis for academic achievement? It is the ability to speak adult language, read, write, spell, perform in mathematics, and obtain information about the past, present, or future. Recently there has been the introduction of affective education into the curriculum, which adds the dimension of helping children develop appropriate self-concepts and interpersonal relationships. The content of elementary and secondary school curriculum guides embraces these academic features. Patterned after the *academic* curriculum, the *preacademic* curriculum includes the acquisition of child language to its adult form as well as readiness skills needed for reading, arithmetic, writing, spelling, and affective education. The long-range educational objectives for these basic skill areas are written into the curriculum guide.

Developmentally Sequenced Behaviors. Teaching content and form in a linguistically modeled program are based on developmental theory and developmental data that have been obtained from normal populations. Although there is variation among children who develop normally, there is also regularity in the increased number of children who acquire the skills and concepts over time. Bangs (1975) recorded the percentage of children who comprehended the meaning of certain words at each six month age level between two and six years of age. The data clearly represent variation among the children yet a fairly consistent regularity of percentage increase over time. (See Table 6–2.)

Teachers select their objectives from checklists (see Appendix 1, Developmental Behaviors) and move the children from their current level of functioning to the next developmental level. For children with language or learning deficiencies, the steps between these levels may have to be reduced and a greater variety of experiences and a greater number of repetitions introduced than would be needed for normally

Table 6-2 Developmental Acquisition of Some Relational Words.

	Percent Correct							
	Age Levels							
	2.0–2.5	2.6–2.11	3.0–3.5	3.6–3.11	4.0–4.5	4.6–4.11	5.0–5.5	5.6–5.11
Quality Words								
Hard	30	60	90	90	100	100	100	100
Soft	30	80	80	90	100	100	100	100
Heavy	30	90	80	90	100	100	100	100
Light	20	70	70	80	100	80	100	90
Position Words								
Top	20	70	80	100	100	100	100	100
Bottom	20	30	50	70	80	80	90	100
in front of	0	40	30	90	90	100	100	100
in back of	0	0	30	80	90	80	90	100
behind	0	20	10	40	60	70	80	80
Quantity Words								
full	30	40	50	100	100	100	100	100
empty	50	70	90	100	100	100	100	100
all	60	80	90	100	100	100	100	100
each	30	40	50	60	80	80	90	80
Size Words								
big	40	100	80	100	90	100	100	100
little	30	80	70	90	90	90	100	100
fat	20	70	60	70	90	100	100	100
thin	20	60	50	60	60	90	100	90

(Bangs, 1975.)

achieving children. Although information related to the sequencing of language and learning behaviors is still in its formative stage, the teacher currently has much research information that will assist in gathering and using developmental data.

Interrelatedness of Content Areas. Oral language and the skills for learning to read, write, and perform arithmetic computations are highly interrelated. Oral language includes vocabulary and the morphosyntactic rules to generate sentences. By the same token, reading, arithmetic, and social and personal skills are dependent upon vocabulary and morphosyntactic rules. The preacademic curriculum guide (see Chapter 9), therefore, is not divided into the reading-readiness curriculum, the language curriculum, or the premathematics curriculum. Rather, the teacher recognizes the overlapping of the instructional content areas and is aware that what happens at any point in the development of one content area is important in influencing the development in another content area. Utilizing this concept, the curriculum guide in this text is based on a *unit* approach to teaching preacademic skills to children.

The *unit* is a designated activity, such as food, transportation, or clothing, which provides real life experiences to assist in developing the content of language or the knowledge children have about the environments in which they live. This knowledge gives them something to talk about which is coded into linguistic form. Within each unit the teacher selects projects, such as art, cooking, or games (see Chapter 8), which supply content and form interractions in a variety of contexts. Furthermore, the projects provide an opportunity for manipulation of objects to discover relationships, practice in developing hand-eye-motor skills and developing feelings of self-worth as well as appropriate interpersonal relationships. The unit approach allows for the instructional content areas to overlap and develop naturally. For example, in the following cooking project from the food unit, class words, relational words, inflectional words, and sentence structure are taught as are the skills needed for reading, arithmetic, and writing competence. This activity also allows for the instructional content areas to overlap and develop in a natural setting.

Roasting peanuts, a two-hour activity which is part of the cooking unit, includes oral language development (content, form, and use) that relates to the basic subjects of reading, arithmetic, and writing. Substantive and relational words are taught, such as *roast*, the noun, and *roast*, the verb, *shell*, *skins*, *unsalted*, and the attributes of the pan that will be used for roasting the peanuts, *square*, *shiny*, *silver*. Morphosyntactic structures and use of language are incorporated into the activity when the children play teacher and ask questions or relate a sequence of events. Reading is introduced when the number of peanuts used in the word problems are written on the board and the children read the numbers. Reading also occurs when the sequence story is written and the children read it. Writing skills are practiced when the children write the numbers on the chalkboard. Arithmetic training is included also. The children watch the clock until the numbers match the teaching clock set for ten o'clock, which is the time to take the peanuts out of the oven. Then they take the correct number of peanuts from the pan and put them into a basket to work a word problem, "I will give Joe two peanuts and Helen three peanuts. How many do they have? Prove it." Social and personal skills are practiced when the children are reminded to take turns and not to interrupt someone who is speaking.

Developing a curriculum guide to meet the needs of the children is the first step in developing an intervention program.

TEACHING STRATEGIES

In general, preschool children learn to talk without an intervention program, and they develop the preacademic skills necessary for entrance into first grade. There are children, however, who for one reason or another do not achieve these skills. For these children, curriculum guides have been developed as well as teaching strategies that will assist them in learning what it is we want them to learn. Most, if not all, of these strategies are used with children who have no difficulty learning to talk, but perhaps these techniques can be applied in a more forceful or repetitious, yet judicious, manner for children who need special programs to meet their language and learning needs. It may be that by carefully integrating a variety of teaching strategies, language- and learning-handicapped children will be helped in the acquisition of oral language and preacademic skills. What kind of interactive behavior should take place between teacher and children? As of mid-1980 there is no research to demonstrate that one strategy is more powerful than all the others; it is probably the teacher's background of experiences and educational guesses that will help in the selection of the most appropriate teaching strategies to meet the language and learning needs of handicapped children. These strategies are discussed under the topics of procuring and maintaining attention, eliciting verbal responses from the children, and creative teaching.

Procuring and Maintaining Attention

Children are selective about what they attend to because of the many factors in their environment that may inhibit or enhance their ability to pay attention. Without appropriate attending skills, children will neither store information nor induce language rules. They will not learn what it is we want them to learn. What, then, are the factors that help to procure and maintain a child's attention?

Physical Health. It is apparent that children who suffer from poor nutrition, are tired, have low grade infection, or any other physical ailments will not be attentive to the task at hand. Physical health is, therefore, a prime asset to learning.

Audition and Vision. Hearing and vision are basic ingredients to the acquisition of oral and written language. They must therefore be constantly monitored by the teacher, who may be the first to suspect that a child is impaired in one or both sensory modalities. For the child who has a fluctuating hearing loss, the teacher should select appropriate seating arrangements and make certain that the child is comprehending what is being said in the classroom. By the same token, the teacher should accommodate for any visual defects the child may have, for example, distant vision, near vision, peripheral vision.

Arousal Techniques. The teacher may set certain ground rules to secure the children's attention. When she says, "Boys and girls," for example, all children stop what they are doing, look at her, and attend to what is coming next; or a time clock may be set to attract the attention of the children, and when the bell rings, a new activity is to begin.

Altering Prosodic Features of Teacher's Voice. Prosody includes variation in stress, inflection, pause, and duration during the speaking act. The effectiveness of variations in prosody as an aid to procuring and maintaining attention is not a new tool for teachers. They know that children attend better to a person reading a story if there is variation in loudness, length of pauses, and inflectional change of voice. Raising one's voice to a greater loudness level is sure to command attention.

Materials. Attention is likely to be directed toward the task at hand if the materials interest the children. There is no problem today in locating toys, games, books, and special educational materials from school supply stores. What is important is that these materials be used to teach children new concepts, increase vocabulary, develop language structure as well as hand-eye-motor skills and not just to entertain them.

Activities. The activities that best serve to develop the concepts that make up the content of language come from everyday experiences. The curriculum guide in this text makes use of this plan by teaching from units to be scheduled throughout the year; a unit on the home, or clothing, or farm animals. Changing units from time to time allows for vocabulary development, variations in the room decor, special field trips, and a general increase in information about the world in which the child lives. Because young children like routine, teachers should schedule certain classroom projects to occur at approximately the same time and in the same sequence from day to day (see Chapter 9).

More Successes than Failures. If children are to maintain interest in what is to be learned, they should be given more successes than failures during a school day. Specific plans to generate feelings of success may be accomplished in the following ways.

Teachers often use the sandwich method, which intersperses a failure between two successes. Billy, who can select two objects from a set of five but cannot select three is asked to select two, then three (a failure), then two (a success).

If a child has not learned to hop on one foot, he should not be forced to demonstrate his failure every day. He can jump on two feet and hop on one with the help of the teacher.

Some children's manuscript and cursive writing deteriorates as they move across a page. The insightful teacher will cut the paper in half and give credit for half a page well done. With time and practice, the width of the paper should be increased.

Allowing children justifiable work time may motivate them to complete an otherwise unsuccessful assignment. Children cannot work at the same rate in a classroom any more than unselected groups of children can finish a race in the same length of time.

The teacher who presents tiny steps each day toward a distant goal will find the students maintaining interest. Giant steps are meant for a limited number of children, and those left behind soon pall because they cannot succeed when bits are omitted.

Communicating on the Child's Level. Communicating on the child's level is another way to maintain interest. Just as an adult soon loses interest in listening to a conversation in a foreign language, so do children shift their thoughts to other than the task at hand if they are not comprehending what is being said. When the teacher asks, "Did you bring the note from mother?" and the child does not respond, the teacher asks, "Did you bring the piece of paper from mother?" The vocabulary the teacher uses as well as the sentence types must be in the child's language repertoire. Closely allied to this aspect of communication is the Piaget concept that children will not learn a task if the experiences presented demand thought processes that are more advanced than their current level of functioning.

Eliciting Verbal Responses from Children

Through verbal responses children practice language form, discover their errors, and often self-correct; they provide teachers with language samples for evaluative purposes; and, of course, they learn how to use language by communicating with others. How do we get children to talk? Teachers use a variety of verbal interactive behaviors to elicit speech from children, and no one technique has been demonstrated to be more successful than others for all children. Each, no doubt, has its appropriate place in the teaching-learning environment. The following techniques have been described frequently in the literature.

Imitation. Through imitation children learn to count by rote. They listen to the phonograph recording of "One little, two little, three little Indians . . ." and imitate what they hear. In like manner, they hear the "Alphabet Song" and imitate the sequencing of letters to learn their A B C's. Teachers find that some children will respond better by choral singing or speaking than by making a response on their own. Children may first have to be encouraged to talk by responding with the group.

Slot Fillers. With this technique the teacher gives all but one word, and the child must fill the blank, for example: "Your name is _____ ", "Brother is a boy and sister is a _____ "; or, in a phonics lesson, "A word that starts like fish is _____ ." In the teacher's repertoire of teaching strategies, slot fillers provide a change of pace.

Questions. Questions are used to test the child's memory of what has been learned. After reading the story of Peter Rabbit, the teacher may use *Wh* questions to check retention of information as well as comprehension of the various question forms. "*What* were the names of the rabbits? *Where* did they go? *When* did they go? *Why* did Peter

Rabbit go into Mr. McGregor's garden patch? *Who* didn't feel well? *Why*?" To avoid *yes* and *no* answers, teachers remember to structure their questions to obtain answers in phrases or sentences. Instead of "Do you like eggs for breakfast?" the teacher requests, "Tell me all of the things you did before coming to school."

Repetition. Repetition of the stimulus in a variety of contexts is a basic tenet of learning to generalize. Language learning is facilitated by increasing the number of exposures to what a child is expected to learn. To teach one-to-one correspondence, the teacher has her children count the number of sheets of paper needed to accommodate each child. The same routine is repeated for the number of cups needed for juice and the number of children to be drinking the juice. Another teacher selects three or more pictures which in sequence tell a story. John develops one oral sentence for each picture and then retells the story. Mary tells it a little differently. Children who have difficulty generating sentences or finding words are chosen last. They will have listened to a variety of words and statements from which to choose.

Ample Time to Respond. Not all children are quick to provide an answer or make a statement. For those who need more time the teacher may say, "Susan wants to think about her answer. Let's wait until she is ready." If no response is given, prompting may be used.

Spontaneity. Taking advantage of a planned or natural disaster in the classroom may elicit responses from children who are not prone to speaking. The teacher quickly asks, "What happened? Tell me about it."

Asking for the Impossible. A more devious way to elicit responses is to ask a child to color her picture but not to provide a crayon. Ask another child to pour the juice into the glasses when no juice is in the pitcher. Another child could be asked to draw a picture and then cut it out, but no scissors have been provided. Such situations may prompt a child to speak.

Sustained Discourse. In general, preschool children do not initiate and sustain a dialogue. There are techniques, however, that will help them generate connected discourse that will later be used in conversation. Because sustained discourse is difficult to measure, it is not advisable to use this skill as an objective. It is of importance to note that children speak more fluently with their peer groups or with younger children than they do with adults. With this in mind the teacher may say, "Kelly, tell your friends how you get dressed in the morning" or may send a child to the window and ask her to tell her friends what she sees.

Creative Teaching

Teachers vary in their creative abilities, but each demonstrates originality in the way activities are conducted, materials are used, or individual needs of children are met.

Varying the Objective of a Favorite Activity. Some activities are so well liked by the children that they are used often, but the procedures could be changed to meet a variety of objectives. Musical chairs is one of the favorite activities, and the creative teacher uses it to teach the relational words *first–last*, that is, the *first* person out and the *last* person out. In an attending activity children could keep walking while the tape recorder plays the sounds of noisemakers and sit only when they hear the sound of the sleighbells. Similarly, children may be told to keep walking as the teacher calls out a list of words and to sit only when they hear a word that begins like *fish*.

Utilizing the Teacher's Talents. Teachers vary in their special talents. Some sing well, some are creative with arts and crafts, and others have no special artistic talents. One teacher may employ singing effectively to teach certain language skills, and another may use her talents in art to accomplish the same objectives. Those teachers with no special talents probably use a greater variety of approaches in helping children meet the objectives.

Providing Feedback. Expansion, modeling, and prompting as feedback techniques have been used by teachers and parents to assist children in their discovery of the content, form, and use of language. How children absorb and utilize this feedback has not been well researched, and it is not clear whether one or the other should be used exclusively. In spite of the lack of data to prove or disprove the techniques of expansion, modeling, and promoting, teachers may be creative in their use of one or more of these methods.

The expansion technique is exemplified by the following. If the child utters a telegraphic statement, "Daddy bye car," his or her mother, using an expansion technique, will reply, "Daddy is going bye-bye in the car." The underlying principle is for the child to discover how the two statements are related and, with repeated listening experiences, to produce the correct form. The modeling technique is somewhat different. Dan, whose expressive language consists of single- and two-word utterances, brings a ball to school for Show and Tell. The teacher says, "Tell me about your ball, Dan" to which he replies, "Dan ball." She responds with, "A ball. A big ball. Dan brought a big ball." The modeling technique comments on what was said instead of on trying to improve the child's statement, as in the expansion examples. An expansion reply to the child who said "Daddy bye car" could be "Yes, Daddy is going to go to his office." The response to Dan's two-word utterance, "Dan ball," might be, "You can kick a ball. You can throw a ball. You can bounce a ball. You don't eat a ball." Prompting begins with a question, "Where is Daddy?" If the child does not answer, the mother might say, "Daddy is where?" The prompting question might be "Are these the same?" and when the child does not answer, the teacher could say "Are these the same size?" To the question, "How are a dog and a cow alike?" the prompting may be, "A dog and a cow both _____." The effectiveness of the expansion, modeling, and prompting strategies may vary with the level of language acquisition as well as with style of learning.

Utilizing Teaching Materials on a Limited Budget. If a substantial budget is available, teacher A may purchase a name stamp at the local print store for each child to use during the school year. With a limited budget, teacher B uses the school duplicating equipment to make several copies of the children's names typed on standard-sized typing paper. These names are cut into rectangles, and each child has an envelope that contains enough personalized rectangles to be used throughout the school year. Instead of stamping her name, Mary will take one of her name papers from her envelope and paste it on her seat work papers. Teacher C, who has no money available, asks each parent to print or type several pages of his or her child's name to be cut and kept in an envelope until needed.

Recognizing Individual Developmental Levels. The children do not always have the same motor skills, but they may be equal in their prereading skills. The teacher presents a card with the letters A, K, R and asks the children to copy the letters. Bill who has superior writing skills copies the letters. Irene who is less adept in writing skills is provided a template from which she chooses the correct letters and writes them. Jimmy with poor hand-eye-motor skills is given a group of letter cards and asked to choose the correct letters, which are pasted on his paper.

Tape Recordings. The creative teacher uses the tape recorder in numerous ways. A tape can be made of the teacher's reading a story from a book that each child has. When a page is to be turned, there is a sound of a noise maker on the tape. Each child should then turn the page. The teacher may chart the names of the children who attended the most times. Periodically, a teacher tape records the children during a Show and Tell activity. Improvement in communication skills over time can be noted and select sections may be played for parents during an individual conference or for the supervisor or principal of the school.

Experienced teachers often can determine empirically which teaching strategy is best for individual children or groups of children. It is this judgment that earns a teacher the respect of parents and colleagues as an outstanding teacher.

PROGRAM ORGANIZATION

Implementing a preacademic program for language- and learning-disability children includes personnel utilization, appropriate class placement for the children, a room with functional space and furnishings, and parent involvement.

Personnel Utilization

Certified teachers may perform a variety of educational services including teaching in a self-contained classroom, instruction in a resource room, and team teaching. No matter what, where, and how they teach, they are fortunate if they have access to support personnel.

Teachers. The certified teacher is viewed as the planner who sets the goals, formulates the objectives, prepares and executes the lesson plans with a balance between the teacher's direction and the child's initiation. In this respect, teachers are responsible for measuring the effects of their teaching program — did the children learn what the teacher purported for them to learn and are the evaluative data available? Teachers are effective in their job assignments if they meet the time worn standards of appropriate teacher training, personal integrity, patience, dedication, and acceptable personality traits. Studies related to desirable and undesirable personality traits of teachers have not been very productive. However, there is general agreement that it is easier to change or improve the teaching skills of teachers and to train them to use appropriate techniques than it is to change undesirable personality traits of teachers.

Support Personnel. Preacademic programs for language- and learning-handicapped children base their success in large part on the diagnostic expertise of a variety of professionals who identify the problem areas of each child. Many of these experts are also available to serve as support personnel to the classroom teacher who is responsible for the preacademic achievement of the children. Speech-language pathologists, counselors, physical therapists, rehabilitative audiologists, and teacher aides may play important roles in the total programming of each child.

The speech-language pathologist, in a narrow definition, is the professional who serves as a resource person in the treatment of disorders of articulation, voice, and fluency (stuttering). The treatment may be accomplished in a resource room, but, certainly, what is taught in individual or group therapy must be translated to the classroom teacher who is advised as to those procedures to use to enhance the results of the therapy. In a broad sense, the speech-language pathologist is also a specialist expert in the field of acquisition of child language to its adult form and expert on how language on a preacademic level relates to reading, writing, arithmetic, and affective education. Speech-language pathologists may work with individuals or groups of children or serve as consultants to the classroom teacher.

The kindergarten teacher of nonhandicapped children was concerned because one of her students was unable to comprehend any of the reading-readiness tasks as presented in the reading series used in her school. The teacher submitted a request for William to be seen by a team of experts in areas including psychology, medicine, and social service. Instead, the speech-language pathologist was asked to consult with the teacher. An analysis of the reading series revealed that the structure of sentences used to give children directions was not in William's language repertoire. He was not learning phonics and other reading skills because he did not understand the directions. The specialist was able to translate the directions into a simplified language form which enabled William to catch up and keep up with his peers.

Counselors may be psychologists or social workers who are trained to meet the affective needs of the children. These specialists may work with groups of children, as described in the Magic Circle Program (Bessell and Ball 1972) or may help the teacher design individual or group programs for modifying unwanted behaviors (see Appendix 6, Behavior Modification Program for a Kindergarten Class).

The physical therapist is one of the new specialists on the educational team, added in compliance with Public Law 94-142 Education for All Handicapped Children Act. This professional's job description includes improving motor functions and preventing deformities. The treatment may be conducted outside of the classroom, but, certainly, the teacher is advised as to how physical therapy principles and techniques may be integrated into classroom activities.

The rehabilitative audiologist is another newcomer to the team, again as a result of Public Law 94-142. This person is knowledgeable about the selection, use, and maintenance of hearing aids, the methods of teaching auditory training and speech reading skills, and the optimum listening environments for hearing-impaired children. Many rehabilitative audiologists are trained to work in oral, aural, manual, and total communication programs (oral plus signs). The rehabilitative audiologist works closely with the classroom teacher and provides support services when indicated.

Teacher aides are either volunteers or paid employees of the school who perform many nonprofessional duties. Standards and the lines of demarcation between instructional and noninstructional tasks, however, are not always clearly defined. State Departments of Education have attempted to classify aides according to their training and their years of experience as aides, and they are classified according to pay grades. The important issues, however, include the job description and who is qualified to fulfill it. The advantages of having a teacher aide in a classroom are apparent. The teacher is freed from many of the noninstructional tasks, such as making materials, housekeeping chores, and paper work. Furthermore, with appropriate guidance from the teacher, the aide may take over some of the individual or group instruction, while the teacher is engaged in activities that require more in-depth training than an aide may have. Four advantages of incorporating aides into school programs are: (1) teachers have more time to meet individual needs of students, (2) more and better instructional materials may be produced, (3) more children may be served in a classroom, and (4) better control of behavior problems may result. The disadvantages of employing teacher aides are related to parents who are concerned about having their children under the tutelage of a noncertified person and the lack of guidelines in many school districts specifying what an aide may and may not do. Appropriately utilized, aides are a definite asset to the teacher.

Class Placement

For a preacademic program designed for children in the developmental range of three years to first grade, three suggestions for class placement will be discussed: (1) self-contained classroom, (2) resource room, and (3) mainstreaming.

Self-Contained Classroom. A self-contained classroom for children with language and learning deficiencies is managed by one teacher who develops the objectives for each child, teaches, and pre- and posttests to determine if the objectives have been met. The advantage of a self-contained classroom over team teaching, which involves instruction from several specialized teachers, lies in the opportunity to teach more than one, if not all, basic skills in a single activity, such as a cooking project, a field trip, or a Halloween party. The curriculum guide in this text makes use of the concept of a self-contained classroom where the teacher is in control of the curriculum, the learning, and progress of the children. The size of the group and its composition according to individual needs may be different from school to school. However, the principle of grouping children according to their developmental ages in their language and learning skills and to their chronological ages seems logical. The number of children to be included in a class should be made on the basis of their needs and their ability to conform to the group. Only five may be enrolled in a class if the children are extremely hyperactive or destructive. On the other hand, a group of ten four-year-olds may be ideal if all are manageable. Fifteen hearing-impaired children who have had previous training may constitute a group, if the primary goal is to prepare them for a regular first grade classroom where the numbers often exceed twenty. The ability to learn in a group of fifteen classmates is very different from that in a class of only four to six peers. There is no magic in numbers, just logic.

Resource Room. Specialists who serve handicapped children, such as the speech-language pathologist, counselor, physical therapist, and rehabilitative audiologist, may be called upon to provide either individualized or group instruction in the resource room outside of the self-contained classroom. Here the children receive in-depth instruction in areas that cannot be met in the classroom. The key to resource teaching is, of course, generalizing what is learned in the resource room to the self-contained classroom and the home environment. A modified version of the resource room is learning stations within the self-contained classroom where children work with the teacher aide or with the teacher on specialized instruction which will meet individual needs. Such a program is presented in Chapter 9.

Mainstreaming. Public Law 94-142 legislates appropriate education for handicapped children in the least restrictive environment. An interpretation of this mandate can mean that, whenever possible, handicapped children should be *mainstreamed,* the term used to describe the integration of handicapped children into regular classrooms for as much of the day as is profitable. There are problems with the concept of mainstreaming. The definition of profitable has not been clarified, and little is known about the effects of mainstreaming on preschool handicapped children. Few preschool children who are provided free and appropriate education through Public Law 94-142 have an opportunity to be mainstreamed in a public school setting with nonhandicapped children, for such classes do not exist in most instances until the kindergarten level. For this reason, parents are often urged to enroll their language- and learning-disability children in nursery school programs with nonhandicapped youngsters, as a supplement to the special education classes in the public schools. Two distinct advantages of mainstreaming are: (1) the handicapped child perceives the everyday behavior of nonhandicapped children and is exposed early on to the kinds of coping skills that will have to be developed to succeed in mainstream education, and (2) nonhandicapped children will develop an understanding of handicapped children and how best to relate to and communicate with them. It is, in essence, a two-way street and should be encouraged in the early preschool and elementary years.

In one school district the statement was made that the highest percentage of emotionally disturbed children in secondary education was the group of hearing impaired. Traditionally these deaf children had been taught in self-contained classrooms with little opportunity to mingle with their normal hearing peer group. The acceptable coping skills that the hearing-impaired children utilized within their own group as compared with their lack of appropriate coping skills in a normal

hearing peer group were apparent. Neither set of children had been prepared for the other, and it was not surprising to find many hearing-
impaired children who could not handle the emotional problems
brought on, perhaps, by late mainstreaming.

Not all of the problems of mainstreaming relate to just the children. Parents and teachers often voice the following complaints:

> We as regular classroom teachers are not trained to work
> with handicapped children and do not know how to integrate
> them with the other children.

> Teachers are already overworked and cannot take on an
> additional burden.

> The handicapped children cannot keep up with the "normal"
> group.

> The addition of handicapped children will disrupt my class
> and also lower the level of achievement.

> Deaf children often require an oral or manual interpreter,
> which is costly.

> Parents of the nonhandicapped children will object. They will
> be heard to say, "I don't want my child to talk like that" or "I
> don't want my child to use the infantile behavior of the retarded."

As with other areas of education, there is a critical need for long-
range follow-up studies of the mainstreaming process to determine the
educational advantages as well as the affective advantages of children
with handicapping conditions.

Physical Attributes of the Room

Classrooms often reflect instruction procedures. Most teachers
prefer an interesting environment to a sterile environment. All make use
of functional teaching materials, but they may differ in their choice of
seating arrangements.

Average vs. Sterile Environment. The average classroom has bulletin boards on the walls and perhaps an uncompleted mural which the
children are painting. There are instructional materials, flowers, and
items for Show and Tell. The not-so-average classroom is either over-
crowded with materials, giving a cluttered appearance, or is a sterile
environment. Knowing that hyperactive, distractible children have
difficulty learning in regular classrooms has led to the notion that the
amount of stimuli in a room is directly related to the child's ability to
learn. Cruickshank and others (1961) and Strauss and Lehtinen (1947)
are proponents of small classrooms with reduced background stimuli,
plain walls in a neutral color and cubicles to be used by the children
who are extremely distractible. They contend that this environment

allows for the highlighting of what the children are to learn. To place preschool children in such an environment, however, would limit their opportunity to see relationships that can be represented on bulletin boards or murals and would limit the teacher's ability to use visible materials to show specific examples in teaching a concept or linguistic form. True, there may be a need for highly structured and sterile environments for some children, if it can be demonstrated that they learn best in such an environment. There are no valid studies in the literature that specify who these children are or that they do learn better in the restricted environment.

Desks, Tables, or Cubicles. The manner in which children are seated in a classroom is dependent upon many factors: age of the students, size of the room, behavior of the children, physical problems, and, most of all, the teacher's judgment of what is best. One teacher may choose to have tables which measure approximately 8' × 2½' arranged in an L shape. Others may arrange the tables in a U shape or distribute them to various areas of the room. Another teacher may find that individual desks with separate chairs are a more satisfactory arrangement so that the children may be less distracted by classmates. In addition, that teacher may like the idea of storage space in the desks and the ease with which they may be moved about the room.

Cubicles probably are not warranted for children in most pre-academic preschool programs. At this stage of development, children must learn to conform in groups and to make use of their skills within the group. To isolate them at this age is not normal, because it deprives them of the opportunity to learn to develop self-discipline with peers and adults. In a readiness, first grade, or nongraded class, the need for cubicles may be very realistic for some children. At this level they are beginning to do independent seat work, which requires them to attend to tasks for a longer period of time. Three or four cubicles at one end of the room probably will be adequate for a class of eight to fifteen children. Only those who need to develop powers of concentration, or who apparently are unable to study except under conditions of minimal visual and auditory distraction, will require isolation. The use of a cubicle, then, becomes not much more than what it means to the adult who prefers to study in a quiet library or in a carrel in the library.

Materials. To provide an environment conducive to learning, a teacher will need motivational materials to hold the child's interest and should have no problem locating games and toys that will command attention during a learning situation. Motivational materials in school are used to assist the development of new skills or to impart information; they are not primarily for entertainment. Hours outside of school should be spent in the kinds of amusements that help children gain satisfaction through the repetition of tasks already mastered. During conference hours, parents should be told which games the children can play well. Suggestions should also be made as to the best kind of instructional and creative toys and materials parents may purchase.

Parent Involvement

Early childhood programs for language- and learning-handicapped children are often parent centered. Schaefer (1975) reviewed research related to the influences of the vast network of relationships among family members and their effects on children. He concluded that there is much evidence to demonstrate that children's intelligence and academic achievement are related to the quality of parental acceptance, the emotional milieu, language stimulation, and family support for academic achievement. Furthermore, the research he reviewed indicated that during the early childhood years children's intellectual development can be influenced when parents are involved in programs for handicapped children. There is general acceptance that the children have needs, but it is not always clear that parents also have needs on both the feeling level and the educational level. Bangs (1979, pp. 111–142) devoted a chapter to parent-centered programs that offer two formats: (1) a program that will help parents cope with their feelings about having a handicapped child and (2) techniques for training parents to carry over into the home what the children learn at school. The purpose of the parents' group program on the feeling level is to help parents overcome the periods of denial, guilt, blame, and anxiety that may pervade the family lifestyle and to guide them on to a period of acceptance and constructive action. The purpose of the parents' group program on the educational level is to teach parents how to apply the teaching skills used in the classroom or resource rooms to the environment outside of the school. The success of a program for handicapped children, then, is measured not only by the child's progress but also by the progress parents make as teachers. Helping parents on the feeling and the educational level is accomplished in a variety of ways: group and individual conferences, critiquing parents' activities in the classroom, and buddy systems.

Conferences. Teaching parents techniques and providing them with information related to language and learning skills is accomplished primarily through group and individual conferences.

Group conferences are scheduled at a specific time on certain days. In general, the younger the children and the shorter the class sessions, the greater the number of conferences. The objectives for group conferences include announcements, assignments, discussions of relevant topics, and a question and answer period.

Held early in the school year, *announcements* lay the ground rules for the teacher and parents and may include:

> Parents or the person who cares for the child must attend the conferences if maximum preacademic gains are to be expected.
>
> Teacher aides will carry out a prepared activity while the teacher is conducting conferences with parents. Parents are assured that their children are in a learning environment as opposed to a baby sitting environment when the teacher aide is conducting class.
>
> Schedules of school holidays and field trips are circulated.
>
> The teacher or parents, or both, provide answers to the following questions: Will the children have birthday parties at school? Will presents be given? Are parents allowed to give teachers gifts during the school year? Are parents to call the teacher by the first or given name, or does it matter? Will the teacher accept phone calls at home, or should there be a time schedule when the teacher may be reached at school?
>
> During the school year the teacher may: Suggest pertinent outside reading; recommend an important lecture including the date, time, and place; recommend a pertinent community sponsored program for children including the date, time, and place.

In general, *assignments* are concerned with transfer of training which is the ultimate payoff for the children. When they can grasp a concept and apply that knowledge to a new situation, we say transfer of training has occurred. Gagne (1965) discussed two types of transfer: horizontal and vertical. Horizontal refers to using information of the same difficulty in a new situation, while vertical learning refers to using knowledge to develop new concepts and skills. An example of horizontal learning is that of the kindergarten child who has learned to read numbers at school. Parents are given assignments to help transfer this learning outside the classroom. They may ask their children to read numbers on license plates, telephone numbers, and a list of numbers that represent the ages of their friends. A striking example of vertical learning was undertaken by a classroom teacher of the hearing impaired (Lewis, 1976). The pilot program was designed for a group of twelve hearing-impaired children who had specific vocabulary deficiencies in words of quality, quantity, position, and size. Each parent was given a prescriptive program according to the child's individual vocabulary needs. Ms. Lewis designed the program further to demonstrate, with the use of pretest and posttest data, each child's vocabulary gains and how the gains were related to the degree of the parents' involvement. Utilizing the Vocabulary Comprehension Scale (Bangs 1975), pretests were administered to individual children, and the test results were discussed individually with each parent. The parent was given home training suggestions as to how to teach her child and was asked to fill in a typed form each week that included the parent's evaluation of which words had been learned and how they were taught and reinforced. These specific words were only incidentally used in the classroom; there was no intentional teaching of the words. At the end of six months, Ms. Lewis inspected the posttest data to determine percent gains and placed the children into three distinct groups: Group I who had the highest percent gain and the highest percentage of forms returned by parents; Group III who had the lowest percent gain and the lowest percentage of parents returning the forms; and Group II who were in between (see Table 6–3). A most significant finding was the high degree of correlation between the percentage of completed assignments (parent participation) and the child's gain in vocabulary comprehension. The results of this pilot study indicate that hearing-impaired children, in the presence of consistent, goal-oriented participation by parents, made significantly better gains than the hearing-impaired children who lacked such parental involvement.

The third aspect of group conferences, *discussion of relevant topics*, is a cooperative venture between teacher and parent. The teacher prepares a list of topics that parents may be interested in discussing. This list is given to parents who are asked to add topics of their choice not included in the typed list. Then they are asked to rank order the topics according to preference. Examples include:

What is meant by preacademic skills?
How to read to a preschool child.
Home activities: Opening the mail can be fun and instructional.
Lessons in sequencing: What comes next and after that what happens?
Stages in language development.
How do children learn?
Increasing a child's vocabulary.
Social behavior: What to expect of the preschool child.
Verbs: Don't criticize "I shutted the door" "I ringed the bell."

The *question and answer period* is provided to encourage parents to seek and clarify information that is both school and home related.

Individual conferences serve as an adjunct to the group conferences. The behavior of parents in a group conference often varies as much as the behavior of children in a classroom. One parent may need more detailed information than warrants the time it would take in a group conference. Some may need constant support for their efforts; others may need answers to questions that apply only to their children. For these reasons individual conferences are held at the discretion of the teacher who may decide to schedule a specific number of meetings with each parent during the school year or schedule at the request of a parent.

Table 6-3 Performance of Hearing-Impaired Subjects on the Vocabulary Comprehension Scale

Group	% Completed Assignments	Pretest Mean Score	%	Posttest Mean Score	%	Mean Gain	% Gain
I 4 children	90.8%	10.3	16.9	44.8	73.4	34.5	68.0
II 6 children	51.3	15.2	24.9	36.7	60.2	21.5	46.9
III 2 children	3.1	19.0	31.1	21.0	34.4	2.0	4.8

(Lewis 1976)

Parent Observation. Parents should be encouraged to visit the children's classroom. Drop-in visits are seldom enjoyable to either teacher or parent, however; it is, therefore, more efficient to have a special time set aside when parents know they are welcome and the teacher has planned a specific lesson for the parents to observe. The teacher knows that parents are usually interested in the part of the program that looks most like a traditional school setting, such as reading-readiness activities, teaching relational words, or activities that relate to mathematical concepts. Parents' observations are designed, of course, to show parents how to meet the performance objectives developed for their children. Booths adjacent to the classroom with one-way vision windows are ideal for observations. Parents are asked to observe from a booth specific aspects of teaching which may be helpful in planning home training programs as well as in gaining a better understanding of their children. Neither visitors nor parents should be permitted to observe a classroom procedure without a competent person to explain the basic educational philosophy and the purpose of the activities being observed. Without such explanations, observers may view the program as a glorified nursery or play school or misinterpret the teacher's purpose underlying each activity. Therefore on the assigned day for observation, each parent should be given a sheet of paper with specific questions to be answered, for example:

What new vocabulary word was introduced today?
In how many different activities was it presented?
How can you reinforce vocabulary building at home?
What successes did your child have today?
What were the failures, if any?
If there were failures, how did the teacher handle them?

The answer sheets are collected, and the parent's comments may be discussed in group or individual conferences.

Critiquing Parent Activities. Critiquing parents' activities in the classroom is another way to involve parents. Some parents, however, are reticent about demonstrating their teaching skills before others. Fear of failure may be very real with parents who do not normally work with groups of children. The astute teacher will allow a parent to choose the activity and the number of children to be involved in the activity. In general, parents are innovative in the classroom and appreciate the opportunity to demonstrate their skills as well as accept constructive criticism.

> Ms. Mauzy utilizes the many talents of her students' parents, most of which she does not possess, tumbling, music, arts and crafts, flower arranging. Parents volunteer to be in charge of a program for Club Day which may include four different activities: preparing lunch, tumbling, arts and crafts, and playing the zither. The teacher prepares the children for the Club Day and allows them to choose a club. She prepares the parents with objectives to be met and other specific help they might need. She observes portions of each group performance and offers constructive comments to each parent.

Buddy System. The buddy system may be used as a supplement to the previous suggestions for parental involvement. Parents whose children have been enrolled in a program for one or more years are often willing to serve as a "buddy" to a newly enrolled parent. The purpose of the buddy system is to provide an interchange of information between two parents who share similar basic feelings and problems related to their handicapped children. One of the parents should have a background and experiences not yet attained by the novice. A parent-to-parent discussion of what is happening now and what the future may hold adds a dimension to a parent's emotional and intellectual growth that may not be accomplished through parent-teacher conferences.

SUMMARY

Instructional programming includes a generic curriculum guide that contains what is to be taught and the sequence in which it is to be taught. For this text the curriculum content is made up of language acquisition (form, content, and use) and the relation of language to the preacademic subjects of reading, spelling, arithmetic, writing, and affective education. There is recognition and use of the cognitive skills that underly the language-learning process. Instructional programming also includes the talents of diagnosticians, teachers, support personnel, and, last but not least, parents.The teacher is responsible for the instruction and keeps children progressing according to their rate and style of learning. Specialists in such areas as speech-language pathology, counseling, physical therapy, and rehabilitative audiology are utilized as needed. An instructional program needs both a system and flexibility.

REFERENCES

Auerbach, A. B. *Parents Learn Through Discussion: Principles and Practices of Parent Group Education.* New York: John Wiley, 1968.

Bangs, Tina E. *Birth to Three: Developmental Learning and the Handicapped Child,* Chapter 5. Boston, Mass.: Teaching Resources, 1979.

Bangs, Tina E. *Vocabulary Comprehension Scale.* Boston, Mass.: Teaching Resources, 1979.

7

program
design process

Part I of this text, Chapters 1 through 6, described the foundations for instructional programming: acquisition of oral language, preacademic and affective education, cognitive skills basic to language learning, techniques of testing and reporting, and basic principles of program design. Part II, Chapters 7 through 10, relates these foundations to the instructional programming process using the same definitions and educational philosophy in meeting the needs of language- or learning-handicapped children.

The instructional programming process in oral language, like its foundations, includes three dimensions: content, form, and use (Bloom and Lahey 1978). Content relates to the knowledge children have about the world in which they live and the concepts they develop through activities of daily living, all of which provide the semantic base for what it is they will listen to and talk about. The form of language is the symbolic representation of the knowledge children have. It includes their lexicon which is made up of substantive, relational, and inflectional words as well as the syntax or word order for generating connected discourse. Use of language reflects the child's intent for speaking and the strategies used to influence the listener. The preacademic sub-

146

jects include reading-, arithmetic-, and handwriting-readiness skills. Reading, the counterpart of oral language, cannot be accomplished until children have developed the content, form, and use of language found in the basal readers. Therefore, reading readiness includes the acquisition of content, form, and use of language. Arithmetic readiness includes the areas of counting by rote and rational counting, number concepts, and number facts, all of which are dependent upon number knowledge and a symbol system to represent numerical relationships. Handwriting readiness includes the drawing of circles, lines, and other printed forms that are the precursors to manuscript writing. The relatively new field of affective education on a preschool level is directed toward the development of a good self-concept and appropriate interactions with people in a nonlinguistic mode as well as acceptable use of linguistic skills.

The instructional process described in Part II is based on the premise that the learning of all of these skills by children with language or learning disorders should not be left to chance. These children need an organized instructional program to ensure that they are developing according to their full potential. The educational philosophy includes a generic approach that allows teachers to use the same curriculum guide and instructional projects for a variety of handicapped children: deaf, hard of hearing, specific learning disability, mentally retarded, environmentally deprived, and multiple handicapped. The instructional program is not designed for the profoundly mentally retarded population who will never obtain the preacademic skill level or for the alleviation of the emtional problems of emotionally disturbed children. The process for organizing an instructional program is outlined in this chapter. The following chapters include projects, a curriculum guide, and a discussion of ways to meet needs through alternative systems of communication.

A CURRICULUM-BASED TEST

How do handicapped children differ from normals in the areas of language and cognitive skills? The question is answered by obtaining from normal populations standardized developmental behaviors in these areas, then relating the performance of each language- and learning-handicapped child to the standardized data. Competence is determined through testing and interpreting an individual's performance. From the psychology of task analysis we know that certain basic skills must be acquired before other skills can be learned. With this knowledge persons currently designing tests for language- and learning-deficient children are choosing test items that sample what the children must learn at different developmental levels in order to succeed in a preacademic curriculum. Many standardized test items have been included in the list of developmental behaviors in Appendix 1 and are used by the teacher in selecting performance objectives.

DEVELOPMENTAL BEHAVIORS

The most practical approach to formulating performance objectives, or what it is the teacher wants the children to learn, is to draw from a pool of sequenced behaviors. Both cognitive and linguistic areas have built-in systems of priorities, and what happens at any point in the development of one of these behaviors is important in influencing subsequent behaviors. If a child, for example, has utterances no longer than three words, one would consider the length of such utterances to be antecedent to more complex and longer sentence structures. The teacher is aware also that knowledge of one part of a system will help her predict information about the other systems. If a child does not have the concept of long-short, then one would not expect the child to use the words *long* and *short* appropriately. Or if a child is deficient in short-term auditory memory, the teacher should give information to the child in small bits.

The following chapters on instructional programming are based on the hypothesis that language- and learning-deficient children must go through the same developmental stages as normal children. The fact that the normal learning process has failed in the population of children with language and learning disorders does not discourage the use of a developmental approach, rather it emphasizes a need for a greater variety of experiences, smaller steps in the developmental sequence, and more repetitions of what is to be learned. These experiences are planned by the teacher. With behavioral baseline data on each child, the teacher will be able to select an appropriate class level.

CLASS LEVELS

Three class levels are included in the curriculum guide in Chapter 9: kindergarten, prekindergarten, and nursery. The kindergarten level curriculum describes the kinds of behavior that normal children acquire between entry into kindergarten and entry into first grade. In many school districts entry is defined as reaching one's fifth birthday before a specified date of the new school year. This means, of course, that some children will be very young five-year-olds and others will be approaching six years of age. The standardized developmental data on this level (see Appendix 1) were obtained from normal children enrolled in private and public schools. The prekindergarten level curriculum includes the types of behavior of normal children in the age range of four years until entry into kindergarten and the nursery level includes the three-year-old children. These standardized behaviors were obtained from children enrolled in nursery schools. All populations included different ethnic groups as well as different socioeconomic levels.

Children with language and learning deficiencies are placed on the level that most closely matches their developmental age levels in the behaviors of language or cognitive skills, or both, with attention given to chronological age. Ten-year-old retarded children functioning on a prekindergarten level, for example, would not be included with five-year-old specific learning disability children who were enrolled in a prekindergarten class. On the other hand, normal hearing four-year-old learning-disabled children may be enrolled with four-year-old hearing-impaired children who have similar language deficits. In large school districts grouping is less of a problem than in school districts with a small population of special education children. Some school districts often develop cooperative programs for which children from many districts can be bused to one location.

CURRICULUM GUIDE

The curriculum guide (Chapter 9) is flexible yet serves as a directive for a teacher's course of action. It presents a plan or a guide for what is to be taught and a format to implement the instruction. The goal, which is a broad general statement that is measurable only through objectives, is the same for all the children — academic achievement according to their individual potential in order that they may become partially or fully self-supporting citizens. The fact that some children will fall short of this goal is less important than the assurance that attempts are being made to reach the goal. Each class level includes units, long-range objectives, lesson plans, and a calendar of events.

Units

The normal course of language learning takes place in a natural environment; therefore, units on such matters as transportation, clothing, and food are used to provide a mechanism for helping children gain knowledge about the world in which they live. For each class level there is a list of units for each month.

Long-Term Objectives

Each level, kindergarten, prekindergarten, and nursery, has long-term objectives which are measurable statements that describe what the children are to accomplish by the end of the school year. These objectives have been selected from the list of developmental behaviors found in Appendix 1. Each teacher will adjust these objectives to meet the requirements of the school district.

Lesson Plans

Each class level has two sample lesson plans that include short-term objectives, projects, and procedures. (See also Appendixes 7 and 8 for *Home Training Hints for Parents* and a format for setting up a *Picture File and Other Training Materials.*)

Short-Term Objectives. Short-term or interim objectives are specific measurable statements that lead to completion of the long-term objectives. These short-term objectives may be selected from the developmental data in Appendix 1. It is more expedient to plan a sequence of interim objectives that fit into the framework of the long-term objectives than to stumble along hoping that the long-term objectives will be met without interim measurements. These short-term objectives form the heart of the curriculum.

Projects. In Chapter 8 is a list of·thirty-three projects, such as art, games, field trips, club day, open house for parents, most of which are used with some regularity sometime during the year for each of the three class levels. Children soon learn to expect a certain project to occur at a specified time during the day or week or month. Again, the structure of the curriculum guide and the total preacademic program is aimed at completing objectives and not at having learning take place by chance. These projects serve as motivating activities.

Calendar of Events

A calendar of events is a monitoring system for recording the events that must take place in order to complete the activities that have been written into the performance objectives. Each class level has a sample calendar of events for a full week and a calendar of projects for the year.

MEETING SPECIAL NEEDS

Chapter 10 includes various teaching techniques and materials that are used for alternative systems of communication, such as sign language for the hearing impaired and conversation boards for children who cannot produce intelligible speech.

SUMMARY

Instructing children with language and learning disorders cannot be left to chance. A flexible yet structured program, which includes a curriculum and measurable objectives of what the children must accomplish to achieve their potential, seems a logical approach to enhancing a child's goal of becoming a well-adjusted, full or partially self-supporting citizen.

8

instructional projects

Coauthor Anne Mauzy

INTRODUCTION

Instructional programming includes the projects the children will engage in throughout the school year. These projects which have specific labels, art, Me Book, object box, are the media through which children acquire knowledge about their environment, have something to talk about, develop a lexicon, discover the rules governing the relationship of words in morphosyntactic form, and learn how to use language effectively. Almost everything the teacher wants the children to learn is developed through the projects. The teacher, therefore, must be familiar with each project in order to develop daily and weekly lesson plans. Although examples for all three class levels — kindergarten, prekindergarten, and nursery — are given, there is, perhaps, a greater emphasis on the kindergarten level because it is easier to look at a higher level activity and translate it to a lower level activity than the other way around. The following is a description of the projects that occur daily, several times in a week, monthly, or only a few times during the school year.

PROJECTS

1. Art (p. 153)
2. Bulletin Boards (p. 155)
3. Calendar (p. 156)
4. Charts (p. 157)
5. Club Day (p. 159)
6. Cooking Projects (p. 161)
7. Expansion Picture File (p. 162)
8. Experience Story (p. 163)
9. Field Trips (p. 163)
10. Finger Plays (p. 165)
11. Games (p. 165)
12. Home Visits (p. 167)
13. Key Words (p. 167)
14. Library Books (p. 168)
15. Lunch (p. 169)
16. Me Book (p. 169)
17. Newspaper (p. 171)
18. Nursery Rhymes (p. 171)
19. Object Box (p. 172)
20. Open House for Parents (p. 173)
21. Phonics Box (p. 175)
22. Records (p. 175)
23. Roll Call (p. 176)
24. Scrapbook (p. 176)
25. Self-Concept (p. 177)
26. Show and Tell (p. 178)
27. Songs (p. 179)
28. Special Events (p. 179)
29. Stations (p. 181)
30. Stories (p. 183)
31. Vocabulary Box (p. 184)
32. Voting (p. 184)
33. Work Tables (p. 184)

1. Art

Art activities are those that allow the children to construct something by cutting, coloring, painting, drawing, folding, pasting, and molding. Some of the spin-offs or purposes of this project for the children are improving hand-eye-motor skills, learning to follow instructions, creating products that can be used to decorate bulletin boards, learning good independent work habits, and providing them a means to communicate with their parents what it is that they have learned at school.

Project: Making a Spider

Materials   Black construction paper, magic marker, chalkboard, paste, scissors, straws, scotch tape

Procedure   The finger play *Eensie Weensie Spider* is introduced. After the children have performed with the teacher, they are told that they will learn how to make spiders. First, a drawing of a spider with body, head, eyes, and legs is shown to the children, and they practice copying it either on the chalkboard or on paper. Then the teacher draws a spider without legs on the chalkboard and asks one child to draw four legs on the right side and four legs on the left side. The children count in unison while the legs are drawn; then the teacher asks questions: "How many legs does the spider have?" "If the spider has four legs on the left side and four legs on the right side, how many legs does he have?" The children rational count the eight legs. The questions shift to other objects: "How many legs does a chair have?" "How many legs do you have?" Questioning is continued until all numbers included in the short-term objective have been used. The next step is to give the children templates of the spider's body and head and have them draw around them on black construction paper. The head and body are cut out and joined with paste. The teacher prepares strips of black paper to be used for spider legs and draws dots on the black construction paper for the children to draw lines between. This will form a strip long enough for two legs. Each child gets four strips. The children take turns connecting the dots to complete the lines that form a strip one-inch wide and long enough for one leg. They cut off the strip and cut it in half to make two legs. They discuss and demonstrate how many legs they will have if they cut each strip in half. The teacher demonstrates how to fold the legs, folding approximately an inch over and back, over and back. As each leg is folded, it is pasted appropriately on the spider's body. While the paste is drying, the children recite *Little Miss Muffett*, and then they play act the poem. One child represents the spider by putting a black cloth around his or her head or using black construction paper for a hat. When the spiders are dry, they may be taped to a straw or a stick for a hand puppet, and Little Miss Muffett can be recited while the children hold their own puppets. These are saved and used on the bulletin board where the poem *Eensie Weensie Spider* has been placed.

Other activities include:

Baker's clay to mold and paint when hardened.

Butterflies. Cut large butterflies and hang from the ceiling.

Chalkboard designs. How many objects can be drawn from a circle? A square? The teacher draws on the chalkboard, and the children copy the figures on paper.

Collages

Cookie cutters. Trace shapes, cut them out, and make a mobile.

Color pens for any artwork. Children may copy a string of beads by drawing circles for the two round beads, one square for the square bead. Then the drawings are colored like the string of beads.

Crayons and wax paper. Shred wax crayon on wax paper, fold over and iron until crayon melts. Frame it for a gift.

Decorations for holidays and special events

Leaves. Make a person out of leaves.

Marshmallows. Make animals from large and small marshmallows. Fashion long and short as well as tall and short animals.

Murals. For a specific unit add something new each day to the mural.

Placemats. Fringe edges, draw circles and crosses in different colors for decorations.

Precut shapes. Children paste cone and circle to make an ice cream cone. Squares, circles, and rectangles are used to form a human body, a wagon, or a house.

Shoe box. Make animal cages with perpendicular bars on the open side.

Snowflakes. Fold paper in a variety of ways and cut to make snowflakes.

Snow scene. Arrange crumpled paper to form hills and valleys then cover with a sheet of cotton. Add a village, sleds, children, and other items to depict the winter season.

Tempera paints to be used at the easel.

Traffic lights made from colored construction paper.

Weaving

2. Bulletin Boards

Bulletin boards may be of any size, shape, or color. They may be trimmed on the outer edge with fluted or other decorative paper, or they may be plain. Usually the boards are placed in the classroom, but they may on occasion be displayed on the corridor walls for sharing with other classes. Decorating bulletin boards is often a burden to teachers, yet if used for teaching purposes as well as decoration, they seem less burdensome. The following are examples of how to use bulletin boards for teaching purposes.

Project: **Numbers Bulletin Board.** This bulletin board is used throughout the year as a referral source for developing pre-mathematics skills, counting, number concepts, reading numbers, and number words.

Materials "Number men" or other items such as pumpkin heads or cars are used depending upon the current unit. These materials may be used as an art project.

Procedure After the first verse of the song, *This Old Man* has been sung, the teacher places on the bulletin board a "number man" with the word *one* and the figure 1 underneath. Additional number men are added each day or week until the last number in the mathematics objective has been met.

Other suggestions for bulletin boards include:

Unit bulletin board. This bulletin board may be used for any of the units, such as the clothing unit. To teach category and class words, all varieties of clothing, such as hats, neckties, and other wearing apparel, can be traced and cut out during an art activity or a Club Day activity.

Seasonal bulletin board. In one part of the room there may be a bulletin board with a seasonal tree which is revamped as the season changes or as the units for fall, winter, spring, and summer are introduced.

Linguistic bulletin board. To teach modification, one bulletin board may have big and small balloons of all colors, some high on the board and some near the bottom or in the middle. The teacher may say, "Who can find the little red balloon that is low on the bulletin board?" On the seasonal bulletin board a large yellow leaf could be on a high branch and a small red leaf on a low branch. To teach double meaning words, the bulletin board may have a picture of a *pear* and a *pair* of shoes.

3. Calendar

It is obvious that the calendar is made up of twelve months, each month displayed on one page with an appropriate title and the days numbered in sequence. The reasons for introducing the calendar during the kindergarten level are to expose children to or teach them the sequence of time, the names of the days and months of the year, and to answer *when* questions. All of these are concepts that truly do not emerge until after first grade for most children but are considered precursors to the acquisition of time concepts. Specifically, the calendar may be used to help children read numbers and add and subtract numbers. Calendars are not appropriate for children below kindergarten age. Other techniques for teaching sequencing and time are used on the prekindergarten and nursery levels. The following is an example of how a calendar may be used in a kindergarten class.

Project: The Calendar

Materials A current calendar and a blank calendar; a date stamp that allows the month, day of the week, and year to be changed as necessary; and printed words and numbers on pieces of paper that can be pasted on the blank calendar

Procedure While sitting in a group, the children look at the current calendar and find the appropriate printed words and numbers to add to the blank calendar. A number is added each day and appropriate words when a new month appears. Seals which represent holidays can be added at the first of each month so the children can count how many days until the special event. A birthday cake sticker is placed on each child's birth date. The children guess at the beginning of each month who will have a birthday.

4. Charts

The teacher develops charts with pictures and words that are representative of a specific unit. A chart for the unit on body parts, for example, will include a picture of a hand on the left side of the chart and the printed word *hand* on the right side. Separate picture and word cards are also made. The picture card should be twice as tall as the word card which allows for the picture card to be placed in the chalk tray or pocket chart and the matching word card to be placed underneath the picture. In addition to the noun charts built around the unit vocabulary, there are also charts that have action pictures with the printed action words, and charts with prepositions such as a picture of a dog *under* a box and the printed word *under*. In like manner, adjectives are utilized. There are additional word cards with other parts of speech such as *to*, *a*, *the*, *and*, plural markers /s/ and /es/, and capital letters.

The purpose of the charts is to help children develop a lexicon and to discover the morphosyntactic rules of language. For the nursery and prekindergarten levels there is vocabulary building, matching classes of pictures, putting pictures into categories, and sequencing pictures to allow for sentence generation. For the kindergarten level, lessons on sentence structure are easy to present in either a picture or word mode. The children improve their oral language skills by playing the part of the teacher, which requires them to use language effectively. After one child builds a sentence with the cards, other children are asked to tell what the sentence says. Word cards such as *can*, *cannot*, and *the* may not be read by the children, but they should be aware that a word is needed in the sentence. Such an approach is helpful for children who use telegraphic speech. For teaching language form and the early basics of reading, these charts with their picture and word cards are used twice weekly in the kindergarten level class.

The following are examples of games that can be played using the charts and the picture and word cards.

Project: Touch Game

Materials Picture-word chart and word and picture cards for the unit on body parts

Procedure Using the word cards, the teacher forms a sentence in the pocket chart: *Touch your foot.* She holds her name in front of the children and touches her foot. "What did the sentence tell me to do?" The children reply, "Touch your foot." Another sentence is presented, and a child performs. The picture and word cards can be clipped together to make the game move faster when the children are acting as teacher. To change the procedure, the word card *my* is added and the procedure becomes, "Touch *my* foot. Touch *your* foot." Or, the number cards 1, 2, 3 with plural marker /s/ are used to elicit the responses "Touch 1 foot, Touch 3 feet. Touch 2 hands."

What Can Do It Game. The teacher puts the verb picture card "wave" in the pocket chart. She waves. She puts picture card "cry" in the pocket chart, and the children pretend to cry. The teacher may add word cards *can* and *cannot.* She places a body part picture in the pocket chart and adds the word card *can.* "Feet can ____." The children find the word *run* to complete the sentence.

Find It Game. Picture cards for the body parts chart are scattered over the room but in conspicuous places. Children are asked to find the body part that represents the word card that the teacher has placed in the pocket chart. They can refer to the body part chart which is in front of them. The picture and word cards for *find* are clipped together. The teacher makes these sentences in the pocket chart: "Find the arm"; "Find the hand"; and the like. Jean's name is drawn from the name basket, and she must search for the correct card. While Jean is searching, the teacher asks one of the boys to answer quietly the question, "What is Jean supposed to do?" He replies, "Find the arm."

Another version of this same game is to change the *find* card to the *found* card and structure a sentence in the pocket chart to read, "____ found the arm." "____ found the hand." The teacher asks, "Who found the arm?" and the children take turns remembering which name was in the blank. They reread the sentences once they are completed. Those who did not get a turn can play teacher for the next game. A story may be written for the scrapbook telling who found what body part.

Match Pictures and Words Game. Picture cards are placed on the chalkboard ledge, and the picture chart is used as a dictionary. Joe's name is drawn, and it is his turn to perform. He looks at the chart, finds the word that matches, finds the picture, and puts the word card in front of the picture card. The teacher says the word and the child repeats it. Children who play teacher have an opportunity to initiate words.

Everything You Can Think of Game. The children are asked to tell everything they can think of that can "wave." Their responses are listed on the chalkboard: *boy, girl, flag, hand.* Then they name all of the things they can think of that can "turn." The answers are also listed on the chalkboard: *car, truck, boy, page.* The children are helped to make a sentence using one of the words, then two words, then three words. Generating a sentence from two words — car, turn — is not accomplished by most children until first or second grade. The exercise, however, is designed to help children discover syntactic rules.

Matching Pictures of Same Class Game. The "expansion file" pictures are placed on the chalkboard with magnetic clips. The children are asked to choose a picture card from the basket and put it under the same word. The child is asked, "What is it?" and the teacher waits for a response. There may be a lunch basket and a wastebasket or a rocking chair and a straight chair. An adaptation of this game is to draw a name, and that child must respond to: "Take down the picture of the basket with a handle" or "Take down the picture of the basket we use to carry a picnic lunch." The children can serve as teacher.

5. Club Day

Club Day is scheduled weekly and includes the participation of a parent, the aide, the teacher, and three groups of children each in a different one hour activity called clubs — Arts and Crafts Club, Tumbling Club, Music Club. The purpose of organizing clubs is to use the many talents that parents and aides may have that are not in the teacher's repertoire of skills. In addition, the children are given opportunities to take instruction and perform for persons other than the teacher. The teacher and parents select the names of the clubs, and each parent chooses the clubs and the days when she would like to conduct them. Parents are given a list of the short-range objectives and are asked to submit to the teacher in writing their procedure and the materials they will need. Early in the year the parents may need assistance, but it is rewarding to observe their improved planning and teaching skills over time. Each club is held in a specific part of the classroom, partitioned by dividers if needed. Materials are furnished by the school or the parents. Each club leader (a parent, the aide, and the teacher) has the names of the children in her group. At the end of the one-hour period the children will have something they have made to show the children from other clubs, or they will demonstrate what they have learned. Nothing is taken home unless all the children have something to take home.

Project: Selecting a Club

Materials   The children's name cards in a basket and magnetic clips

Procedure   The manner in which children select a club is a teaching and a learning situation. Three clubs named the Drawing Club, Puzzle Club, and Paint Club were selected for a Club Day. The name of each club was written on the chalkboard and an explanation of what would transpire in the club was given to the children without mentioning the leader's name. Then the question was asked, "How many children are here today?" "Thirteen." The teacher drew five lines under one club and four lines under the others. The children were asked to count the lines, which indicate a one-to-one relationship between the line and a child's name. Each child knew that when the lines under one club were filled with names, no others could join that club. In a basket were the children's name cards, each with a magnetic clip. The teacher drew a name, and the appropriate child stood up. If he or she could not read the name, it was placed back in the basket. The last child did not have a chance to choose but was complimented for being such a good sport. The first child to choose was called *lucky* and the last child *unlucky*. Each club leader called her group to the specified part of the classroom.

Other Club Day activities include:

Drawing Club. Mary will lie on the wrapping paper while the parent draws around her with a magic marker. Then she is asked to look into the mirror and decide what parts of her body she wants to color. "I want blue chalk to color my eyes." Each child has his or her silhouette drawn and colors it appropriately. These are to be cut out later and used for parent night.

Music Club. If space away from the classroom is available, a parent teaches the children a new song and accompanies their singing with a zither or other musical instrument.

Puzzle Club. The children select a picture from a coloring book, such as Little Miss Muffet or a doll with several pieces of clothing, and describe what they have chosen. The entire page is covered with paste, which is an unusual procedure so there is a discussion as to why the page must be covered. The teacher draws curved and straight lines on the picture so that the finished puzzle will have five or six parts. The children trace these lines with the magic marker, and, with the help of the leader, they cut out the segments. The children decide how to keep the puzzles from getting mixed up: giving them all the same number or stamping the owner's name on each piece then putting the pieces in an envelope. These puzzles will be used later during a daily event called arrival table.

Paint Club. Each child selects a page from a "Paint with Water Book" and describes the picture. The aide demonstrates how to use the paint brush so that only a small amount of water flows from the brush. Each child may paint a picture, or the group may do one together. Individuals in the group must make a sentence describing what it is that they want to paint.

Other Clubs. Other Club Day projects include making macaroni bracelets, zoo animals, and valentines; playing games of Old Maid, Bingo, and Lotto; creating Indian headdresses for acting out "Ten Little Indians"; and designing a TV show from a box and a roll of paper to tell a story with pictures. For the TV show the children tell the story as the pictures are being shown; this project is saved for the open house for parents. Other projects include a collection of pictures taken around the school for a bulletin board display and planting seeds.

6. Cooking Projects

A cooking project may involve cooking on the stove, in the oven, mixing ingredients that do not have to be cooked, or something as simple as cutting an apple to see the star inside. The teacher directs, but the children measure or cut as much as their capabilities permit. The purpose is to introduce children to culinary aspects of living, to develop hand-eye-motor coordination skills, to follow directions, and to communicate.

Project: Decorating a Gingerbread Boy

Materials A gingerbread flavored sheet cake, knife, pattern for gingerbread boy, candies, icing in tubes, picture and word cards for body parts chart

Procedure The teacher cuts the figures from the cake by cutting around the pattern of the gingerbread boy. The children sample the pieces of cake that are cut away. Before decorating a figure with the tube of icing, each child has to know which part to decorate by reading the word card presented by the teacher. A word is drawn out of the basket, for example, *wrist.* The child points to the appropriate body part. If correct, that person can use the icing tube to outline the wrists. If there is an error made, the child is referred to the chart for body parts. A counting exercise is used to select and place candies for buttons. For younger children, pictures of body parts are drawn from the basket; these must be named and then matched to the same body part on the gingerbread boy.

A follow-up activity includes acting out the story of the gingerbread boy. Each child wears a picture of the appropriate person or animal from the story. The children practice the "play," and a final cast is selected to be photographed so a story can be made. In addition, a tape recording of their remarks are made. Another class may be invited to watch the play "The Gingerbread Boy" and to share the gingerbread boy refreshments. The teacher may want to play the tape recording while the children act, because they often are not willing to talk in front of newcomers.

Other cooking activities follow:

Boiling an Egg. While the water is getting ready to boil, the teacher discusses the number of eggs in one carton and uses problem stories that meet the objectives. The remainder of this lesson is designed to demonstrate cause and effect, how one substance can change to another. This is accomplished by watching water turn to steam and disappear, observing the texture of the egg white and egg yolk before and after cooking, noting that the egg can be cut with a knife only after cooking, feeling how the boiled eggs can be changed from hot to cold by placing them under cold running water, and seeing that an egg slicer can change a whole egg into pieces and that egg shells can be turned into a mosaic. A follow-up activity is to have the children draw or trace a picture of an egg, cover it with glue, and fill it in with the crumbled pieces of egg shells. These mosaics may be used for bulletin board decorations.

Making Cookies. Use different sized spoons, such as long–short, big–little, for measuring and mixing. Cut cookies into shapes that children must learn to name, such as circle, triangle, square, and rectangle.

Other cooking projects include making orange juice, jello, popcorn, cookies, candied apples, cinnamon toast, scrambled eggs, instant pudding, ice box pie, lemonade, vegetable soup, and potato soup, changing whipping cream to butter, and even glazing doughnuts.

7. Expansion Picture File

This file contains pictures that expand the meaning of the pictures and words found on the charts. For example, a shoe may be a boot, sandal, slipper, moccasin, or loafer. The file could also have unusual items, such as booties, suspenders, or a garter. If there are duplicate pictures, irregular plurals can be taught, *foot-feet.* Pictures relate to clothes worn during the four seasons as well as to what different people wear, like a firefighter, doctor and nurse. These expansion picture files become treasures for the teacher whose intention is to make teaching a career. (See *Picture File and Other Training Materials*, Appendix 8.)

8. Experience Story

Experience stories are written summaries of places, people, and events that have been experienced by the children in the class. After an activity at school, such as popping corn, the children are asked to tell what happened or to answer specific questions such as "What did we cook?" When the child replies "popcorn," the teacher asks for a sentence about popcorn so that she can write a story for the scrapbook. The reasons for writing experience stories are many. It requires the children to attend to facts in order to recall the events; it gives them practice in hearing complete sentence forms and in generating sentences; and it allows them to reread at a later date what was written. Children like to hear about their own experiences such as "Jane took the lid off the popcorn popper." If the teacher writes the sentences as the children dictate them, they see the relationship of letters and words to what they have said. It is interesting to hear them say, "That sure was a long sentence" or "I see my name in the story."

9. Field Trips

Field trips are carefully planned, executed, and documented and are followed by an activity that will reinforce what was learned on the trip. The trip can be away from the school grounds or as simple as going to the school yard to find an ant hill. The teacher should visit the chosen place before the children go. The mode of transporting the children must be carefully planned in accordance with the school's rules, and the field trip should be coordinated with the unit for the week. Parents and sometimes school officials may need to be sold on the value of field trips for young children. Firmly written objectives often help to get approval of the program. The fact should be stressed that children learn through experiences, many of the rich experiences being outside the classroom. Field trips provide common experiences for the children and since the teacher knows what the children have experienced, provides him or her a starting place to learn more about the subject.

Project: Fire Station

Materials Pictures and books of fire stations and fire equipment

Procedure In preparation for the field trip to the fire station, the teacher contacts the appropriate person at the station, discusses the ages of the children, and their reasons for wanting to visit the station. She also obtains information regarding what the firefighters will show and tell the children. Permission to take pictures is also requested. Several days prior to the trip, the teacher reads the children books and shows them pictures of the equipment and activities that are a part of a fire station. While on the bus, the teacher has a list of vehicles that the children may see while traveling: passenger car, taxi, truck. The children are asked to call out the kind of vehicle they see, and the teacher makes tally marks. At the fire station the teacher makes a list of new vocabulary words, takes pictures, and writes notes of what happened from the beginning to end of the visit. On the return bus trip, the children recall things they saw and things they learned.

As a follow up to the field trip, the teacher writes the names of the vehicles and how many of each were seen. She introduces them to the system of tallying by fives, a cross mark across four lines. She asks, "Which vehicle was seen the *most* times? The *least* number of times? Were there *less* trucks or *less* taxis?" All new vocabulary words are defined by the teacher and then by the children. An experience story is written for a book which may be titled "A Trip to the Fire Station." Pictures taken on the trip and an illustrated cover complete the book which is added to the class library and can be checked out by the children.

Another field trip could be a visit to a mail box. The children walk to the mail box near the school just before the letter carrier arrives. While walking they are asked to comment on things they see, and the teacher makes notes for the sequence story. Songs may be sung or poems recited until the letter carrier arrives. The letter carrier has previously been asked to tell the children what he or she does with the mail. The children ask questions and, if permitted, take his or her picture. As a follow up, the children write an experience story. They may assemble mail trucks using a corrugated box and basic parts to be pasted on the box, such as wheels or a door. They may make a mail bag from a round piece of fabric that has a plastic string threaded through holes on the outer edge of the circle. Children can be taught how to make envelopes. They cut rectangles and squares to be used for letters. They draw a square for the stamp and address the letter to themselves, copying their name, address, and city.

Other field trips include going to the grocery store to buy vegetables for a cooking unit or going to the zoo; taking a spring walk with
paper sacks to collect treasures or harmful objects; visiting a child's
home; having a picnic in the park; going to the library to check out
books, to the nurse's office to weigh, and to the airport. The airport
trip can be followed up by playing pilot, stewardess, and passengers in
the classroom.

10. Finger Plays

Finger plays are poems or verses that can be said while using the
fingers and body movements to act out the poem. The purpose is to
provide selected sentence structures that will be repeated over and
over, to introduce new vocabulary words, and to help children develop
good self-concepts about a task they have accomplished. Books with
finger plays are available in teacher supply stores.

11. Games

In addition to the usual games of Hide and Seek, Red Rover, or
running a race, table games are excellent projects. The games are played
at the table or with the children seated on the floor. The materials
include picture cards that relate to the unit of the week or to a specific
project. The advantages of using table games as a teaching device include learning rules and how to follow them, discovering how to be a
good winner as well as a good loser, learning acceptable language structure by repeating statements called for in the rules, increasing attention
span if one wants to win at least part of the time, and having an opportunity to learn acceptable interpersonal relationships with peers.
Another advantage is having the opportunity to teach the game to
family members which gives the child good feelings about the self as
well as helps the child to develop communication skills.

Project: Lotto Game
Materials   Poster board approximately nine by nine inches with
    six equal squares drawn on the finished master card, six
    separate squares of poster board that match the master card
    squares, appropriate pictures for each game
Procedure   Several master cards that contain pictures of items
    included in the clothing unit are given to each child. The
    game can be played in a variety of ways. A leader may draw
    a card from a box and ask, "Who has a hat?" The appropriate
    child receives the hat and covers the matching picture on the
    master card. The routine may be changed to "Who has some-

thing to wear on feet?" The cards may also be hidden around the room, and the children must find the cards to fill their master card. The one who has covered the master card first is the winner. The game is over when the last person's card is filled. Any unit may have a Lotto game in it and can include not only pictures of nouns, verbs, and plurals, but also number words, numbers, or letters.

Rhyming Words. Although most children do not discover the rules for rhyming words until first or second grade, rhyming games may be introduced in kindergarten. One game requires several four-by-eight-inch poster cards, separate four-by-four-inch cards that contain words or pictures that rhyme, such as man–pan, sun–gun. Place one of the pairs on the left side of the four-by-eight-inch poster card and one on the four-by-four-inch card. Appropriate sets of cards should be kept in boxes making sure that only one set of words that rhyme is included. For instance, do not have man–pan and can–fan in the same box. Place the separate cards in a basket and the four-by-eight-inch poster cards in the middle of the table. John selects a card, names it, and places it in the appropriate spot on the poster card. If he makes an error, he returns the card to the basket. If he is correct, he keeps the card. The winner is the one who has the most cards.

Go Fish Game. Fish about the size of regular playing cards are cut from poster board. Letters of the alphabet, number words or pictures are printed or pasted on the fish. The same item will appear on four fish. For learning to read numbers, each child is dealt four fish cards. The remainder of the cards are placed on the table. Mary asks Karen to give her all of her 3's. If Mary receives one or more 3's, she makes a "book" of two 3's and puts it in front of her. Mary may continue to ask for specific cards until she fails to receive what she needs. When she asks John for his 3's and he has none, he says "Go Fish." The turn goes to the next child on her left. The winner is the one with the most "books."

What's Missing Game. Cut one part from each of many pictures: back of a chair, leg of a table, wheel of a car. Give each child a mutilated picture and ask, "Who has a picture of a chair? What is missing? Who has the missing part?"

Feed the Animals. One child is an animal. The older children in turn throw the animal three fish, one bone, two heads of lettuce. The objects could be made from cardboard.

Five Questions. The teacher and children ask a child five questions in an effort to discover what is in his or her sack.

Hit the Balloon. Each child is given a balloon to blow up. Those that are successful will have the teacher knot the stem of the balloon, and all are placed out of reach. An area is designated in the room where the game will be played; the in-bounds area is marked by a small round or square rug or a small circle drawn on the floor with chalk. The teacher presents the rules and the children repeat them at least twice after being told. The rules are: stand in the middle of the circle (or rug) and do not step outside of it, hold one hand behind you, hit the balloon with the other hand, do not let the balloon touch the ground, do not let it touch the ceiling, stop if you hit the balloon twenty times. John's name is drawn from the name-card basket. He gets into position and begins to hit the balloon. The children count in unison. When a rule is broken or the count of twenty is reached, John selects from the number cards the number of times he hit the balloon and tells how many times he hit it. If he cannot do this, he refers to the number chart. The number is written on the chalkboard. The same procedure is followed for each child. The winner takes two balloons home and the others take one home. The children discuss who hit the balloon the most times, and that number is underlined on the chalkboard. With such a procedure, the children begin to see the relationship of numbers to events. This activity is a favorite of the children and is useful when they are restless and need to move around.

12. Home Visits

A home visit is scheduled for a specified time at the parent's convenience, and the purpose of the visit is discussed with the parent ahead of time in order to make it nonthreatening. The visit lets the children see the teacher as a person outside the classroom and lets the teacher see the child who is host in the home. The suggestions may have been made to the mother that the child show his or her toys, pets, play yard, or even introduce neighborhood playmates. If the parents wish, lemonade and perhaps cookies that the child helped make could be served. The parent knows how long the teacher will visit. The teacher remembers what occurred during the visit and, if pictures were taken, includes the recollections and pictures in the child's Me Book.

13. Key Words

Key words are used to introduce children to phonics. A simple word such as *fish* is chosen to represent the 'f' sound. A picture of a "fish" is pasted on a card and the letter /f/ is written under it. This key word card is left on the bulletin board as a reference for teaching the phoneme-grapheme relationship. Key words should be introduced with a flourish so that the concept of relation of sound to letter makes an early impact on the children. The key words can be introduced at the rate of one a week through motivational teaching techniques.

Project: Make a Ring

Materials A key word card with a picture of a ring and the letter /r/ written under it, a pipe cleaner for each child, beads or macaroni, scissors or wire cutter

Procedure The /r/ key word card with the picture of the ring is presented to the children, and they are asked what they think will be made today. After they respond with *ring*, the teacher presents the materials to be used and each is discussed in detail. For example, "How does the pipe cleaner feel? What else feels fuzzy [caterpillar, velvet dress]? Can you bend a pipe cleaner? A pencil? Can you twist a pipe cleaner? Show me." The children are given an explanation of how they will string the beads or macaroni on the pipe cleaner to produce the ring. If the pipe cleaner is too long, it may be cut in *half*. "How many pieces do you have if you cut it in half?" "How many rings will the pieces make?" When the ring is completed, the teacher says, "Think of a word on our picture charts that starts like *ring*. Look at the picture chart on the chalkboard tray. Does anyone have a name that starts like ring?"

Later in the day, when there is time, the teacher says, "Let's play the contrast game with the key words *ring* and *leg*. I am thinking of something that gives you light to read by. Yes, *lamp*. Does it start like *ring* or *leg*?" The teacher works toward the day when she can say, "Name a color that starts like *ring*" when nothing has been said that day about the key word.

14. Library Books

Children should be encouraged to go to the library on a regular basis to help form good reading habits. Most schools do not like to have the young children using the school library. One alternative to this problem is for the teacher to borrow twenty or more books from the library. Each child selects one of these books to take home overnight, except over the weekend. Each book should be put into a manila envelope with the child's name and the date stamped with the personalized name stamp and the date stamp. The same information is to be stamped on the library card and filed in the library book file box. The next day the books are returned in the same envelope. The names of the books each child has read can be recorded in their Me Books.

Other suggestions are to have a permanent library book shelf in the classroom which also will include Me Books and the class's newspapers. For teaching concepts of height, the shelves may be arranged so that only tall books will fit on one shelf and very short books on another.

15. Lunch

Different schools and classrooms have varying limitations on the preparation and serving of lunch by the children. If the school has a kitchen for the children's use, a group of three to four children can prepare many simple menus for lunch under the teacher's direction. A second group can set the table, while a third cleans up after the meal. The rest of the children may be involved in an activity led by the aide, for example, listening to a story or creative play in the block corner or playhouse.

In the absence of a kitchen, the classroom can be used to assemble sandwiches, cut vegetables or fruit, and open cans. Lunch can be served in the classroom, on the playground, or on a field trip. A variety of seldom-used food should be selected to give opportunity to use new vocabulary. A lunch of steamed corn on the cob, crab meat salad on crackers, unpitted Queen Anne cherries, and pear nectar to drink could stimulate a discussion of how corns are husked; what crabs look like, where they are found, the number of legs they have; what seeds are; or how pears are made into nectar. Cans and boxes from the lunch preparation are kept to provide stock for the grocery store unit. Good table manners are taught with positive reinforcement for those who comply. Other spin-offs from the lunch activity include folding napkins into different patterns, sorting eating utensils, and inviting a guest, such as the school secretary or the principal. Sample lunch menus include:

1. Tuna Fish Sandwich
   Orange Slices
   Fortune Cookies
2. Vegetable Soup
   Peanut Butter and Jam Sandwich
   Pineapple Juice
3. Melon
   Peanut Butter and Crackers
   Roasted Marshmallows
4. Peach and Pear Salad
   Toast and Jelly Strips
   Chocolate Milk

16. Me Book

Me Book is a book that each child continues to make throughout the school year. The pages are usually completed after large group activities have been conducted. All Me Books are on display during parents' night and taken home at the end of the school year. If covers are made early in the year, the Me Books may periodically be placed on the library table to be read during the assembly period.

Project: My Face and Hair

Materials A piece of paper (page) that has a blank space at the top and the following story at the bottom of the page: My eyes are _____ . My eyelashes are _____ . My eyebrows _____ . My hair is _____ .

Procedure The teacher asks each parent for the color word they use to describe the above body parts so that there will be no confusion as to what is used at home and what is used at school. These color words are written on pieces of paper that will fit the blanks. One by one the children stand before the mirror and say in response to the appropriate question, "My eyes are brown." The teacher gives the color word strip to the child to be pasted on the appropriate line. After this exercise, the children are asked to draw their face on the top of the page and color their eyes appropriately. The same procedure is followed for filling in the remaining lines and coloring the picture.

My Height. Joan stands at the chalkboard under her name card, which is held by the magnetic clip. The teacher draws a horizontal line at the top of Joan's head. A piece of string is measured and cut to the same length as her height, and she puts it around her neck for future use. The yardstick is used to measure her height and the appropriate number is written on the chalkboard by the horizontal line. The same procedure is followed for each child, and, when the process is completed, the teacher asks each child to stretch out his or her string on the floor, from the longest to the shortest. By looking at the strings, the children can see which one is longer and whose it is. The one with the longest string is the tallest in the class and the one who has the shortest string is the shortest in the class. The children look at the chalkboard and find the highest mark indicating the tallest child. They are taught the relationship between long and tall.

This activity is recorded in the Me Book with the following story to be completed: We measured with a _____ . We cut string the same as our _____ . I am _____ inches tall. We measured all the strings. _____ is the shortest in the class. _____ is the tallest.

The teacher has sheets of words that are appropriate for the blanks, and these same words are on the chalkboard beside the picture of the word, for example, a ruler and the word *ruler*. With the number stamp, the appropriate height is recorded in the Me Book. These numbers also can be arranged from least to most for children to see height in another perspective.

For the prekindergarten level stick figures may represent the tallest and the shortest child, and the figures should be used in the Me Book.

The Balloon Game. After the children have played the balloon game, the following experience story is written in the Me Book. I hit the balloon _____ times. _____ was the winner. He hit the balloon _____ times. He got to take home _____ balloons. I got _____ to take home.

Other Me Book suggestions for prekindergarten and nursery levels are:

My Teacher	My Thumb Prints	My Family
My School	My Hands	My Pet
My Address	My Weight	My Home
My City	My Birthday	My Toys

17. Newspaper

The class newspaper is published monthly and consists of eight to ten pages for one month's activities. The children through a voting activity select from a list of titles the one of their choice. The cover sheet with the title and an illustration remains the same throughout the year. Children participate in placing the pages in numerical order. Names and dates are stamped or pasted on the cover, and the final product is taken to the copy machine. The newspaper is stapled together and sent home to the parents on the last day of the month. The newspaper informs the parents of the activities that have transpired during the month, and the children are given an opportunity to read to their parents or describe the pictures and activities to them. The following are sample topics for the newspaper.

Club Day — Group 1 — Making Indian Headdresses
Club Day — Group 2 — Making Tom-Toms
Club Day — Group 3 — Making the Thanksgiving Cornucopia
Cooking Project — Making Pumpkin Pie
Field Trip — Visiting an Ant Hill in the School Yard
Good Citizen Award — Won by _____ .
John pulled his tooth at school on _____ .
Mary went to the rodeo last Sunday.
Jim has a new baby brother.

18. Nursery Rhymes

Nursery rhymes are poems that have been handed down from generation to generation, and children apparently like them because of the sing-song nature during recitation. Many nursery rhymes have been set to music. The purpose of introducing nursery rhymes into the preacademic program is to increase vocabulary, discover morphosyntactic rules by repetition of many different sentence types, and to improve the child's self-concept by positive reinforcement from the teacher when a rhyme is learned or is play acted well. Some nursery rhymes help children learn arithmetic skills.

Project: "Ten Little Indians" (Song)
Materials Indian headdress, number cards 1–10, and number chart 1–10
Procedure Each child receives an Indian headdress by answering the teacher's question, "What do you want?" and each child receives a number card. The teacher points to 1 on the number chart and shows the child holding number 1 where to stand. The other children line up in the correct order. When this is accomplished, the children are told to face the front of the room, sit down (in random number order), and to hold their number cards in front of their chests. As the teacher slowly sings the song, "*One* little, *two* little, *three* little Indians," the appropriate child stands when the number is heard. The children change number cards, and the procedure is repeated. After several practice sessions, they can perform with a record or tape recording of the song.

The children learn a variety of nursery rhymes and then play act them.

---

19. Object Box

There is a continual collecting of small objects to be added to the object box to be used by the children for concept development and language games. With the objects children can categorize and classify or learn relational terms: heavy–light, tall–short, long–short. They can identify objects by function or give the function of an object.

Project: What Is It Used for Game
Materials Tools such as saw, hammer, wire snipper, screwdriver, stapler, needle, staple remover, hole punch
Procedure As each object is removed from the box, the children are asked, "What is it used for?" They may demonstrate first and then give an answer, or they may reverse the procedure. The action can be demonstrated by the group as they chant "Tap, tap, tap goes the hammer. Snip, snip, snip goes the

snippers. Sew, sew, sew goes the needle, and saw, saw, saw goes the saw."

Other object box activities include the following:

Where Do You Wear It? One child is asked to find something "to wear on your waist." If the word *waist* is not known, a doll's waist is shown. "Give me something to wear on my earlobe." The same procedure follows until all of the items have been selected.

Sandpile. Sand is poured into shoe boxes, and objects are buried in it. The children are asked to "Find one we ride in. Sleep in. Drink out of."

Unit Objects. A collection of objects for the units will provide many ways to teach oral language and preacademic skills.

20. Open House for Parents

The open house should be held in the spring; the specific time and date should be cleared with the school principal. Arrangements should be made for doors to be open and for completed housekeeping chores such as appropriate building temperature and clean rooms and corridors. The purposes of an open house are twofold: (1) to bring parents and friends together to learn and to see what the children do at school and (2) to provide learning experiences for the children. This consists of planning a carnival which necessitates making invitations and developing a program which may include (1) fish pond, (2) post office, (3) balloon game, (4) gingerbread boy story, (5) cake walk, (6) slide show, (7) refreshments, and (8) display of the children's work in the classroom.

Invitations. The invitations are made at school by the children who generate the sentences. The teacher completes the final format for the invitation and makes copies for each parent. The children fold the paper appropriately to fit the envelope and address the envelope by copying their parents' names and addresses, or the teacher may print the address for the younger children. If the field trip to the mailbox is planned during this week, the children can use this opportunity to mail their invitations.

Program for the Carnival. As a group the children select the kinds of activities they would like to participate in as well as the materials they would like to have displayed in the classroom, and the teacher writes the list on the board. If too many items appear, there will be a voting activity. There will be decisons also about the color of paper to be used and what kinds of art work might be appropriate. The teacher completes the program and makes copies to be given to the parents the night of the carnival.

Fish Pond. The purpose of the fish pond is to demonstrate to parents that the children can read numbers and match numbers. Prior to the open house, the children will have had a phonics lesson "Find the picture that starts like *fish*" and one of the clubs may have had a lesson related to magnets. The children are given instructions as to how they can make the fish, each having a number on it as well as a paper clip which will make it possible for the parents to catch the fish with their magnet at the end of the fish line. A cardboard box may be used to hold the fish, and one or more children will sit by the fish pond to read the number on the fish that is caught. This number will be matched with the number on the prize that has been won. The numbered prizes are located on shelves behind the fish pond. Shelf one may have two or three very special items, such as a plant or a box of homemade cookies. Shelf two may have safety pins, emery boards, and rubber bands, and shelf three may have candy, gum, and small bags of popcorn. The children who play behind the scene must read the number on the fish that was caught and find the matching number on the prize, which is given to the person fishing. For younger children, pictures instead of words may be used. They may match the picture to the object on the shelf or to a class or category of items.

Post Office. The purpose of the post office is to demonstrate each child's handwriting skills. The children will discuss what is to be said in the letter. The letter may be as simple as "THANK YOU. LOVE, HELEN" or it may include more words, "THANK YOU FOR COMING TO MY CLASS. LOVE, JOE." The children choose what they wish to write, and the teacher provides models for them to copy. During the evening of the carnival, the post office will be open at a specified time and operated by one or two children. Each parent will receive a letter that has been placed in a mail slot. For younger children a drawing may be included with the child's name stamped underneath.

Balloon Game. The balloon game, a favorite of the children, and described in the section on Games, is played by the parents. The purpose is to demonstrate to the parents how the children can present rules of the game. If there are five rules, then each of the five children will announce one rule before the game is to begin. In place of writing the number of times the parents hit the balloon, everyone counts aloud and the winner is the one who hits the balloon the most times with no errors. The children may want to provide a prize for the winner.

Gingerbread Boy Story. The gingerbread boy play described in the section on Cooking Projects will be produced by selected children either for small groups during the evening or for all of the guests at one showing.

Cake Walk. The purpose of this activity is to demonstrate that children can read numbers or match pictures, and also that they relate well with their classmates as well as with adults. The young children enjoy the cake walk, which is played as follows. If the children can read numbers through ten, tags with numbers one through ten are printed and one number is attached to each chair. Cards with numbers one through ten are placed in a draw box. Ten guests sit on the chairs that form a circle and when the music begins, they stand up and walk, one behind the other. When the music stops, they find a seat. One child draws a number from the draw box and reads it aloud. The person sitting on that numbered chair is awarded a cake. Three cakes or even several frosted cupcakes made by the children on Club Day will allow the cake walk to be played several times. For younger children, pictures may be used instead of numbers. These may be pictures of dogs, a collie, a dachshund, and other breeds that the children may have at home.

Slide Show. The slide show consists of pictures that have been taken at the school and made into slides. The children view the slides and practice describing them. When they are quite fluent, the teacher turns on the tape recorder, and each child has an opportunity to record his or her description of a slide. This presentation is made by the teacher on the night of the carnival.

Refreshments. Refreshments can be made the week of the open house during a cooking project. Lemonade and frosted cookies would be simple to prepare. Two or more children serve the punch and cookies at a specified time.

Display of Children's Work. The children make decisions as to what work they would like to have their parents see. In general, the children like to display the class scrapbook, special bulletin board exhibits, and the Me Books. Labels may be placed on the "arrival tables," "stations," and other areas of the room where parents can view the format of the daily schedule.

Because the teacher has used the parent night as a unit for preparing the carnival, her work is not an extra-curricular activity and the children have continued to be in a learning environment.

21. Phonics Box

The phonics box contains pictures that are filed under the initial sound: "fish" under /f/ and "nut" under /n/. Pictures such as "circus" are not included in the phonics box because they begin with letters that make more than one sound. The teacher may have a set of such pictures in her desk drawer to introduce as needed.

22. Records

Appropriate phonograph and tape recordings teach children new vocabulary, provide listening experiences for different sentence types, and add variety by having children follow directions in a classroom activity. (Instructions are often included on commercial recordings, which require attention from the children and are an asset also to the teacher who has not had an opportunity to memorize the directions.)

23. Roll Call

The purpose of roll call is to keep attendance. However, there is much language that can take place during this activity.

Project: Hello Song

Materials Name cards in a basket

Procedure The morning begins with the "Hello Song." The teacher and the children sing, "Hello. Hello. Hello. How are you today?" Then the teacher holds up the name of a child who stands and sings, "I'm fine. I'm fine. I hope that you're fine too." The children place their name cards on the chalkboard ledge. When each has had a turn, the teacher asks who is absent, and after their reply they are asked to read the name or names of absent children whose name cards or pictures are placed a bit removed from those who are present. Visually and by counting, the class can solve the problem. "If there are fifteen children in the class and two are absent, how many are present?" The children rational count.

Other suggestions include the teacher's use of cowboy jargon, such as "Howdy, Jennifer" or "Is pardner Joe here?" Other variations include the use of Spanish phrases or other foreign language phrases.

As the children's names are called, the girls go to one side of the room and the boys to the other. The leader for the day may rational count the number of boys and the number of girls, and the teacher will ask, "Are there more boys or more girls?"

24. Scrapbook

The class scrapbook consists of written experience stories with the children providing sentences, ideas, answers to questions, or words to fill in the blanks. The teacher includes correct sentence structure, regular and irregular plurals and verbs, new vocabulary words, and punctuation. These stories are written as a follow-up activity to Club Day, art, Me Book, or games. Incidental happenings are also included, such as a story or picture brought from home, the name of the child who lost a tooth at school and a height or weight graph. When the story has been written on the lower portion of the page, the children are given a piece of paper equal to the size of the space on the top of the page and are asked to "illustrate the story with a drawing." The children vote on the one that is to be used, but the teacher always makes sure that every child has a picture on a page several times during the year. No mention is made, of course, about the poor quality of some of the drawings. The story is read by the children with the help of the teacher, is dated, given a page number, and placed in the scrapbook. The children often ask for stories from the scrapbook to be reread. It is shown to visitors as a chronicle of class activities and is on view during the open house for parents. Once a month pages from the scrapbook can be selected to make up the class newspaper.

25. Self-Concept

A good self-concept is essential to developing feelings of self-worth. Children who feel good about themselves will say, "I can do it" or "I will try to do it." Children learn to accept things about themselves such as "I can't run as fast as Tom." The more they learn about themselves and their interpersonal relationships, the more apt they are to deal well with successes as well as failures. The teacher can develop many activities in the classroom that will help children develop good self-concepts.

Project: The Throne. The throne is a very special stage setting where one child becomes the center of attention among the classmates.

Materials Whatever the furniture or clothing, it should remain the same throughout the year. There may be a special drape to cover a chair, a robe for the children, and a crown.

Procedure Each child in the class will be selected at least once during the year to sit on the throne. It may be on a birthday or on the day the leader of the class is chosen. The child's picture is taken and while the children are focusing on him, the teacher asks, "What can we tell about Joe who is on the throne today?" The children describe his hair, eyes, and say that he is the fastest runner in the class and many other compliments. The teacher leads the discussion to emphasize positive statements. Remarks from the children are written and made into a story that will be included in the scrapbook. For example, "This is Troy. Troy is a boy. Troy has on white shoes. He lives in Pasadena. He has a red yo-yo. He has one sister. He has striped pants. He lives on Heart Street. He is a good citizen in the class. He opened the door for the teacher today. He has a friend named Dale. Dale lives next door. He has four people in his family. He is six years old. He has a swing. His address is 1213 Heart Street." The children like to hear things about themselves and to read about themselves either in the scrapbook or in the Me Book. The pictures may be used on the covers of the Me Books which are displayed at the open house for parents. Other suggestions follow.

Feelings About Myself and Others. The children sit in a circle and the teacher makes a statement about how she feels, "I am happy when I hear good music." Then she presents slot filler statements that allow children to express their feelings.

I am happy when _____.
I am afraid when _____.
I love _____.
I don't like _____.
A good wish from a fortune cookie would be _____.
I help my mother by _____.
I like it when my daddy _____.

The statements may be tape recorded and added to each child's Me Book under a title of "My feelings."

Good Citizen of the Week. The children gather in a circle at the end of the day, and the teacher announces that it is time to vote for our Good Citizen of the Week. "Let's nominate three people who have been good citizens this week. I have one to nominate. Nominate means to name. I nominate Kenneth because he opened the door for me when my hands were full of books. That's being a good citizen. Let's put his name on the chalkboard. Who else? Someone nominate a good citizen." Betsy says, "I'll nominate Jane, because she was a friend to me when I got my dress wet. She helped me wipe it off with a paper towel." The procedure continues until three are selected. Everyone votes on the child of choice by placing his or her name card under the nominated good citizen. The children count the votes and determine who has the most. The winner is John who is given the Good Citizen of the Week badge, and it is stapled to his collar so that he can wear it home. An experience story is written about him with three statements as to why he was voted good citizen.

26. Show and Tell

Show and Tell is held each Monday for a short period of time. The children are asked to take turns telling anything they want to talk about or show something they have brought from home. All items brought from home are placed on the teacher's desk and are not used except for the Show and Tell period. The purpose of this activity is to encourage children to use language for communication, by explaining, inviting comments, and sharing experiences. The teacher may wish to audio-tape what the children say at the beginning, middle, and end of the year to demonstrate improvement in communication skills both quantitatively and qualitatively.

27. Songs

Songs, like nursery rhymes and experience stories, provide a new vocabulary, experiences with a variety of sentence structures, and help to develop good interpersonal relationships.

Project: Looby Loo

Materials   Chart and word card for body parts

Procedure   After forming a circle, the children begin to sing "Here we go Looby Loo. Here we go Looby Light. Here we go Looby Loo. All on a Saturday night." A child selects a card from the basket and reads the word or refers to the chart if the word cannot be read. If the word is *hand* the children sing, "I put my right hand in, I take my right hand out. I give my right hand a shake, shake, shake and turn myself about." The procedure continues until each child has had a turn for as long as there are words in the basket. This song may be written and placed in the Me Book, in the scrapbook, or sent home in one of the class newspapers. Younger children can learn the song which they can later use in the above-mentioned procedure.

---

28. Special Events

Special events include birthdays, mother's day, father's day, Halloween, Valentine's Day, Thanksgiving, and religious holidays. The teacher includes these days in a unit or as an instructional project.

Project: Birthday party

Materials   Paper plates, cups, juice, napkins, cupcakes, candles

Procedure   The cupcakes have been baked and frosted the day before in a cooking project. The birthday child's mother has been given a list of objectives that will be used during the birthday party. The children will rational count the candles, count the children and the number of plates needed, always teaching the one-to-one correspondence. Each child could bring an inexpensive gift or a homemade gift and the game of clues could be played as the presents are opened. Activities for other birthday parties include: The teacher places birthday candles upside down in a styrofoam dish and asks, "What is wrong?"

Children draw pictures of cupcakes with the appropriate number of candles.

Valentine's Day. Valentines can be made of different textures with a variety of colors. The children trace around a cardboard heart, cut out the drawing, fold it in half, and apply seals. To _____ and From _____ are printed on the inside of the valentine. On another heart the children draw a face and paste a hat on the top for the boy and yarn pigtails for the girl. Valentines are hidden about the room, and the children must find the one that matches the valentine the teacher gives to them or they must find a *tall* and a *short* valentine, or one that is *between* the two books on the shelf. A large box with a slot in the top is decorated for the valentine mailbox. This could be a Club Day activity.

Thanksgiving. Pine cones and pipe cleaners are basic media for making turkeys for table decorations. The children help set the table. The children dress in pilgrim costumes for the Thanksgiving party at school. They each make a sentence with the words, "I am thankful for _____ ." Placecards can be made for each child. They copy their own names on their cards or use their name stamp or seal. The menu is planned by the teacher with the help of the children.

Halloween. The children cut out various sized pumpkins for the store. Each is marked with a price and the children purchase them with play money, or they are asked to select the biggest and smallest pumpkins. They may take the pumpkin home after they have drawn in the eyes, nose, and mouth. Costumes are worn to class, and the teacher stresses such vocabulary as *mask, friendly, scary, ghost, skeleton,* and *witch.* A simple chart of each child's costume will help the class remember what each wore at the Halloween party. A playhouse made from a paper box large enough for the children to enter is a good motivational technique to practice trick or treat. One child stays in the box to give out the treats. Another dons a costume, goes to the door, and says, "Trick or treat." Cat masks are made from black paper, and the children paste on the whiskers. Each child in turn pretends to be a friendly cat or a scary cat.

29. Stations

One day a week for a forty-five-minute period the children are grouped according to their abilities and needs and assigned to either Station 1, which is taught by the teacher, Station 2, taught by the aide, or Station 3 for independent work. The purposes of the stations are to provide individualized instruction by working in small groups and to promote independent work habits. Objectives are written for each child, and the teacher and the aide provide experiences that will lead to the accomplishment of these objectives. The children working at Station 3 are given an envelope of materials with designated activities to be accomplished within the time period. Each successive week the children move to the next higher station and those in Station 3 move to Station 1.

Project for Station 1:   Constructing a Group Picture. The objective toward which the children are working is to read their house number and street names and to be able to give them orally when asked.

Materials Poster board for the picture, precut shapes of large rectangles, small rectangles, large squares and small squares, large and small diamonds, small triangle, long rectangle, glue, crayons, small cards with each child's house number, small cards with each child's street name, and a chart of each child's name and address.

Procedure The teacher holds up one card with a street name and asks, "Who lives on this street?" By referring to the chart a child can find his name and match the street name. When this is accomplished, the child receives the street name card, and the procedure continues until each has a card. Then the house number cards are introduced. The teacher asks, "Where do you live?" and "Where do you find the house number?" and "Where do you find the name of the street?" The children are ready now to construct a big picture where they can take turns placing their street sign and house numbers in the appropriate spots. "We are going to construct a house. Helen, find a large rectangle. Paste the corners of the paper. How many dots will be needed to have a dot on each corner? Paste the square in the middle of this piece of poster board. Joe, choose a large rectangle and paste it in the middle of that one. Draw a small circle on the right-hand side. Now we have made a door." The teacher continues to give directions and assists the children when they need help. The house is completed with the various shapes. Someone draws the lines for the sidewalk, the street, and the skyline, and a tree is drawn. The children guess what a diamond may be used for and decide on a kite. When the picture is completed, it is put on the chalkboard ledge, and the children take turns in placing their street name and house number in the appropriate spots. The children read the numbers and the teacher explains that house numbers may be 1004 and read 1-0-0-4, or as 10-0-4, or as 1,004, but kindergarten children are only asked to name each number.

Younger children may construct the same picture but on a less sophisticated level. They will match numbers if they cannot read them, and they will match shapes if they do not know the names.

Project for Station 2: Bowling. The objective toward which the children are working is to develop the concepts of adding and subtracting and to add and subtract within sets of one through six.

Materials Six plastic bottles or bowling pins, a lane made with a wide sheet of plastic, a ball, a counting frame with six beads on the left side (a coat hanger can be opened and six beads put on it, then closed), the number chart with numbers one through six, cards with numbers in domino dots, chalkboard and chalk, a room divider.

Procedure The divider is needed to separate this active game from the view of children at Stations 1 and 3. The lane is put into place and the bowling pins are placed at the end with three in the back, two in the middle and one in front. The children are asked to name the shape formed by the pins. An explanation of how to play the game is given as well as the rules. Each child has a turn when his or her name is drawn from the basket. Susan bowls first and knocks down three pins. She goes to the counting frame and moves three beads to the far right. The teacher presents the problem, "You had six pins standing, you knocked down three, how many are still standing? Prove it." If there is time, the problem is written on the chalkboard using the numbers and subtraction or addition signs. The score is kept on the chalkboard and at the end of the period, the children, with the help of the teacher, determine who was the winner.

Visualization of arithmetic problems may be very helpful when children are asked to add and subtract with pencil and paper. They have a reference similar to the concept of the key word.

Prekindergarten level children may play a table game of Lotto that teaches categorization.

Nursery level children play a Domino game that matches pictures to pictures.

Project for Station 3: Find the Picture that Starts Like the Key Word. The objective toward which the children are working is to match sounds to pictures.

Materials Three separate pages with a different picture pasted on the top. Page one has a picture of a "ring" and underneath the picture "rope" has been stamped with the picture stamp set. Pages two and three have different pictures but the same format. The picture stamp set is on the table.

Procedure The children stamp on each page as many appropriate pictures as they can find. Because they have had previous experience in correcting each other's work, they will know how to exchange papers and check for correct pictures.

Prekindergarten level children have a story read to them and are asked Wh questions about the story.

Nursery level children use the object box to describe objects by their function as well as to find objects by their function.

30. Stories

Stories can come from books, from the teacher, or from the children. Children enjoy hearing the same stories over and over, and the teacher can take advantage of this fact by using the story to teach a variety of language and preacademic skills as well as to provide children with new information.

Project: Story of "The Three Billy Goats Gruff"

Materials A chair is placed at each end of the long table so the children can climb on the table (bridge) and walk across it.

Procedure The teacher reads the story of "The Three Billy Goats Gruff," and the children choose which characters they want to be. The Troll hides under the table.

Other projects include: Reading stories on children's age levels and making costumes and sets for play acting. Stories such as those about the circus are read. The opaque projector is used to show a series of the circus acts and the children describe what they see.

31. Vocabulary Box

This file box contains new words which occur incidentally during class. For example, when singing about Barbara's striped dress during the self-concept activity, someone points out Deanna's dress is striped too. Actually it is plaid. The word *plaid* is written on the file card and used in a sentence. Children are asked to bring a piece of plaid material to class if they can or to find a picture of a plaid dress in a magazine. The parents may need to assist in this request. The children discover that it is fun to bring new words to class, and sometimes they are presented in Show and Tell. Periodically words from the vocabulary box are used for an activity of defining words.

32. Voting

Allowing children to choose is an important part of the pre-academic curriculum guide. Although the teacher is responsible for structuring the lessons in order to meet objectives, there are many opportunities for the children to make choices individually or as a group. Voting on favorite activities, food, toys, or scents helps children know that it is all right to have different choices than those of their friends. Voting, a kindergarten level activity, is used also in developing number concepts, adding and subtracting, and generating sentences for the newspaper or Me Book.

33. Work Tables

Two rectangular tables that seat eight children each are designated as work tables. Each morning between 8:30 and 8:45, these tables have familiar materials on them, such as library books, puzzles, or color designed cards to be reproduced on peg boards. After the children have been greeted by the teacher, have placed materials from home in appropriate baskets, and hung up their coats, they select a table where they will sit and work. The rationale for work tables includes: (1) allowing the teacher time to greet each child, (2) providing a quiet time for the teacher to get her early morning desk work completed, (3) giving the children time to relax before beginning the day's activities, and (4) teaching children to be creative and work independently. The aide is in charge at the tables, and each table must be in order before the children can leave. Materials are changed daily with an effort to find equally motivating materials for each table. If the children are creating a product, they may choose to take it home or throw it away, or the teacher may suggest, if it is appropriate, that it go into the Me Book.

SUMMARY

This chapter has presented thirty-three projects, each with specific examples of how the teacher can develop a curriculum through these motivational techniques. The relationship between Chapters 8 and 9 will become apparent to the reader as the design of the curriculum is presented.

9

curriculum
guide

Coauthor Anne Mauzy

INTRODUCTION

The curriculum guide is basically the same for the three developmental levels: kindergarten, prekindergarten, and nursery. It is designed to teach oral language and the basic skills in preacademic and affective education. The kindergarten level differs from the lower levels primarily in its emphasis on reading readiness. All levels follow the same daily events with some differences in the time frame for each. The teachers at each level draw from the instructional projects in Chapter 8 and the developmental behaviors found in Appendix 1. Each project is marked by an asterisk and can be located in Chapter 8 by checking page 153. Sample lesson plans are included for each level and acquaint the reader with the procedures for utilizing the instructional projects. A calendar of events for one week is presented for each level, and a final calendar lays out the classroom projects for a full school year. There is structure to the curriculum guide because the authors believe that young children like and need a certain amount of structure. In addition, the teacher does not want learning for handicapped children to be left to chance.

SCHEDULE OF EVENTS

The following schedule taken from the kindergarten level is an example of the structure of daily events.

8:30– 8:45	Arrival		10:00-10:45	Projects
8:45– 9:00	Assembly		10:45-11:15	Follow-up Activities
9:00– 9:45	Sequenced Instruction		11:15-11:45	Fine Arts
9:45-10:00	Break		11:45-12:00	Dismissal

Operational definitions of these events follow and asterisks provide an exercise in coordinating Chapters 8 and 9 (see pp. 153–184).

Arrival

Arrival refers to the first part of the morning when the children arrive one by one or in a group from another room in the building. At this time the teacher greets each child, the children place their books or other items brought from home into the teacher's basket, hang up their coats, and choose a *work table where they will be involved until assembly period. Greeting each child at the door serves several functions. Just making eye contact with a friendly "Hello" or "Good Morning" is important to each child. The teacher also uses this time to notice if any of the children appear sick, if hearing aids are on and working, if glasses are on, and whether or not a child has shoes on the wrong feet. The remainder of the time allows the teacher to attend to administrative duties and prepare for the next activity. Arrival time extends for a fifteen minute period for kindergarten and prekindergarten levels, but the time allotted the nursery level children is thirty minutes. They require a longer time to hang up their coats and a bathroom break is often needed upon arrival.

On Monday the materials at the *work tables are always *library books. The children select one they wish to check out and take home. This may be done during the assembly period.

On Tuesdays they are required to return their *library books and place them in the teacher's basket. The aide is responsible for checking books in and out of the classroom. All books are carried home in large manila envelopes, each having the child's name printed on the envelope or, for the younger children, their own picture stamp instead of their name.

On Tuesday through Friday there is new material at each *work table for each day.

Assembly

Assembly is the first group activity of the day and is programmed to include sitting in a semicircle on the rug, saluting the flag, answering to roll call, marking the attendance book, marking the calendar (for kindergarten level only), and selecting a leader for the day. This person's responsibilities are to lead the line any time the children leave the room and perform any chores in the classroom, such as watering plants and handing out papers. The leader is selected by drawing a name card or a child's picture from the basket. Each child is to be leader before all the name cards or pictures are put back into the basket. However, a child may be a leader on his or her birthday. It is a treat to be the leader, and efforts are made to build the child's feelings of self-worth.

On Monday the new unit is discussed and the *bulletin boards are "read." *Show and Tell is the activity for the rest of the period. The nursery level children, however, may have "Show and Tell" anytime during the week. This is one of the best activities for helping nursery level children develop good feelings about themselves and practice communication skills.

On Tuesday the teacher presents a *self-concept project, such as throne or a slot filler activity.

On one Wednesday a month the *newspaper is assembled and made ready to be sent home to the parents. On the other Wednesdays a *scrapbook story may be chosen by the leader, and the children may read it, or the teacher may read it to them. Perhaps an appropriate *song could be learned that relates to the unit or to a picture on the *bulletin board. Nursery and prekindergarten level children use pictures or objects in place of words. They are not expected to read.

On Thursday the *field trip is discussed during the assembly, and discussion continues, if necessary, until time to leave for the field trip.

On Friday the *clubs, to be held later in the day, are described and the children make their selection.

Sequenced Instruction

This is the period of the day that closely resembles a traditional classroom program, with teaching of oral language, reading-, arithmetic-, and writing-readiness skills, and psycho-social development.

Monday is *chart day. The children bring their chairs to the chalkboard and sit in a semicircle. In place of *charts the nursery level may use the *expansion picture file and a slot chart or objects from the *object box.

On Tuesday the children go to one of the *stations. The *key word is introduced to the kindergarten level children. The younger children use the *expansion picture file and *object box for language development.

On Wednesday the *key word which was introduced on Tuesday is reviewed by the kindergarten children and the *phonics box is used for games. The nursery level children work on relational words and pre-mathematical skills with pictures and slot charts or with objects.

On Thursday basic skills are taught with *charts for the kindergarten and prekindergarten levels. The nursery children may use the slot charts. Once a month on Thursday the parents are invited to observe the children and confer with the teacher while the children are on a break. Parents like to observe a period when the children are taking part in the most traditional appearing school activities, when they are being taught the basics. This can be effectively accomplished with charts. Also, Thursday is chosen as a parent day because it is a field trip day, and they may be needed to provide transportation. If a behavior modification program is under way, this period is the one best suited for charting behaviors.

On Friday the children sit in chairs at the chalkboard and play *games that develop oral and preacademic skills.

Projects

Projects which have been described in Chapter 8 are different each day of the week.

On Monday the project is the *Me Book.

Tuesday is for *key word activities for kindergarten children, and the younger children have projects that relate to the unit.

Wednesday is set aside for a *cooking project. Two rectangular tables used in the classroom are put together to make one long table where the children eat what they have prepared.

On Thursday the project is a *field trip. Once a month a simple lunch is served in combination with the field trip. The *cooking project from the previous day is planned for the Thursday lunch.

Friday is *Club Day

Follow-Up Activities

This period provides time to follow through with a previous activity.

Fine Arts

The fine arts period includes *art, *finger plays, *games, *nursery rhymes, *records, *songs, and *stories. They are chosen to reinforce what is being learned in the unit. On Friday the fine arts period is short so the children can form a circle on the rug and cast *votes on the Good Citizen of the Week or engage in a favorite *self-concept project. The week's activities are reviewed and there is a discussion of plans for the following week. Twice yearly the entire period is spent on developing a sociogram (see Chapter 5, p. 102).

Dismissal

Dismissal requires only that amount of time necessary to get coats and any papers or projects to take home and a "lining-up" activity that the teacher chooses. It is referred to as "call to the door." This activity may involve being exposed to the ordinal number words *first, second, third*, or to *first–last* or to attributes in such phrases as "The boy with the red hair, brown eyes, and green pants go to the door." As a forerunner to a sociogram, the teacher may ask Karen, leader for the day, to be first and to call her best friend. Each child, then, calls his or her best friend until the line is formed. Nursery level children may be asked to crawl *under* a table to get to the door or to give their first name on request before leaving the room.

KINDERGARTEN LEVEL CURRICULUM GUIDE

The following kindergarten curriculum guide, although designed for and field tested with a specific group of children, may be altered to accommodate varied numbers of children. The class may include children with only a single handicap, such as deafness or mental retardation, or may include children with a variety of handicaps or even multiple handicaps. The resource teacher will find that many of the activities are appropriate for teaching specific skills to children on a one-to-one basis or in small groups. The purpose is the same for any group: acquisition of oral language and the skills needed for preacademic and affective education. The teacher will use, when needed, the resources of such specialists as a speech and language pathologist, physical therapist, rehabilitative audiologist, psychologist, and social worker.

Description of the Class

Fifteen children in this field-tested, half-day program were enrolled in a public school, self-contained classroom with one teacher and one aide. Fourteen of the children had normal hearing and were described as having language and learning disabilities. One boy was moderately hearing impaired and wore a hearing aid. Within the group of fifteen, five had articulation problems, four were hyperactive, and four exhibited mild to severe emotional problems including disruptive behavior.

The classroom was the size, usually found in primary or elementary grades, that will accommodate approximately thirty children. In place of desks, the teacher preferred chairs and two rectangular tables with washable surfaces, each table seating the children in groups of seven and eight. A nine-by-twelve-foot oval rug for the children to sit on during certain group activities was kept in one part of the room. This classroom had running water, a hot plate for *cooking projects, and folding screens to partition the room for activities that involved only small groups. There were three adult chairs, a teacher's desk, *bulletin boards, and cabinets to store from view the toys and materials not currently in use. There was a magnetic chalkboard, which allowed for the use of magnetic clips to display materials. Other items included a pocket chart, record player, tape recorder, and a camera. A *phonics box was in the room as were several baskets used to hold the children's name cards, finished work, things to be taken home, and whatever was brought to the teacher from home. There was a set of picture stamps for making specific *games as well as ink stamps with each child's name. Although no refrigerator was in the classroom, the teacher had access to one in the teacher's lounge.

Units

The following units are only suggestions. They are subject to change because of geographical location or any other variables that may suggest change. Units may be added or deleted.

September	School Routine (materials used, the people at school, special rooms in the building, and school activities, such as fire drill) Fall, Weather
October	Family, Home, Circus, Halloween
November	Transportation, Thanksgiving
December	Toys, Winter, Health
January	Fruit, Travel
February	Valentine's Day, Famous People, Parents' Program
March	Library, Yard, Spring, Farm, Vegetables
April	Money, Grocery Store
May	Weather and Temperature, Mother's Day, Park, Summer

Schools may differ in their long-range objectives. The following were used for the kindergarten class described in this section.

Before entry into first grade, the children will meet the following objectives as measured by appropriate tests:

Comprehend the meaning of 90 percent of the relational words presented during the year

Correctly use sentence types found in first grade readers

Recognize their own printed name from among ten other printed names

Define 80 percent of a list of affective words presented during the year

Tell five positive things about self

Read ten printed words spelled phonetically

Read ten printed words that are not spelled phonetically, words that were learned through the sight reading method

Read ten printed "words" spelled phonetically that are not real words; *nis, bate, nav, riz*

Add and subtract within sets of five

Write upper case letters from dictation

Write lower case letters from dictation

Print and correctly spell own name

Write numerals 1–10 from dictation

Daily Schedule

8:30– 8:45	Arrival
8:45– 9:00	Assembly
9:00– 9:45	Sequenced Instruction
9:45–10:00	Break
10:00–10:45	Projects
10:45–11:15	Follow-Up Activities
11:15–11:45	Fine Arts
11:45–12:00	Dismissal

Sample Lesson Plans

The following lesson plans for the kindergarten level are structured according to what is to be taught, but the teacher uses his or her knowledge and talents to develop the teaching strategies that will teach or expose children to what it is they are to learn.

SAMPLE LESSON PLAN I – KINDERGARTEN LEVEL
Unit – School
Date: September 17, Monday

SHORT-RANGE OBJECTIVES:

By ————(date) the children will meet the following objectives as measured by appropriate tests:

1. Comprehend the meaning of the following words: weigh, measure (the children are weighed and measured during the first week of school and a page with their height and weight is included in their *Me Book), *same-different, absent-present, sounds like, good citizen, earn*
2. Add and subtract within a set of three
3. Read numbers 1 through 5
4. Rational count through 10
5. Maintain or lower all behavior modification scores to a minimum of ———— points

MATERIALS

*Library books   Number *chart
Materials for making number men   Numbers and word cards

PROCEDURE

8:30– 8:45	Arrival	The children go to the work tables and check out *library books
8:45– 9:00	Assembly	Roll call is taken using the words *present* and *absent*. "Is Katie *present* or *absent*?" For *Show and Tell the children have brought an object from home or will talk about something they would like to share with their friends.
9:00– 9:45	Sequenced Instruction	The numbers *chart with the number and word cards are used to teach the children to read numbers and to match number words with numbers and numbers with sets of objects. The children are asked to find numbers that are the *same*, *different*. The find it game is played as a *chart activity.
9:45–10:00	Break	
10:00–10:45	Projects	The Behavior Modification Program (see Appendix 6) is presented and will continue for six weeks. Step 1 in the program is the activity for this day.

10-45–11:15	Follow-Up Activities	A sequence story is written for the *Me Book and includes a list of the attributes of a good citizen.
11:15–11:45	Fine Arts	The children construct the number men *chart that will be placed on the number men *bulletin board. They will sing and play act the *song "One Little, Two Little, Three Little Indians."
11:45–12:00	Dismissal	In a call to the door activity the aide records on the sociogram tally sheet the rank order in which each child was called.

SAMPLE LESSON PLAN II – KINDERGARTEN LEVEL
Unit: Circus
Date: October 17, Wednesday

SHORT-RANGE OBJECTIVES

By —————(date) the children will meet the following objectives as measured by appropriate tests:

1. Identify and name the following words:

acrobat	loud speaker	tight rope
announcer	midway	trainer
audience	parade	trapeze
band	program	trick
bareback rider	ringmaster	first-last
cannon	safety net	ahead of-in back of
circus	souvenir	in front of-behind
coliseum (tent)	spot light	largest-smallest

2. Name two attributes of an object
3. Find a picture that starts like ring
4. Add and subtract within a set of four
5. Copy numbers 1 through 4

MATERIALS

*Chart for body parts   Peanuts
Body parts cards and words   Pan

PROCEDURE

8:30– 8:45	Arrival	The children go to the *work tables where they will find the *Me Books of each child and choose which ones they would like to look at.
8:45– 9:00	Assembly	As the roll is called each child, with the help of the teacher, is asked to "Make a sentence with a word from the unit vocabulary." Pledge to the flag takes place, and the children are shown the new picture on the *bulletin board that starts like *ring*.
9:00– 9:45	Sequenced Instruction	The body parts *chart is introduced, and the children play the find it game with the picture and word cards. Following the game the children discuss the circus animals and how their body parts differ.
9:45–10:00	Break	
10:00–10:45	Projects	See roasting peanuts lesson that follows.
10:45–11:15	Follow-Up Activities	See roasting peanuts lesson that follows.
11:15–11:45	Fine Arts	The teacher reads a circus *story and includes all of the vocabulary words that appear in the short-term objectives. Questions are asked and the children point to the appropriate pictures, or make appropriate verbal responses
11:45–12:00	Dismissal	The room leader, Mike, is called to the door. Helen is called and asked to stand *behind* Mike. The next child is asked to stand *in back of* Mike. When the line is completed, the teacher asks, "Who is *in front of* Joe? *In back of* Jean? *Behind* Karen?"

Roasting Peanuts Lesson

The teacher has a sack of raw peanuts and asks the children to guess what is in the sack. "I will give you a *clue*. You buy them at the circus. . . . They have shells." When they have guessed correctly, the peanuts are put into a basket and the question is asked, "Are they raw or roasted? . . . *Raw, roasted*. Those words start like our key word. Who can remember the key word? Yes, it's *ring*. *Raw* starts like *ring* and *roasted* starts like *ring*. If we are going to roast the peanuts, what do we have to do *first*? Yes, put them into a pan. What do we do *second*? Yes, put them into the oven but be sure to turn it on." While the oven is warming, the teacher holds up the pan and asks the children to tell something about it. As they give their answers, the teacher writes them on her portable chalk slate: *silver, shiny, has a tag on it, bake a cake in it, put water in it.* In this activity, the children name twenty different attributes. As the teacher reads back each attribute, the children count, 1, 2, 3 . . . 19 "Yes, and there is one more, and that will make ____?" With the teacher's help the children generate sentences using the words as modifiers: "That is a shiny, square pan." Several raw peanuts are kept in one basket and the remainder to be roasted are put into the pan. The teacher asks, "Who can name a word that rhymes with *pan*?"

While the peanuts are roasting, the children engage in an arithmetic activity, utilizing three baskets and the raw peanuts. For example, Jim is given one basket that contains two peanuts and one basket that is empty. A third basket full of peanuts is held by the teacher who says "If I give Jim two peanuts (place in second basket) and he has two in this basket, how many will he have?" Joan, who cannot see the peanuts, answers. If she says, *"four"* then she must prove her answer. Jim places all the peanuts in one basket, and the children count aloud. The game continues with all number facts in sets of one to four. Subtraction is practiced in the same manner and the last go around can be played for "keeps." The children form a line. If they give a correct answer, they keep the peanuts, if an incorrect answer, they go to the *end* of the line.

An elaboration of the roasting peanuts activity includes:

A discussion of how peanut butter, peanut brittle, and peanut soup are made.

When a correct answer is given to an arithmetic problem, a child is asked to point to the number on the numbers men *bulletin board.

One child is the Peanut Man or Peanut Woman at the circus and sells the peanuts. With play money the children buy peanuts and make change when necessary.

The camera is used to take pictures of the activity for purposes of retelling and writing a sequence story. This story may be used in the *scrapbook or *Me Book. Modifiers are used.

Peanuts tied to strings are attached to the bottom of a twig to represent a peanut plant. The peanuts (roots) are buried in a dirt pot. There is discussion and demonstration of how peanuts grow.

Classification of nuts may be done with pictures or real nuts, like peanuts, walnuts, pecans. There are also pictures to show that most nuts grow on trees, but peanuts grow underground.

CALENDAR OF EVENTS FOR ONE WEEK: KINDERGARTEN LEVEL

MONDAY

Time	Leader	Period	Activities
8:30- 8:45	Teacher Children Aide	Arrival	Greetings *Work Table Check Out *Library Books
8:45- 9:00	Teacher	Assembly	*Show and Tell
9:00- 9:45	Teacher	Sequenced Instruction	*Charts
9:45-10:00	Aide	Break	
10:00-10:45	Teacher	Project	*Me Book
10:45-11:15	Teacher	Follow-Up Activities	*Me Book
11:15-11:45	Teacher	Fine Arts	*Art
11:45-12:00	Aide	Dismissal	Call to the Door

TUESDAY

Time	Leader	Period	Activities
8:30- 8:45	Teacher Aide Children	Arrival	Greetings Check In *Library Books *Work Tables
8:45- 9:00	Teacher	Assembly	*Self-Concept: My Feelings
9:00- 9:45	Teacher Aide Children	Sequenced Instruction	*Station 1 *Station 2 *Station 3
9:45-10:00	Aide	Break	
10:00-10:45	Teacher	Project	*Key Word
10:45-11:15	Teacher	Follow-Up Activities	*Key Word
11:15-11:45	Aide	Substitute *Self-Concept for Fine Arts	Throne Activity
11:45-12:00	Aide	Dismissal	Call to the Door

WEDNESDAY

Time	Leader	Period	Activities
8:30- 8:45	Teacher Children	Arrival	Greetings *Work Tables
8:45- 9:00	Teacher	Assembly	*Newspaper

Time	Leader	Period	Activities
9:00- 9:45	Teacher	Sequenced Instruction	*Key Word with *Phonics Box
9:45-10:00	Aide	Break	
10:00-10:45	Teacher	Project	*Cooking
10:45-11:15	Teacher	Follow-Up Activities	*Cooking
11:15-11:45	Teacher	Fine Arts	*Finger Play, *Songs
11:45-12:00	Aide	Dismissal	Call to the Door

THURSDAY

Time	Leader	Period	Activities
8:30- 8:45	Teacher Children	Arrival	Greetings *Work Tables
8:45- 9:00	Teacher Aide	Assembly	*Field Trip Preview
9:00- 9:45	Teacher Aide Teacher	Sequenced Instruction	*Charts Charting Behaviors Parents' Observations Parents' Conference
9:45-10:00	Aide	Break	
10:00-10:45	Teacher Aide	Project	*Field Trip
10:45-11:15	Teacher Aide	Follow-Up Activities	*Field Trip
11:15-11:45	Teacher	Fine Arts	*Songs
11:45-12:00	Aide	Dismissal	Call to the Door

FRIDAY

Time	Leader	Period	Activities
8:30- 8:45	Teacher Children	Arrival	Greetings *Work Tables
8:45- 9:00	Teacher Aide	Assembly	*Club Day Selection
9:00- 9:45	Teacher	Sequenced Instruction	*Object Box; *Games
9:45-10:00	Aide	Break	
10:00-10:45	Teacher Aide Parent	Project	*Club Day 1 *Club Day 2 *Club Day 3
10:45-11:15	Teacher	Follow-Up Activities	*Club Day Assembly Write and Read *Scrapbook *Stories

Time	Leader	Period	Activities
11:15–11:45	Teacher	Fine Arts	*Games *Vote
11:45–12:00	Aide	Dismissal	Call to the Door

CALENDAR OF EVENTS FOR CLASS ROUTINE: KINDERGARTEN LEVEL

DAILY

Break	Choose Leader	*Self-Concept
*Calendar	*Roll Call	*Work Tables

OFTEN BUT NOT NECESSARILY DAILY

*Art	*Games	Sequence Stories
*Expansion Picture File	*Nursery Rhymes	*Songs
*Finger Plays	*Scrapbook	
*Experience Story	*Records	

TWICE WEEKLY

*Charts

WEEKLY

*Bulletin Boards	*Me Book	*Show and Tell
*Club Day	*Library Books	*Stations
*Cooking Project	*Object Box	Units
*Key Word	*Phonics Box	*Voting
*Field Trip		

MONTHLY

*Lunch	*Newspaper	Parents' Observations and Conferences

TWICE YEARLY

Pre- and Posttesting Objectives

YEARLY

Behavior Modification Program
*Home Visits
*Open House for Parents

PREKINDERGARTEN LEVEL CURRICULUM GUIDE

The following prekindergarten level curriculum guide although designed for mentally retarded children is just as well suited for children with other handicaps, such as deafness, environmental deprivation, or multiple handicaps. The key to success is found in forming groups that are similar in the developmental levels of oral language and learning skills and chronological age. The purpose is the same as for the kindergarten level: acquisition of oral language and the skills needed for preacademic and affective education. The teacher will use, when needed, resource specialists such as a speech and language pathologist, rehabilitative audiologist, psychologist, physical therapist, and social worker.

Description of the Class

This prekindergarten class is designed for a group of twelve retarded children in the chronological age of six to seven years but functioning developmentally on the prekindergarten level. There is one teacher and one aide. The classroom is similar to that described for the kindergarten children except there is no need for the *phonics box.

Units

The following units are only suggestions. They are subject to change because of geographical location, ethnic groups, and any other variables that may suggest change. Other units may be added.

September	School Routine
October	Home, Furniture, Halloween
November	Food, Thanksgiving
December	Weather, Toys
January	Health, Grocery Store
February	Valentine's Day, Workers, Review
March	Safety
April	Parents' Program, Farm
May	Circus, Zoo, Mothers' Tea

Long-Range Objectives

Before entry into kindergarten the children will meet the following objectives as measured by appropriate tests:

Comprehend the meaning of 90 percent of the relational words presented during the year

Comprehend the meaning of possessive nouns
Identify singular and plural noun pictures (s, z, uz)
Identify objects in categories (toy, fruit, vegetable, person, animal)
Identify and name at least three numbers and three letters
Name all colors red through purple and black and white
Rational count to twelve
Answer *Why* questions (Why do we go to the store?)
Fold a six inch square of paper (1) into a smaller square and (2) a double triangle after watching the operation

Daily Schedule

8:30- 8:45	Arrival
8:45- 9:15	Assembly
9:15- 9:45	Sequenced Instruction
9:45-10:00	Break (1) Bathroom and Drink
10:00-10:45	Project and Follow Up
10:45-11:15	Break (2) Snack and Play
11:15-11:45	Fine Arts
11:45-12:00	Dismissal

Sample Lesson Plans

The following lesson plans for the prekindergarten level are structured according to what is to be taught, but the teacher uses his or her knowledge and talents to develop the teaching strategies that will teach or expose children to what it is they are to learn.

SAMPLE LESSON PLAN I – PREKINDERGARTEN
Unit: – Workers
Date: February 2, Monday

SHORT-RANGE OBJECTIVES

By _____ (date) the children will meet the following objectives as measured by the appropriate tests:

1. Comprehend the meaning of the following words:

top–bottom	*firefighter*	*letter carrier*
forward–backward	*police officer*	*pilot*
up–down	*nurse*	*dentist*
	doctor	

2. Rational count to six
3. Name at least four colors
4. Answer *Why* questions
5. Comprehend possessive nouns

MATERIALS

Cardboard cutouts of the workers
Opaque projector
Cookies

PROCEDURE

8:30– 8:45	Arrival	Children go to the *work tables, select the books they want to take home, and check them out with the aide.
8:45– 9:15	Assembly	*Roll call is taken by calling each child for *Show and Tell. After this activity the teacher asks "Who is not here?" The children are asked to count as the teacher points to each child.
9:15– 9:45	Sequenced Instruction	The various cardboard workers are clipped to the chalkboard where they will remain throughout the unit. The children count the number of workers and name them and the color of their clothing. The teacher uses the opaque projector to show pictures of workers taken from story books or from the *picture expansion file. The children discuss the kinds of clothing the workers wear, what they use when on their jobs, what it is that they do, and why they do it.
9:45–10:00	Break (1)	Bathroom and drink
10:00–10:45	Project and Follow Up	From a set of mimeographed pictures, each child chooses one of the workers. From another set of mimeographed pictures the children select the items that go with their worker: firefighter — hat, ladder, hose; doctor — thermometer, stethoscope, and bottle of medicine. These pictures are pasted with the worker's in their *Me Books. The teacher provides a sentence strip that is pasted at the top of the page which may read "This is a firefighter." The children answer the question, "Why do we have firefighters?"
10:45–11:15	Break (2)	The teacher and the children count the number of children and then count the number of

cups. She has one extra cup and makes the statement "This one is left over. There is no child for it." Two stacked cookies are presented to each child. "Do you want the *top* one or the *bottom* one?"

11:15–11:45	Fine Arts	With clay the children mold a firefighter's hat, a ladder, and a firehose. From the *object box the teacher selects a firefighter and asks the children to put him *high* on the ladder (which is pressed to paper and put in a vertical position) then *low* on the ladder. Another child is asked to take the firefighter *down* the ladder and *up* the ladder. They also are asked to point to the *top* and *bottom* of the ladder.
11:45–12:00	Dismissal	The children are called to the door by name. Before dismissal they pretend they are a fire engine with the leader being the driver. The driver says "Move the truck *forward*" and the children move in that direction. "Move the truck *backward*" and they do.

SAMPLE LESSON PLAN II – PREKINDERGARTEN LEVEL
Unit: Pets
Date: March 15, Friday

SHORT-RANGE OBJECTIVES

By _____ (date) the children will meet the following objectives as measured by the appropriate tests:

1. Comprehend the meaning of the following words: *tall-short, each, beside, between,* and all unit words.
2. Identify at least three letters
3. Rational count to ten
4. Understand number concepts to six
5. Add one and one
6. Describe an event

MATERIALS

marshmallows
toothpicks
film strip on pets and their care
picture cards of pets with printed name
animal crackers

tall and short paper cups

sound effects record and Lotto cards for the song *Old MacDonald Had a Farm*

PROCEDURES

8:30– 8:45	Arrival	The children go to the *work tables where they will make a dachshund like the sample on the table. They will construct them out of the big and little marshmallows and toothpicks that are on the table. The dog is made out of five big marshmallows for his body and one for his head. Two small ones are strung on tooth-picks for each leg.
8:45– 9:15	Assembly	The children are told that instead of club day one of the mothers is bringing the family's pets, which are two dogs. One dog is the mother and the other is the mother's baby or puppy. The film strip on "Pets and Their Care" is shown. The teacher asks Wh questions after showing the film strip. "Why do you wash a dog? What do you feed a dog? Where does a dog sleep?"
9:15– 9:45	Sequenced Instruction	Pictures with identifying printed names of a cat, dog, fish, horse, and bird are placed in the slot chart. The teacher has pictures of many different breeds of these pets, and the children take turns classifying them under the appropriate pet on the slot chart. They count the pets and give the teacher the number of pets she requests. They play number games, "If I have one cat and I give you one more, how many will you have?" After the child answers, he or she must prove the answers by rational counting. The teacher asks how a dog and a cat are alike, how different. She asks the children to identify a capital letter by name.
9:45–10:00	Break (1)	Bathroom and drink
10:00–10:45	Project and Follow Up	This activity is in lieu of club day. The mother brings to the classroom Wendy, the mother sheep dog, and Buff, her puppy. In general, the period flows as follows: The children are allowed to pet the dogs and then are asked to sit in a semicircle on the rug. Mrs. Wilson explains who is the mother and who is the baby. She tells how old they are and their names. Then she asks them to name the mother's baby, the baby's mother. Next

she passes a picture book of dogs to the children, and they locate Wendy and Buff as well as a picture of their own dog, if they have one.

The discussion proceeds as to what the dogs must eat. Mrs. Wilson feeds the baby dog vitamins with a dropper and then asks the children if they take vitamins. She shows them the kind of dry food they have and tells them how many feedings a day for each day.

The question is asked, "Why do you brush your teeth?" "Do dogs brush their teeth?" Mrs. Wilson goes on to explain that dogs chew on bones or hard biscuits because this helps keep food away from their teeth. She shows the children what the dog's teeth look like and asks the children if they are the same or different from their teeth. A discussion follows.

The last part of the demonstration is the tricks the dogs can do and the children decide why Wendy does better than Buff.

10:45–11:15	Break (2)	Tall and short plastic glasses are placed on the table. Each child is asked to point to the short one and the tall one and then name the one they want.

After the juice is served, the teacher presents a box of animal crackers and asks, "Do you want two or three? Four or six?" The children answer and select the appropriate number. Each child names his or her animal and tells three things about it.

11:15–11:45	Fine Arts	Each child is given a Lotto card with six pictures of animals, fish, and birds. A sound effects record is played and the children identify the sounds. The child who has that picture on his or her Lotto card covers it with a chip. The one who covers the pictures first is the winner. The children are given large pictures of the animals represented in the song *Old Mac-Donald Had a Farm*. While singing the song, the child with the appropriate animal stands up and remains standing until all of the children are standing.
11:45–12:00	Dismissal	The leader for the day calls the children to the door, one by one, and asks one of the children to count how many are in line. The teacher asks, "Who is standing *between* Kathy and Joan?" or "Who can point to a *tall* girl, *short* girl?"

CALENDAR OF EVENTS FOR ONE WEEK: PREKINDERGARTEN

MONDAY

Time	Leader	Period	Activities
8:30- 8:45	Teacher Aide	Arrival	Greetings *Work Tables
8:45- 9:15	Aide Teacher	Assembly	Check Out*Library Books *Show and Tell
9:15- 9:45	Teacher	Sequenced Instruction	*Charts
9:45-10:00	Aide	Break (1)	Bathroom and Water
10:00-10:45	Teacher	Project and Follow Up	*Me Book
10:45-11:15	Aide	Break (2)	*Bathroom, Snack, Play
11:15-11:45	Teacher	Fine Arts	*Art
11:45-12:00	Aide	Dismissal	Call to the Door

TUESDAY

Time	Leader	Period	Activities
8:30- 8:45	Teacher Aide	Arrival	Greetings *Work Tables Check In *Library Books
8:45- 9:15	Teacher	Assembly	*Self-Concept: My Feelings
9:15- 9:45	Teacher	Sequenced Instruction	*Station 1 *Station 2 *Station 3
9:45-10:00	Aide	Break (1)	Bathroom and Water
10:00-10:45	Teacher	Project and Follow Up	A Unit Project
10:45-11:15	Aide	Break (2)	Bathroom, Snack, Play
11:15-11:45	Teacher	Fine Arts	Game
11:45-12:00	Aide	Dismissal	Call to the Door

WEDNESDAY

Time	Leader	Period	Activities
8:30- 8:45	Teacher Aide	Arrival	Greetings *Work Tables
8:45- 9:15	Teacher Aide	Assembly	*Newspaper
9:15- 9:45	Teacher	Sequenced Instruction	Listening Activities
9:45-10:00	Aide	Break (1)	Bathroom and Water
10:00-10:45	Teacher	Project and Follow Up	*Cooking

Time	Leader	Period	Activities
10:45-11:15	Aide	Break (2)	Bathroom, Snack, Play
11:15-11:45	Teacher	Fine Arts	*Finger Play and *Songs
11:45-12:00	Aide	Dismissal	Call to the Door

THURSDAY

Time	Leader	Period	Activities
8:30- 8:45	Teacher Aide	Arrival	Greetings *Work Tables
8:45- 9:15	Teacher	Assembly	*Field Trip Preview
9:15- 9:45	Teacher	Sequenced Instruction	*Charts Behavior Modification Parents' Observations Parents' Conference
9:45-10:00	Aide	Break (1)	Bathroom and Water
10:00-10:45	Teacher	Project and Follow Up	*Field Trip
10:45-11:15	Aide	Break (2)	Bathroom, Snack, Play
11:15-11:45	Teacher	Fine Arts	*Songs
11:45-12:00	Aide	Dismissal	Call to the Door

FRIDAY

Time	Leader	Period	Activities
8:30- 8:45	Teacher Aide	Arrival	Greetings *Work Tables
8:45- 9:15	Teacher	Assembly	*Club Day Selection
9:15- 9:45	Teacher	Sequenced Instruction	*Object Box: *Games
9:45-10:00	Aide	Break (1)	Bathroom and Water
10:00-10:45	Teacher Aide Parent	Project Follow Up	*Club Day 1 *Club Day 2 *Club Day 3
10:45-11:15	Aide	Break (2)	Bathroom, Snack, Play
11:15-11:45	Teacher	Fine Arts	*Games
11:45-12:00	Aide	Dismissal	Call to the Door

CALENDAR OF EVENTS FOR CLASS ROUTINE: PREKINDERGARTEN LEVEL

DAILY

Two Breaks	*Roll Call	*Self-Concept
Choose Leader	*Work Tables	

*Art	*Records	*Scrapbook
*Expansion Picture File	*Experience Story	Sequence Story
*Finger Plays	*Stories	*Games
*Vocabulary Box	*Nursery Rhymes	

WEEKLY

*Bulletin Boards	*Me Book	*Show and Tell
*Club Day	*Library Books	*Stations
*Cooking Project	*Object Box	Units
*Listening Activities	*Field Trip	

MONTHLY

*Lunch	*Newspaper	Parents' Observations and Conferences

TWICE YEARLY

Pre- and Posttesting Objectives

YEARLY

Behavior Modification Program	*Home Visits
*Open House for Parents	

NURSERY LEVEL CURRICULUM GUIDE

The following nursery level curriculum guide although designed for hearing-impaired children is just as well suited to children with other handicaps, such as mental retardation, environmental deprivation, and multiple handicaps. The key to success is found in forming groups that are similar in the developmental levels of language and learning and chronological age. The purpose is the same as for the kindergarten and prekindergarten levels: acquisition of oral language and the skills needed for preacademic and affective education. The teacher will use such resource specialists, when needed, as a speech and language pathologist, rehabilitative audiologist, physical therapist, psychologist, and social worker.

Description of the Class

This nursery level class is designed for a group of eight hearing-impaired children in the chronological age of three to four years. Their nonlinguistic skills are on age level, but their linguistic skills range between eighteen and twenty-four months. There is one teacher and one aide. The classroom is similar to that described for the kindergarten children except there is no need for the *phonics box.

Units

The following units are only suggestions. They are subject to change because of geographical location, ethnic groups, and any other variables that may suggest change. Other units may be added.

September	School Routine
October	Family, Home, Halloween
November	Body Parts, Thanksgiving
December	Clothing, Toys
January	Review, Food, Books
February	Valentine's Day, Farm Animals
March	Planting, Yard
April	Pets, Zoo
May	Circus, Mothers' Tea

Long-Range Objectives

By the end of the school year the children will meet the following objectives as measured by appropriate tests:

Comprehend twelve basic phrases
Comprehend the meaning of the unit vocabulary words
Comprehend the meaning of the pronouns *I, my, mine, me, you, your, he, his, him, her*
Comprehend *in, on, under, off, big, little, small*
Identify six objects by function
Know number concepts to two

Daily Schedule

8:30- 9:00	Arrival
9:00- 9:15	Assembly
9:15- 9:45	Sequenced Instruction
9:45-10:00	Break (1), Bathroom and Drink

10:00–10:30	Project and Follow Up
10:30–11:10	Break (2), Snacks, Walks, Rest
11:10–11:40	Fine Arts
11:40–12:00	Dismissal

Sample Lesson Plans

The following lesson plans for the nursery level are structured according to what is to be taught, but the teacher uses his or her knowledge and talents to develop the strategies that will teach or expose children to what it is they are to learn.

SAMPLE LESSON PLAN I – NURSERY LEVEL
Unit: Home
Date: October 15, Tuesday

SHORT-RANGE OBJECTIVES

By _____ (date) the children will meet the following objectives as measured by the appropriate tests:

1. Name five pieces of furniture found in a home
2. Comprehend the meaning of *I, my, mine, me, your*
3. Comprehend the meaning of *in, on, under, big, little, small*
4. Identify two objects by function
5. Sort furniture into classes and subclasses
6. Comprehend basic phrases: Give me the ____. Go get the ____.

MATERIALS

beads and strings	five pictures each of beds, chairs, tables
necklace of beads for the teacher	pegs and peg boards
three shoe boxes	snacks
doll house and furniture	picture book about home
	sixteen paper napkins

PROCEDURE

8:30– 9:00	Arrival	Children go to the *work tables that are set up with big and little beads and strings. The aide holds up a big bead and says, "Find a big one, a small one, a little one."

		The procedure continues by changing the size of the beads until a string of beads is long enough for a necklace. The children wear their necklaces to assembly.
9:00- 9:15	Assembly	The teacher is wearing a necklace of beads. She calls roll by saying, "Karen, stand up. Show me *your* beads. Show me *my* beads." "Sit down." For the next child she says, "Show me *my* beads. Show me *your* beads." The children present their Show and Tell objects. When finished "talking" about their objects, the teacher asks them to place them *in* the box, *on* the chair, *under* the chair.
9:15- 9:45	Sequenced Instruction	The children go to one of the specified *stations where they receive instruction to meet their special needs. *Station I teaches identification of objects by function, using the *object box, the *picture expansion file, and a Lotto *game. Station II teaches pronouns. Using peg boards, the teacher gives directions to individual children. "*I* want a peg. *You* may have a peg. Show me *my* peg. Show me *your* peg. Show me *mine*." *Him, his*, and *her* may also be included even though not a part of the objective. Station III has for each child a box containing pictures of furniture; a variety of chairs (rocking, straight back) as well as other pieces of furniture. Each child classifies the furniture and when completed, passes the box to the next child.
9:45-10:00	Break (1)	
10:00-10:30	Project and Follow Up	The teacher has pictures of five chairs, each different in appearance, for example, a rocking chair, straight chair, high chair. There are also five pictures each of beds and tables. From a set of pictures the children are asked to "Find one chair. Find two beds."
		By turn the children match the furniture according to subclasses on the slot chart. Then the teacher says, "Go get what we sit on. Sleep in." The children may be asked to select a *big* table, a *little* table, a *small* table from pictures of big and little tables. They may select a *tall* and *short* table. Although not in the objective, children may be exposed to words beyond their language age. For another activity the children reach into a bag of toys and through feeling select one and name it. The teacher tells where to place it, *in* the box, *under* the box, or *on* the box.
10:30-11:10	Break (2)	Before snack time the children visit the teacher's lounge, the kitchen if one is in the school,

and the nurse's room. They identify and name household belongings that would be in their home, such as chairs, sofa, stove, bed, sink. During snack time the teacher again uses the pronouns, "*I* want a cookie. *You* take a cookie." This period ends with bathroom and rest period.

11:10–11:40	Fine Arts	The teacher selects a picture book about the home and "reads" it to the children. Then they are asked to identify and name the objects in the book. For another activity the teacher demonstrates how to fold a square and a triangle. The children fold the napkins into these patterns and sort them, and the teacher puts them away for snack time during the rest of the week.
11:40–12:00	Dismissal	The children are dismissed as follows: "Billy, go to the door. Helen and Karen go to the door. Brett and Judy go to the door." When the children are in line the teacher points to one child and says, "Here we have one boy." Then she points to two girls and says, "Here we have two girls."

SAMPLE LESSON PLAN II – NURSERY LEVEL
Unit: Clothing
Date: December 2, Wednesday

SHORT-RANGE OBJECTIVES

By _____ (date) the children will meet the following objectives as measured by appropriate tests:

1. Comprehend pronouns: *she, her, he, his, him*
2. Identify four objects by function
3. Comprehend the following basic phrases: Pick it up. Throw it away. Where is the ___? Open it. Close it.
4. Name six articles of clothing

MATERIALS

Precut place mats	Two pitchers
Crayons	Eight styrofoam cups
Boy doll (cardboard)	One teaspoon
Girl doll (cardboard)	One long-handled spoon
Set of clothes for each	Crackers
Lemonade	

PROCEDURE

8:30- 9:00	Arrival	At *work tables the children will find pre-cut place mats and crayons. They are to draw colored circles and crosses to decorate their place mats. The picture seal that represents their name is pasted on their place mat.
9:00- 9:15	Assembly	The teacher calls roll by pointing to a child and asking "What's his or her name?" Then the teacher asks each child who has brought something for Show and Tell "What is it?" and expects an answer. Then she asks all the children to name the objects. The teacher draws the objects on the chalkboard, and the pictures are named.
9:15- 9:45	Sequenced Instruction	Each parent has been asked to bring a small suitcase or a box with four articles of clothing that belong to the child. The children take turns showing their clothing. The teacher stimulates language comprehension with the following questions and statements: "Open it. Open your suitcase. Where is your *hat*? *Shoes*? *Shirt*? *Socks*? Which one do you wear on your head? Feet?" The other children are asked to name the clothing. The teacher takes a pair of shoes from Mary's box and a pair from Jim's box. She holds up a pair of shoes and asks, "Are they *his*? *Hers*?"
9:45-10:00	Break (1)	
10:00-10:30	Project and Follow Up	The project for the day is making lemonade. The teacher has a large empty pitcher, a pitcher full of water, and the packet of lemonade that has been emptied into a bowl. The teacher stimulates language comprehension and expression by asking questions and giving directions. "What is this [pitcher]? What is this [spoon]?" The children take turns putting the lemonade powder into the empty pitcher. Some put in one teaspoonful and some put in two. The water is poured into paper cups and the children empty their cups of water into the lemonade pitcher. They stir. Each activity has an oral direction or requires an oral response. The teacher reinforces productions of two-word utterances. The next step is to set the table. The teacher gives directions, "Go get *your* place mat. Put it *on* the table." From the set of eight cups one child is asked to take two. Give one to *him*. Give one to *her* (a boy and girl are sitting side by side). When the table is set, the children are ready for break 2.
10:30-11:10	Break (2)	Crackers are served, and each child is asked to take two. The teacher asks such questions as

		"Which one do you drink out of? Do you eat?" A bathroom break and rest period follow.
11:10–11:40	Fine Arts	Two paper dolls, a boy and a girl, are placed on the table with a box of clothes including a hat for each doll, a dress and a boy's suit, shoes for each. The teacher asks, "What do you wear on your head? Find one. Show me the boy, the girl. Is it *his*? *Hers*? *She* wants some shoes. *He* wants some shoes." When the dolls have been dressed, their clothing is pasted on them, and the finished product is tacked to the *bulletin board. The children are asked to "Go wash your hands"; "Sit down."
11:40–12:00	Dismissal	The children are dismissed as follows, "Louise, stand up. Go get *your* coat." When all children have their coats, they line up at the door for dismissal. The teacher says "Good-bye" to each by name.

CALENDAR OF EVENTS FOR ONE WEEK: NURSERY LEVEL

MONDAY

Time	Leader	Period	Activities
8:30– 9:00	Teacher Aide	Arrival	Greetings *Work Tables Bathroom if necessary
9:00– 9:15	Aide Teacher	Assembly	Check Out *Library Books *Show and Tell
9:15– 9:45	Teacher	Sequenced Instruction	*Charts
9:45–10:00	Aide	Break (1)	Bathroom, Water
10:00–10:30	Teacher	Project and Follow Up	*Me Book
10:30–11:10	Aide	Break (2)	Snack, Walk, Rest
11:10–11:40	Teacher	Fine Arts	*Art
11:40–12:00	Aide	Dismissal	Call to the Door

TUESDAY

Time	Leader	Period	Activities
8:30– 9:00	Teacher Aide	Arrival	Greetings *Work Tables

Time	Leader	Period	Activities
			Bathroom if necessary
			Check In *Library Books
9:00- 9:15	Teacher	Assembly	*Show and Tell
			*Self-Concept: Birthday
			Child
9:15- 9:45	Teacher	Sequenced Instruction	*Station 1
			*Station 2
			*Station 3
9:45-10:00	Aide	Break (1)	Bathroom and Water
10:00-10:30	Teacher	Project and Follow Up	Unit Activity
10:30-11:10	Aide	Break (2)	Snack, Walk, Rest
11:10-11:40	Teacher	Fine Arts	Story
11:40-12:00	Aide	Dismissal	Call to the Door

WEDNESDAY

Time	Leader	Period	Activities
8:30- 9:00	Teacher	Arrival	Greetings
	Aide		*Work Tables
9:00- 9:15	Teacher	Assembly	*Newspaper
9:15- 9:45	Teacher	Sequenced Instruction	*Object Box
9:45-10:00	Aide	Break (1)	Bathroom and Water
10:00-10:30	Teacher	Project and Follow Up	*Cooking
10:30-11:10	Aide	Break (2)	Snack, Walk, Rest
11:10-11:40	Teacher	Fine Arts	*Finger Play
			*Music
11:40-12:00	Aide	Dismissal	Call to the Door

THURSDAY

Time	Leader	Period	Activities
8:30- 9:00	Teacher	Arrival	Greetings
	Aide		*Work Tables
9:00- 9:15	Teacher	Assembly	*Field Trip Preview
9:15- 9:45	Teacher	Sequenced Instruction	Charts
			Parents' Observations
			Parents' Conferences
9:45-10:00	Aide	Break (1)	Bathroom and Water
10:00-10:30	Teacher	Project and Follow Up	*Field Trip
10:30-11:10	Aide	Break (2)	Snack, Walk, Rest
11:10-11:40	Teacher	Fine Arts	*Songs
11:40-12:00	Aide	Dismissal	Call to the Door

Time	Leader	Period	Activities
8:30- 9:00	Teacher Aide	Arrival	Greetings *Work Tables
9:00- 9:15	Teacher	Assembly	*Club Day Selection
9:15- 9:45	Teacher	Sequenced Instruction	*Object Box
9:45-10:00	Aide	Break (1)	Bathroom and Water
10:00-10:30	Teacher Aide Parent	Project and Follow Up	*Club Day 1 *Club Day 2 *Club Day 3
10:30-11:10	Aide	Break (2)	Snack, Walk, Rest
11:10-11:40	Teacher	Fine Arts	*Games
11:40-12:00	Aide	Dismissal	Call to the Door

CALENDAR OF EVENTS FOR CLASS ROUTINE: NURSERY LEVEL

DAILY

Two Breaks
*Show and Tell (anytime
   child brings something)

Roll Call
Choose Leader

*Self-Concept
*Work Tables

TWICE WEEKLY

*Charts

OFTEN BUT NOT NECESSARILY DAILY

*Art
*Expansion Picture File
*Finger Plays
*Object Box

*Records
*Experience Story
*Stories
*Nursery Rhymes

*Scrapbook
Sequence Story
*Games

WEEKLY

*Bulletin Boards
*Library Books
*Object Box

*Me Book
*Stations
*Units

*Club Day
*Cooking Projects
*Field Trip

216

MONTHLY

*Lunch   *Newspaper   Parents' Observations
                                                and Conferences

TWICE YEARLY

*Pre- and Posttesting Objectives

YEARLY

Behavior Modification Program   *Home Visits
*Open House for Parents

SUMMARY

This chapter has included a format for structuring a preacademic program for children in nursery, prekindergarten, and kindergarten level
classes. The format serves as a guide for teachers who wish to develop
objectives and a sequenced program for the full school year. The description of the instructional projects in Chapter 8 plus the home
training activities for parents found in Appendix 7 will supplement this
chapter. Such a curriculum guide will help to avoid leaving language
learning, acquisition of preacademic skills, and affective education to
chance.

10

meeting
special needs

INTRODUCTION

Communication requires interaction of at least two individuals, and in the traditional mode this takes place through oral language. The basic purpose of communication is to transmit one's thoughts, questions, feelings, and needs to another person and to receive some kind of feedback from that person. People, who for different reasons are unable to speak or understand, or both, are at risk of being excluded from participation in the social interaction of society. Fortunately for some communicatively handicapped children, speech therapy or a special language program will partially or totally alleviate the problem. For others, prosthetic devices have been developed which serve to assist the defective part to function more normally. Among these are obturators to improve velopharyngeal closure in the case of cleft palate, hearing aids, and glasses. With these devices and the aid of speech and language pathologists many children speak well, are able to participate in mainstream education, and develop feelings of self-worth and self-esteem. Unfortunately, there are some children who do not learn language through the same channels that normal speakers learn language. Such children may be found among populations of the deaf, retarded, and autistic. For these youngsters alternative systems of communication are needed, such as manual language, or programs employing pictographs and other symbols for teaching the content, form, and use of language. There is yet another group of children who comprehend what is said to them but are partially or totally limited in their speaking ability due to a dysfunction of the speech mechanism. The most common categories are the dysarthrias and apraxias, both resulting in poor speech intelligibility. For some of these children manual language or communication boards may be helpful. For those who have additional motor handicaps that limit the range of motion of both arms and hands, manual language is not feasible. To use communication boards some of these children must resort to technical aids, such as pointer sticks attached to the head or electronic switches that require minimal hand pressure to activate a device that will help the child select the appropriate stimuli.

The development and use of alternate systems of communication for nonoral children made its greatest impact in the early 1970s (Lloyd 1976). It became apparent during this period that there was great heterogeneity not only among the user group but also among the instructional systems and the technical aids to augment instruction. Different populations of children needed different software and different hardware. For example, the school age, intellectually normal, nonverbal cerebral palsied child, with limited range of motion in the upper extremities required a different instructional program and different technical aids than the three-year-old child with the same handicaps. Federal funding was available to create model programs for these children, but progress was slow because it took years of work to develop and field test the innovative ideas. Parents became anxious, but it was difficult for them to form pressure groups to promote alternate systems of communication for their children because of the small number of children involved and their lack of homogeneity. However, with the impact of Public Law 94-142, which provides public school education for many children who previously have been denied school enrollment, we can expect an additional influx of innovative hardware and teaching strategies to help these children function at their full potential. The following sections include a description of some of the alternate communication systems and technical aids for augmenting the various systems now in use, suggestions for evaluating the needs of the children, criteria for selecting alternative instructional systems and technical aids, and a discussion of research needs.

ALTERNATE SYSTEMS OF COMMUNICATION

Communication systems for the nonverbal child in the range birth to first grade are not particularly new. Manual language and communication boards have been around for some time. What is new, however, are such concepts as that manual language can become a communication system for populations other than the deaf and that logographic systems with a linguistic base can be developed for teaching the content, form, and use of language. Although there are no current programs that meet the needs of all children or perhaps all the needs of one child, there is a current thrust to develop ideal communication systems for all nonverbal children. In general, these techniques fall into the categories of oral and manual, orthographic, and logographic systems.

Oral and Manual Systems

Three general approaches to teaching language to deaf children are oral and aural, signs, and total communication. In the late 1960s and early 1970s there were, and there continue to be, confrontations among the oralists (oral and aural), the manualists (signing only), and Total Communication specialists (oral and aural plus signing). The oralists firmly believe that all deaf children should be introduced to the oral and aural method from the very beginning, and manual language should be taught only as a last resort to those children who fail to learn enough language to communicate in a hearing world. This educational philosophy has angered the manualists and total communication specialists. They maintain that it places a stigma on those children who for one reason or another could not learn to communicate orally; they are tagged as an inferior group in society. The manualists would like to have deaf children become bimodal in their communication skills, but, if necessary, happily settle for a system of signs, which provides an alternate system of communication. The manualists cite the many deaf children who have been enrolled for years in oral programs and during their teen years still have no serviceable method of communication in either a deaf or a hearing community. The manualists believe that had these children been taught sign language early, they would not be in this dilemma. The advocates for Total Communication argue that a combination of manual and oral and aural teaching is the answer to meeting the objective of communicating in a hearing world. They contend that if children do not become oral, they have the alternate system of manual language. The discussion continues, and these issues will not be settled until further research, particularly longitudinal studies, determine which children should be trained by which method and at what period of time in their language-learning program. Until more definitive data become available, the choice of methods should be made by the diagnostic team, including the teacher and the parents.

While all methods recommend using hearing aids to make the best use of the child's residual hearing, the question of whether two hearing aids are better than one has not yet been resolved. The evidence is in favor of binaural amplification (Libby 1980). The audiologist is the one who determines the need for one or two hearing aids and is the most qualified professional to coordinate the procedure for selecting a hearing aid (Northern and Downs 1978). In addition to advocating hearing aids, all methods include training in speech reading (lip reading), which is the ability to comprehend speech by learning to observe and interpret the movement of the speaker's oral mechanism.

Oral and Aural Method. The combination of what the deaf person hears and what she or he can speech read is the foundation upon which the oral and aural approach has been structured. As mentioned previously, proponents of this method believe that intellectually normal, properly trained hearing-impaired children can become oral and live and communicate in a hearing society without the restrictions imposed by manual methods only.

To avoid some of the problems encountered in speech reading, Cornett (1967) developed Cued Speech, a system of hand movements that differentiates phonemes that look alike on the lips, such as /p/, /b/, and /m/, yet have distinctive sound features, such as, voiceless, voiced, and nasal. The hand movements made close to the speaker's face are not considered signs, but only an aid in identifying the distinctive sound features of the phoneme, hence improving speech intelligibility. Clark and Ling (1976) suggest that Cued Speech may have some advantages for children who have failed with a traditional speech reading approach, but they caution that the visual burden imposed by the variety of hand cues may draw the child's attention away from the auditory and speech reading cues. Certainly more research is needed in this area.

The major alternative system to teaching communication skills to hearing-impaired individuals is manual language, which is a broad, generic term to mean language of signs and finger spelling. Manual language for the deaf includes at least the following: American Sign Language (ASL), Seeing Essential English (SEE 1), Signing Exact English (SEE 2), Rochester Method, and Total Communication.

American Sign Language (ASL). One of the oldest manual languages used by many deaf adults is the American Sign Language, often referred to as ASL or Ameslan. It is a system of signs and finger spelling that is widely used by deaf adults who usually teach the same system to their hearing-impaired children. There are two distinct disadvantages to this method of communication: (1) only those who know ASL can communicate with one another and (2) the morphosyntactic structure is not linguistically compatible with standard English, spoken or written. Therefore, many persons who communicate only with ASL are deficient in reading, written communication, and spelling. All of these become educational deficits that interfere with academic achievement and later with employment opportunities. For an in-depth review of the research literature related to the American Sign Language, the reader is referred to Wilbur (1976, pp. 425–499).

Seeing Essential English (SEE 1). The first attempt in the United States to introduce the morphosyntax of standard English into manual language was a program developed by David Anthony (1966, 1971). Signs were developed for articles, pronouns, tense markers, and other language-enriching features which would have been finger spelled or deleted in ASL. In addition, SEE 1 included signs not found in ASL.

Signing Exact English (SEE 2). An improvement upon SEE 1 was brought about by the development of SEE 2, Signing Exact English (Gustason and others 1972). This offshoot of ASL utilizes the morphologic and syntactic features of standard English, while staying as close as possible to the traditional signs used in ASL. Similar versions of SEE 2 have been developed by committees in state Departments of Special Education. Bornstein and others (1973) developed a SEE 2 version primarily aimed at meeting the communication needs of the preschool child, and later (1975) extended the signed-English program to the elementary school child.

Rochester Method. The Rochester Method (Scouten 1967 and Castle 1974) was developed by a group of educators who believe that English should be signed as it is spoken and that the only avenue for accomplishing this is finger spelling. This orthographic method has not met with much favor due to the difference between the extended time it takes to finger spell a word and the brief time it takes to say a word. Bornstein (1965) found that a comfortable rate of finger spelling for experienced adults is three hundred letters or sixty words per minute. Normal speech is approximately 150 words per minute or about 2½ times as fast as finger spelling. Furthermore, very young children do not have the finger coordination needed to form the letters and are not developmentally ready for the academic subject of spelling inherent in the Rochester Method.

Total Communication. In the last decade some educators of the deaf and clinical researchers have recognized that not all children taught by the oral method speak standard English (Rister 1975 and Vernon and Koh 1971). Some educators became interested in combining methods, which led to the development of Total Communication (Jordan and others 1976). As agreed upon by the Conference of Executives of American Schools for the Deaf, "Total Communication is a philosophy requiring the incorporation of appropriate aural, manual, and oral modes of communication in order to insure effective communication with hearing impaired persons" (Crammattee, 1967). Total Communication includes speech, speech reading, auditory training, reading, writing, and manual language, including finger spelling. The rationale for such a program lies in the theory that early developing concepts can be linguistically coded by simultaneously using the manual sign and the spoken word for the object. Children trained in the Total Communication system are expected to develop a larger vocabulary of signs than most children do of words in the early stages of language learning, simply because signs are more readily comprehended and expressed. This becomes an advantage because the early vocabulary of signs allows the child to communicate needs and feelings to the family, a positive factor in child development. Proponents of the system believe that children eventually will drop signs and develop better oral communication skills if the oral aspect of communication and interaction with normal hearing peers and adults continues to be emphasized.

Oralists who oppose the concept of Total Communication have raised two questions, neither of which has yet been answered: (1) Will profoundly deaf children, who perhaps would be oral in an oral and aural program, find signs easier and, therefore, never become oral? and (2) Will parents and relatives be motivated to learn a program such as SEE 2 in order to provide the Total Communication system outside the school environment? Schlesinger and Meadow (1972) probably come close to summarizing the concept of Total Communication for all its proponents. They believe that since speech and speech reading are difficult for the very young deaf child, oral language will be acquired at a slower rate if a child is limited to only the oral approach. They conclude that children who receive sign language in infancy not only have linguistic advantages but are also more like hearing children in these early years because they can participate in meaningful communication with their families during the critical early years of language development.

The bulk of the studies related to Total Communication have been conducted by proponents of this method, and the results strongly favor introducing both signs and words in the early language development years. A literature critique by Nix (1975), however, cites several limitations of the studies, including poor control of variables and poor research design. These factors suggest the need for a more scientific approach to the evaluation of all systems for teaching language to young deaf children. An educated guess is that no one system is appropriate for all children.

Orthographic Systems

Traditional English orthography (T.O.), a graphic system that utilizes the alphabet for writing, spelling and reading, is considered to be a complex task for normally achieving children and a difficult and sometimes impossible task for children with language and learning handicaps. The use of any orthographic system for very young handicapped children often is not considered because they are not developmentally ready to either write or spell. However as children progress into the kindergarten curriculum, there is a need for a system to translate oral language into a graphic form. It is apparent that blind children will need an alternative form, and children who cannot hear the sounds the phonemes make will have difficulty learning the phoneme-grapheme correspondence. To augment the learning of T.O., at least three special systems have been developed: Braille, finger spelling, and the initial teaching alphabet.

Braille. The universally accepted system of orthography for the blind is Braille developed by Louis Braille in 1824. The basic unit of Braille is the six-dot cell in which the dots are raised or embossed by the use of a Braille typewriter. The reader receives tactile cues by moving his or her fingers across the Braille-typed message, and through this mode learns to read. As with T.O., heavy demands are placed on spelling.

Finger spelling. Another structured system of orthography is finger spelling which is an adaptive motor behavior used primarily by the deaf population. It is a manual alphabet of letters formed by hand-finger configurations. There are twenty-six configurations that correspond to the twenty-six letters of the alphabet. Its use is tied to T.O. and has the same limitations as T.O. for very young children: they do not have the motor dexterity required to finger spell and are not cognitively ready to spell. Signing is the basic communication tool of the young deaf child using manual language, and finger spelling emerges much later as an auxiliary system.

Initial Teaching Alphabet. The initial teaching alphabet (i.t.a.), with a history of development dating back to Isaac Pitman in 1844, made its appearance in the United States in the early 1960s and became widely used through that decade with normal-achieving as well as language- and learning-handicapped children. In general, each i.t.a. character represents only one sound, therefore, each sound is represented by only one character. The purpose of this alphabet is to provide a simpler means of teaching children to read. Clark and Woodcock (1976) report on some of the extensive research conducted in both Britain and the United States and conclude that "The initial teaching alphabet enjoyed great popularity in the 1960s. However, when studies failed to show i.t.a.'s long range superiority over T.O., its use declined" (p. 574).

Logographic Systems

Logographs represent word units or ideas through pictographic or non-pictographic symbols. Pictographs are concrete pictures easily identifiable by children and adults, such as a stick figure of a boy running to indicate the word *running*, or a wheelchair to symbolize the handicapped person. Non-pictographic symbols use abstract signs, such as a form that in no way looks like a dog to represent dog. Logographs are often referred to as rebuses and are classified into three general types: (1) concrete, stick figure of the boy running, (2) relational, an arrow pointing up and an arrow pointing down to indicate the words *up–down*, and (3) a symbol that represents an object or idea yet looks nothing like its counterpart. Complex rebuses combine these three general types to make sentences and often include *ing* and other T.O. markers, a straight line —— representing the word *is* and other abstract signs.

Logographs have become common symbols nationally and internationally in a variety of locations —symbols designating the location of the baggage claim at the airport, and ⋃ indicating a no U-turn at the intersection. Other uses of logographic systems are in teaching English as a second language, teaching beginning reading to children, teaching remedial reading, and in communication boards for the handicapped.

To standardize the rebus forms throughout the world, Clark and others (1974) developed a *Standard Rebus Glossary*, which includes 818 different rebuses plus over 1,200 combinations of rebuses or rebuses with letters. Although anyone can develop his or her own pictographic and nonpictographic symbols, there is a trend to utilize a common glossary. Hence many of the same symbols are used in the following alternate systems of communication: Rebus Reading Series, Peabody Reading Program, Blissymbolics, Non-Speech Language Initiation Program (Non-SLIP), and Minnesota Early Language Development Sequence (MELDS).

Rebus Reading Series. One of the earlier experimental studies with the rebus approach to teaching reading to young mentally retarded children was the Rebus Reading Series (Woodcock 1965). The goal was to teach children to read by using a vocabulary of rebuses that were gradually translated into T.O.

Peabody Rebus Reading Program. The Peabody Rebus Reading Program (Woodcock and others 1968) emanated from the Rebus Reading Series. The goal of this program is to teach children to read using an initial curriculum of rebuses that are gradually translated to T.O. The instructional materials include programmed workbooks, readers, and supplementary materials. This program is primarily a whole-word approach to teaching reading with emphasis upon comprehension ·skills. The logographs are presented in complex form and serve as a link to spoken language, reading rebuses, and eventually reading traditional orthography.

Blissymbols (Formerly Bliss Symbols). Shirley McNaughton, a teacher in the Ontario Crippled Children's Centre in Ontario, Canada, and her colleagues, began the first Blissymbolics program in 1971. They described the program as follows:

> Blissymbolics, also called Semantography, is a symbol system developed by Mr. Charles Bliss as a bridge between meaning and traditional orthography. Mr. Bliss was very concerned about international understanding and was attempting to create an easily learned modern language for communication between all peoples. The symbols were based upon his experience in China during the war. With these symbols he sought to do the same thing for the world that the Chinese written language has done for the people in China: Allow people of different spoken dialects to communicate using a common symbolic language. We discovered Bliss Symbols through our efforts to find a communication vehicle for non-vocal, non-reading children and we thought this system might have a potential for use to the young handicapped children. We have adapted this system somewhat in our program. (McNaughton 1976, p. 85)

The goal of the system is similar to the goals of other systems: to provide an alternative means of communication for children who understand some of what is said to them but are unable to talk due to neuromuscular impairment or retardation. Specifically, the goal includes the following:

1. To more effectively develop concepts by the use of a symbol (stick) figure of a man as opposed to the picture of a man (the latter may connote only one person's father)
2. To use symbols that will generalize in order to promote richer communication with a limited number of symbols
3. To allow for symbols that can express feelings
4. To be used as a transition system for the prereading child to progress to reading readiness and on to reading with T.O.

The Blissymbolic program includes approximately one hundred elements on two-by-three inch cards that combine to form symbols. A few of these symbols are pictographic, but most are abstract and made up of combined elements. (See Figure 10-1). The procedure is implemented on a language board. Newly designed mechanical and electronic devices, however, are now being adapted to the Blissymbolics program, including fairly complicated printers for printouts.

The curriculum content includes most of the grammatical structures of the language, such as nouns, verbs, opposites, negation, numbers, and words of feeling. A summary description of the teaching sequence follows:

1. The child is given a symbol that can be used immediately in conversation with the teacher or aide.

Figure 10-1 Selected Samples of Blissymbols Basic Symbols

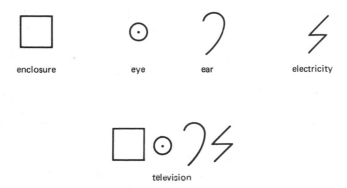

enclosure   eye   ear   electricity

television

Copyright, Blissymbolics Communication Institute 1980,
Toronto, Canada.

2. More symbols are added to build a working vocabulary with an attempt to include functional responses such as yes-no, happy-sad.
3. The concept that one symbol represents a range of meaning is taught.
4. The children are helped to discover strategies for using the symbols efficiently in "connected discourse." (See Figure 10-2.)
5. Strategies to increase speed of communication also are taught.

For detailed information on the Ontario curriculum and how it is implemented, write to the Blissymbolics Communication Institute, 350 Rumsey Road, Toronto, Ontario M46 1R8 Canada. Also from this address obtain information on "Mr. Symbol Man," a film documenting Mr. Bliss's symbols as well as a twenty-minute segment showing the use

Figure 10-2 Blissymbolics provides the user with the capability to communicate in sentences.

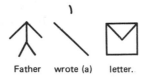

Father   wrote (a)   letter.

Copyright, Blissymbolics Communication Institute
1980, Toronto, Canada.

of the symbols with some of the children at the Ontario Crippled Children's Centre in Toronto.

Non-Speech Language Initiation Program (Non-SLIP). The Non-SLIP program published by Carrier and Peak (1975) is a nonspeech program modeled after Premack's work in teaching language to chimpanzees (Premack 1970, 1971 and Premack and Premack 1972, 1974). Two questions were asked: (1) Can severely impaired, nonverbal children with low probability of success in learning to talk, learn from the Premack system? and (2) Will the geometric shaped symbols, like those used by Premack, facilitate the discovery of the linguistic rules of spoken language?

The goal of the Non-SLIP program is to teach retarded children the tactics for acquiring functional communication responses. That is, the program is designed to teach the children a set of conceptual skills that will lead to functional communication. Although the program was originally designed for children with severe and profound retardation, some success with autistic children has been reported by McLean and McLean (1974). Carrier (1976) reports that the system is also applicable to children with psychoses, sensory impairment including deaf-blind, and mild to moderate cerebral palsy.

Materials for the Non-SLIP program include:

1. Pieces of masonite cut in various abstract shapes that represent words. These shapes which have one or more color-coded dots and the word name in T.O. on each provide the core vocabulary for the instructional program (see Figure 10-3).
2. A tray similar to a chalkboard divided into four inch-wide slots, each slot coded with the colored dots found on the shapes.
3. A set of pictures that match the forms.
4. A set of instructions.
5. Record-keeping sheets.
6. Reinforcers that are appropriate for each child.

It has been recommended that for cerebral palsied children, the shapes be attached to blocks making them easier to be grasped.

The objectives include learning to match shapes with the same number of dots, matching colored dots, and sequencing the number and color cues according to the appropriate slot on the tray. The training proceeds from simple to complex until the children can produce grammatically correct, seven-word sentences of the form: article + noun + auxiliary + verb + preposition + article + object of preposition. The curriculum also includes subprograms.

Minnesota Early Language Development Sequence. The Minnesota Early Language Development Sequence, with the acronym MELDS, was developed by Clark, Moores, and Woodcock (1975) in response to a need for a receptive language program for young hearing-impaired chil-

Figure 10-3 Non-SLIP (Non-Speech Language Initiation Program) symbols. An example of using Non-SLIP (plastic words) to construct a sentence. For instruction the symbols are arranged horizontally on a response tray.

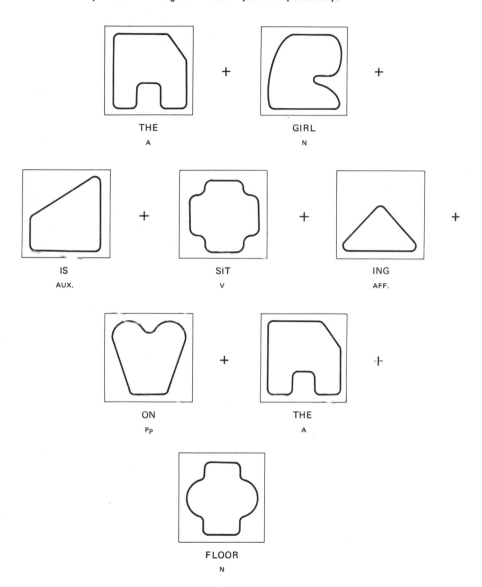

Source: J. K. Carrier and T. Peak. *Non-Speech Language Initiation Program.* Lawrence, Kan.: H & H Enterprises, Inc., 1975.

dren who had little or no language. MELDS combines elements of two visual systems, rebuses and the vocabulary of the American Sign Language (ASL). Although intended for hearing-impaired children as young as two years, the program has been used with severely mentally retarded individuals and children with developmental language delay.

The goal of this program is to facilitate the development of receptive communication skills in young hearing-impaired children and other populations with language and learning disorders. Specifically the goals are aimed at teaching parents to teach their own children and teaching children to:

1. See language spatially as an aid to building many different sentence patterns
2. Obtain practice in decoding printed symbols
3. Learn a variety of reading skills, such as left-right sequencing and ordering of word units which will later translate into T.O.

The instructional materials include a teacher's and a parent's manual of lessons, rebus cards, sentence cards, pocket chart for teacher and parent, and student workbooks. A supplementary publication, *MELDS Glossary of Rebuses and Signs* (Clark and Greco 1973) presents 393 pairs of rebuses and ASL signs utilized in the MELDS program. This publication serves as a reference source for teachers and parents wishing to use rebuses jointly with signing.

There are 120 classroom lessons and 120 correlated parent lessons that require approximately twenty minutes of structured teaching time per lesson. Much of the program grew out of vocabulary and situations suggested by parents. The program is designed to be completed in one academic year and follows a basic sequence in which rebus words or sentences are put into a pocket chart. There are 380 vocabulary words. The teacher or parent points to and says each word and then gives the appropriate signs in combination with the spoken words. As the children learn the vocabulary, they are presented many different sentence patterns. The activities are designed for constant and active involvement of the child in the teaching and learning process. Sets of parent-lesson envelopes are sent home each day with the child. Provision is made for the transition of fourteen rebuses into traditional orthography and five signs into finger-spelled words in the last thirty lessons.

TECHNICAL AIDS FOR ALTERNATE
SYSTEMS OF COMMUNICATION

Alternate systems of communication for nonvocal, physically handicapped children include both software and hardware. The software or instructional systems have already been presented. The following provides samples of the hardware or mechanical and electronic aids that augment the communicative process. The use of technical aids is one more approach to habilitating or rehabilitating nonvocal, motor-handicapped children. Unfortunately, there is no one most appropriate aid that meets the needs of all children. The nature and extent of each child's handicapping condition requires a technical aid that is best suited for the child. Vanderheiden and Harris-Vanderheiden (1976) present three basic approaches for helping children in the visual mode to point to, select, or in some way indicate what it is they would like to communicate to the receiver. These approaches include scanning, encoding, and direct selection.

Scanning involves presentation of the stimulus materials in a sequential manner until the child indicates by a prearranged signal the stimulus he or she is selecting. The simplest form is a head nod or eye blink for "yes–no" responses. The advantage of a scanning technique is its simplicity of operation for children with low cognitive skills or severe neuromuscular problems, or both. The major disadvantage is the time consuming element of stimulus presentation before a response can be elicited. Encoding techniques utilize multiple signals from the child which are presented in a pattern that must be memorized or looked up on a chart. One of the simpler forms is the five by five matrix that includes letters of the alphabet (Z excluded). If the child wants the letter D, he or she holds up four fingers to indicate the column and one finger to indicate the row. This same principle can be accomplished with switches. In a direct selection technique, the child directly selects the desired elements of the message. The most familiar direct selection technique is the communication board. On this board are logographs, words, or letters that the child points to or manipulates to develop communication skills.

Augmentative Devices

A variety of augmentative devices and their combinations as alternate communication systems for physically impaired children is a growing technology. Unaided techniques which involve pointing or looking at the needed item have been used for many years. From this stage we have moved to fundamental aids that require no moving parts, such as the head pointer. More recently, simple electromechanical and electronic devices have been developed as portable and nonportable fully independent communication aids. They include such devices as boards and displays, pointers, and switches.

Boards and Displays. Boards and displays are made by teachers, therapists, and parents or may be designed by mechanical or electronic engineers. These include communication boards and flip charts. The most common is the communication board which is placed on the desk or wheelchair or is used for bedridden patients. Manual, electromechanical, or electronic devices are attached to these boards for children who have limited range of motion. When large vocabularies become unwieldy on communication boards, flip charts are frequently used. Words are arranged into specified linguistic categories and placed in separate flip-type notebooks. The children indicate which flip chart is needed to select words in order to develop their phrases or sentences.

Pointers. For children who have extremely limited use of the upper and lower extremities, pointers may be attached to the head. These pointers are long enough to reach the desired symbols on the communication board. With even greater restricted head movement a light may be attached to the pointer and the communication board placed in an upright position where the beam of light can be directed.

Switches. Due to the neuromuscular involvement of the child, switches may be designed so that they are activated by a very light touch or by a heavy blow. They may be operated by the knee, shoulder muscles, or muscles around the eyebrows. Other switches may be activated by the breath through a "sip-and-puff" technique that uses the sucking as well as blowing muscles.

For an overview of the vast variety of technical aids, their description, and information on where they can be purchased, the reader is referred to the "Masterchart of Communication Aids" (Holt and Vanderheiden 1976).

The State of the Art with Technical Aids

The state of the art in design and field testing of technical aids is still in its infancy. One giant step was taken in 1975 by the Swedish Institute for the Handicapped in collaboration with the International Commission on Technical Aids, Housing and Transportation (ICTA). The purpose was to establish an international cooperative effort to further the knowledge of technical aids for nonvocal, motor-handicapped children. The project has been in progress since 1975, with funds granted by the Swedish Board for Technical Development. A Swedish committee of experts from various fields of knowledge, such as phoniatrics, neurological rehabilitation and habilitation, special education, and technology, has been guiding the project since its inception (Royal Institute of Technology, S-100, Stockholm, Sweden 70). This group, with contributions from international specialists, will be able to:

1. Provide a forum for discussing topics of technical aids
2. Monitor ongoing research in each country and disseminate this knowledge
3. Undertake exchange of relevant information among countries

CRITERIA FOR SELECTING ALTERNATE
SYSTEMS AND TECHNICAL AIDS

The optimum solution to selecting an alternative communication system with a compatible technical aid would be communication skills that would evolve with the progress of the children. As the children reached higher language or cognitive levels, so would they be exposed to higher level curricula and more efficient technical aids. To achieve the optimum requires an in-depth evaluation of each child's motor, sensory, and cognitive skills and an evaluation of the technical aids as they relate to the needs of the user and the receiver.

Evaluation of User's Skills

The evaluation of a nonvocal and often multiple handicapped child requires a cooperative interdisciplinary effort involving at least the following professionals: speech and language pathologists, audiologists, linguists, physical and occupational therapists, social workers, physicians, and engineers in prosthetics, orthotics, and technical communication aids. Through the coordinated efforts of these and other professions, the full potential of the nonvocal child may be realized.

Motor. A complete audit of each child's motor skills is basic to any further assessments. A medical evaluation with input from the physical and occupational therapists will reveal what motor skills the child can currently perform and what improvement can be predicted over time with a program of physical and occupational therapy including prosthetic and orthotic consultation. Specifically, the teacher will need to know the child's range of motion in the upper and lower limbs and to what extent he or she can grasp and release. If the upper limbs are not functional, the decision must be made as to what set of muscles can be used to provide a means for nonoral communication, using lower limbs, shoulders, neck, or sucking and blowing.

Ambulation and posture also need in-depth evaluation. Is a wheelchair or walker to become a permanent part of the child's life, or will full self-ambulation occur over time? Information on posture will help the teacher develop seating arrangements that will allow the child to make optimal use of vision and range of motion during the instructional program. The physical therapist will play a major role in the evaluation of each child's motor skills and use of these skills in the instructional program.

Sensory. Another physical condition that needs assessing is the sensory input, primarily hearing and vision. In the last decade audiologists have devised special tests and techniques for evaluating the hearing of hard-to-test children, like infants, retardates, cerebral palsied, autistic, and multiple handicapped. These techniques have emerged from the development of electroacoustic impedance audiometers, the low cost averaging computer, and the new testing materials for speech audiometry (Northern and Downs 1978). These new technological developments have provided the audiologists with tools that help determine the nature and extent of the hearing impairment of these hard-to-test children and to recommend hearing aids when indicated. Rehabilitative audiologists become a part of the teacher's supportive personnel.

Equally as important as hearing testing is the assessment of vision. Unfortunately ophthalmologists have not been able to devise visual tests that can be administered routinely to hard-to-test children in the doctor's office. Often the physician calls upon members of the therapy and teaching staff to provide descriptions of what they have observed regarding the child's visual problem and how it appears to interfere with his or her functioning. McDonald (1976, pp. 111–112) who has had extensive experience with nonverbal multiple handicapped children, describes the visual problems as follows.

> There are many things therapists and educators can and should observe regarding the child's visual functioning. Children who have neuromuscular problems which effect [sic] control of the extremities often have neuromuscular problems with their ocular motor functions. Strabismus, or squint, is very common. When one eye turns in and one out the child sees double and the human brain does not tolerate diplopia. If the child has double vision, he will suppress the vision in one eye. If he does this long enough, he will lose the vision in that eye. The child who is seeing double may also have a difficult time attending to the kinds of visual stimuli we want to present on his communication board. When a child has difficulty identifying pictures, you can have the child respond while you hold a card in front of one eye and then in front of the other. If he does better seeing with one eye than with the other, you have some helpful information for the eye doctor. Another problem found in some children is hemianopsia, a loss of vision in one half of the visual field. The loss would be on the nasal side in one eye and on the cheek side in the other. If you are working with a child from the side, and it is his blind side, you may get the impression that he is dumb, he is not seeing, or that he is not responding to visual stimuli. The problem is that you are not in his visual field. If he has difficulty with head control and is a very slow reactor, he may have trouble getting his eyes around to where he can see the material. Teachers and therapist should work in front of the child so they can observe him carefully to see how he tries to use his eyes, or turn his head, or manipulate his body to bring things within his visual field.
>
> There are also problems of vertical imbalance, where instead of deviating in the lateral plane, the eyes deviate in the vertical plane, causing visual problems for the child. A very simple procedure for detecting deviations is to hold a little fountain pen flashlight about 30 inches in front of the child's eyes. When the light falls in the center of the pupil of one eye, it should fall in the center of the pupil of the other eye as well. If it falls up too high or to the

side, that is an indication that the child's eyes are probably not functioning in a binocular way. This observation warrants referring the child to an ophthalmologist.

We had in one of our residential centers a very interesting little girl who "went all to pieces" everytime she tried to handle visual material at nearpoint. Her eyes appeared to fly off in several directions and she became quite hyperactive. She was unable to keep herself integrated. Instead of working with her at nearpoint, we got some large pictures and displayed them for her at about 20 feet where her visual axes were parallel. She could identify pictures at this distance and behaved much more normally. We gradually moved the pictures in closer and closer and now she looks at things on a language board with the visual material arranged around the edge of the tray.

Cognitive. Once the examiner knows the child's deficits in the motor and sensory areas, tests of cognitive development can be selected or devised. This is not an easy task when the child has auditory, visual, motor, and language deficiencies. As with the ophthalmologist, the psychologist will call upon other team members for their observations or will devise simple tasks that can be administered by one or more of the team members. Diagnostic teaching discussed earlier in this text is perhaps the best avenue for determining the developmental level of cognitive skills of children with multiple handicaps. For the less-involved children, standardized tests or checklists can be administered.

Language. The cognitive level of the child may provide some insight as to the level of language acquisition. Because these children are, for the most part, nonvocal, tests of language comprehension are administered using an appropriate communication system, whether gestures, manual language, or speech. Both prelinguistic and linguistic features of language will be assessed. Again, the hard-to-test child may be evaluated best in a diagnostic teaching program.

Meeting the Needs of the User and the Receiver

Each nonverbal child should be helped to develop an alternative communication system, however limited it may be, and to express needs and feelings through this system. Members of the assessment, therapy, and teaching teams, knowing the motor, sensory, cognitive, and language skills of each child, will select the appropriate communication system and the appropriate technical aids for each child. Ongoing evaluation will help determine when the children are ready for a change. Not to be overlooked in the total programming are answers to two questions: Are the needs of the user being met? Are the needs of the receiver being met?

Meeting the Needs of the User

Whatever instructional and technical aids are used, they should assist the user in:

1. Learning new behaviors, concepts, and labels that will promote communication skills
2. Communicating as independently as possible under all circumstances
3. Communicating as rapidly and efficiently as feasible
4. Providing interaction with the receiver
5. Maintaining a high level of motivation
6. Gaining personal gratification

Specific questions should be asked such as:

1. Is the equipment acceptable to the user?
2. Is the equipment compatible with the curriculum?
3. Is the equipment always available to the user?

Meeting the Needs of the Receiver

With concern for the receiver's needs, the following questions may be asked:

1. Does the listener receive information about the user's intentions, beliefs, feeling, requests, and even danger signals?
2. Is the receiver motivated to communicate with the user?
3. Is the system acceptable to the receiver?

RESEARCH

Research in the areas of alternative communication systems for children who do not learn language in the traditional mode lag far behind the innovative methods that have been designed and implemented for the children, including both software and hardware. Three concerns are alluded to throughout the literature: (1) the questionable scientific design in much of the reported research, (2) the lack of longitudinal studies, and (3) the need for adapting linguistic features into the alternative instructional programs. People have speculated freely regarding the techniques that might be appropriate and have used intuition and educated guesses. There is now a need for more extensive study and research to determine which instructional and technical aids are best for which children.

SUMMARY

The impact of Public Law 94-142 which provides free and appropriate education for handicapped children has opened doors to a population of young handicapped children for whom few language intervention programs were available. In the late 1960s and early 1970s innovative persons developed or improved upon a variety of alternative systems of communication to meet the needs of the children who could not learn language by traditional methods. Because children often had neuro-muscular problems that interfered with the instructional program, another group of innovators devised mechanical, electromechanical, and electronic aids that would augment the instructional program. The cooperative efforts of these two innovative groups have provided new schemes for helping the neurologically involved and language- and learning-handicapped children develop alternative systems of communication.

DEVELOPMENTAL BEHAVIORS

Obtaining a list of developmental behaviors for specific age groups is a frustrating experience due to the many variables among the standardized norm-referenced and criterion-referenced tests as well as the differences in checklists which have no standardized data available. Some norm-referenced tests provide standard scores that tell how a child responded in relation to other children of the same population on a normal curve, and some norm-referenced tests provide equivalent scores that compare children of different ages or grade levels on a normal curve. Then there are criterion-referenced tests that relate to mastery of operationally defined behaviors that are used to write objectives and measure achievement. Some of the tests use pictures for eliciting responses, some use objects, and others use both. Scoring test items may vary, for example, from a pass–fail on one trial only to two out of three correct responses or three out of five correct responses.

The following list of developmental behaviors has been divided into the categories of Language Comprehension, Language Expression, Reading Readiness, Arithmetic Readiness, Problem Solving (birth to three years), Avenues of Learning (three years to first grade), Social-Personal, and Motor and Self-Help Skills. A brief description of each category precedes the behaviors. The purpose of this list of sequenced behaviors is to describe a child's development in terms of what he has and can do in the above categories (assessment), to select subsequent behaviors from the developmental list for writing objectives, to prepare lesson plans related to the objectives, and to be accountable for what the child was expected to learn (reassessment).

Language Comprehension

The following behaviors represent children's responses to the content and form of language when no verbal reply is required. An attempt was made to include a sampling of children's lexicons and syntactic structures at six-month intervals until kindergarten and then at an approximate twelve-month age spread from kindergarten to first grade. The behaviors have been defined and discussed in Chapter 2 (pp. 23–36) and Chapter 6 (pp. 125–26). All of the language comprehension items were taken from the following criterion-referenced tests, each of which provides an 80 percent cutoff point, that is, 80 percent of the children in the standardization process could perform the test item (Bangs 1975, Kraner 1976, Bangs and Dodson 1979, and Bangs 1980).

0 to 6 Months

Responds to sound:
  bell, snapper

  person's voice

Child becomes active or ceases activity when noisemaker is heard (by one month).

Child ceases activity or coos back when person talks (by two months).

| quieted by voices | Ceases crying when person speaks (by three months). |
| Localizes sound | Turns appropriately to sound source (between three and six months). |

6 to 12 Months

Responds to own name	Child gives appropriate response when name is called.
Recognizes names of pets, familiar persons	Child looks toward pet or person when name is called.
Negation — *no-no*	Child withdraws when caretaker says "no-no."

1-0 to 1-6 Years

Shows piece of clothing on request	Child looks at, points to, or shows clothing.
Comprehends "Go get your ___" "Where is ___"	Child performs request.
Responds to "bye-bye" or "pat-a-cake"	Person gives verbal request (no hand cues) and child responds.

1-6 to 2-0 Years

Responds to "Sit down. Stand up"	Child follows directions.
Responds to two-part command	Puts the doll in the bed.
Identifies two body parts	Identifies from pictures, self, doll, or person.
Points to one or more pictures	Points to pictures from picture book.

2-0 to 2-6 Years

Objects by use: *drink out of, sleep in, sit on*	Which one do we drink out of? Sleep in? Sit on?
Quantity words: *One*	Give me one block, two, one.
Pronouns: *I, my, mine, me, your*	*I* want a cup. I'll give you a cup. Show me *my* cup, *your* cup, *mine*.

2-6 to 3-0 Years

Objects by use: *Write with. Live in*	Which one do we write with? Live in?
Quality words: *light–dark*	Show me the light one, dark one, (black and white squares of paper).
Size words: *big–little–small*	Show me the small ball, big ball, little ball (obvious size difference).
Position words: *in, on, under, out of*	Put the block under the box, in the box, on the box. Take the block out of the box.

Quantity words: *all*	Take one block. Take all the blocks.
Pronouns: *she, her, he, his, him*	*She* wants a cookie. Give *her* a cookie. *He* wants a cookie. Give *him* a cookie. Point to *his* cookie.

3-0 to 3-6 Years

Objects by use: *play with, wear*	Which one do we play with? Wear?
Category words: *animal*	Show me an animal.
Two-part command	Give me the pencil and stand up.
Negation: *is, is not*	Show me the ball is on the table, is not on the table.
Quality words: *hard-soft*	Give me the hard one, soft one.
Directional words: *apart-together*	Take the cars apart. Put the cars together.
Pronouns: *you, they*	You take a cup. They want cups.

3-6 to 4-0 Years

Objects by use: *read*	Show me what we read.
Action agent: *swims, bounce*	Which one swims in the water? Which one do we bounce?
Category word: *toy*	Show me a toy.
Colors: *red, blue, yellow, green*	Child points to appropriate colors.
Quality words: *heavy-light*	Give me the heavy one, light one.
Quantity words: *empty-full, more-less*	Show me the empty, full box. Which box has more-less buttons?
Position words: *around, in front of-in back of,*	Push the car around the tree. Put the car in front of, in back of the garage.
next to	Put the car next to the tree.
Size words: *big-little*	Use objects with less size difference than used for 2-6 to 3-0 year olds or use objects with more properties than a ball, such as a car. Show me the big-little car.
Pronouns: *us, their, them*	Give us a cookie. Give them cookies. Show me their cookies.
Modification: two modifiers	Show me the big, yellow house, the little, red house.

4-0 to 4-6 Years

Objects by use: *eat with, cut with, tells time*	Show me what we eat with, cut with. Show me what tells us time.
Objects by function: *gives us milk*	Show me which one gives us milk.
Category words: *person, building, fruit, vegetable*	Show me a person, building, fruit, vegetable.
Colors: red through purple, black, white	Child points to colors.

Position words: *beside,* *top–bottom,* *highest–lowest*	Put the car beside the tree. Show me the top, bottom of the car. Show me the airplane that is highest, lowest.
Directional words: *backward–* *forward*	Push the car forward, backward.
Size words: *tall–short, short–* *long*	Show me the tall tree, short tree. Show me the short stick, long stick.
Quantity words: *each*	Point to each button.
Quality words: *same–* *not the same*	Look at this picture. Show me one that is the same, not the same.
Time words: *after, when*	After I stand up, give me a pencil. When I stand up, give me a pencil.
Pronouns: *who–what*	Show me who is on the bed, what is on the bed.
Possessives	Show me the mother's baby, baby's mother.
Verbs: *past, future*	Show me the man who fell out of the tree, will fall out of the tree.

4–6 to Kindergarten

Quality words: *same–different*	Show me one that is the same as this one, different.
Quantity words: *more–most–less*	Which coat has more, less, most buttons.
Position words: *high–low*	Put the dog high, low on the ladder.
Directional words: *up–down*	Take the doll up, down the ladder.
Time words: *Before*	Before I clap my hands, stand up.

Kindergarten to First Grade

Position words: *farthest–nearest*	Show me the boy farthest from the tree, nearest to the tree.
Verb tense, passive.	Show me the truck was hit by the car, the car was hit by the truck.
Position words: *in front of,* *ahead of, behind*	Put the dog in front of, behind, ahead of the car.
Position words: *first–last*	Show me the first, last car.

Language Expression

The following behaviors represent children's verbal responses to specific questions and directions and include samples of the categories of spoken form: phonology, morphology, and syntax. An attempt was made to sample children's expressive language including their lexicons and syntactic structures within six month age levels until kindergarten and at an approximate twelve month age spread from kindergarten to first grade. The items are similar to those found in the list of language comprehension behaviors. All of the language expression items were taken from the following criterion-referenced tests, each of which provides an 80 percent cutoff point, that is, 80 percent of the children in the standardization process could perform the test item (Bangs 1975, Kraner 1976, Bangs and Dodson 1979, and Bangs 1980).

0 to 6 months

Vocalizes other than crying	Produces mostly guttural sounds during first month.
Vocalizes two identifiable vowels	Produces vowels by third month.
Vocalizes when adult copies infant	Coos with or back to parent by sixth month.
Laughs out loud	Laughs by six months.
Makes babbling sound and squeals	Produces these sounds by six months.
Vocalizes when alone	Vocalizes when alone by five or six months.

6 to 12 Months

Vocalizes with two identifiable consonants	By twelve months of age children demonstrate these behaviors.
Vocalizes with vowel combinations	
Combines consonants and vowels	
Vocalizes to own mirror image	
Indicates wants by vocalizing, not crying	
Pitch variation when vocalizing	

1-0 to 1-6 Years

Imitates animal sounds	By eighteen months of age children demonstrate these behaviors.
Imitates words	
Uses jargon speech	
Imitates adult's production of la-la-la-, da-da-da	
Says three or more words appropriately	
Verbally labels one or more objects	
Says equivalent of "thank you"	

1-6 to 2-0 Years

Jargon speech	Good inflectional changes, but unintelligible.
Combines two or more words	"More milk." "Daddy bye-bye."
Vocabulary of twenty or more words	Substantive and relational words.
Names one or more pictures	Substantive and relational words.
Responds to speech of others	"Do you want more milk?" Answer, "No milk."

2-0 to 2-6 Years

Asks questions	"What doing?"
Names five or more pictures	Substantive and relational words.
Recites portions of nursery rhymes	Uses telegraphic style or deletes portions of rhyme.
Vocabulary of 275 or more words	Great variation among children in size of lexicon.
Speech is socially oriented	Talks with others.
Refers to self by name	"Jamie go."
Speech is telegraphic but functional	Deletes words as in a telegram.
Nouns, verbs, and adjectives predominate	Word classes vary among children.
Talks about immediate experiences	"Billy push car."
Uses one or more personal pronouns, not always correctly.	"Me push car."

2-6 to 3-0 Years

Mean length of utterance is three to four words	Some utterances include single words and some utterances more than four words.
Uses past tense	"I found kitty."
Uses negation	"No more apple."
Uses plurals	Blocks, dogs.
Carries on simple conversation	Short statements primarily about here and now.
Uses Wh questions	Where is? Who do? Why?

3-0 to 3-6 Years

Action-Agent: *flies, sleeps, bites, swims, meows*	Tell me what flies, sleeps, bites, swims, meows.
Questions: What do you do when: *hungry, cold, tired*	What do you do when you are hungry? Cold? Tired?
Questions: What do you: *eat, wear, drink*	What do you eat? Wear? Drink?
Action-Agent: *burns, bounces*	What burns? Bounces?
Questions: What do you do when: *thirsty, sleepy*	What do you do when you are thirsty? Sleepy?
Questions: What do you: *live in, play with, ride in, sit on*	What do you live in? Play with? Ride in? Sit on?
Plurals: *s, z, uz*	Here is a cup. Here ___ [dogs, houses].

4-0 to 4-6 Years

Objects by function: *cuts, shoots*	What cuts? Shoots?
Action-Agent: *melts, stings*	What melts? Stings?

Colors: *red through purple,* and *black, white*	Names the colors.
Categories: *toy, fruit*	Name a toy, fruit.
Opposite analogies	Sister is a girl, brother is a ____ .
Defines: *shoe, book, pencil*	What is a shoe? Book? Pencil?
Questions, Why: *drink water, eat food, wash hands, go to store, carry umbrella*	Why do we drink water? Eat food? Wash our hands? Go to the store? Carry an umbrella?
Questions, Why: *houses, stores, eyes, ears, books, cars*	Why do we have houses? Stores? Eyes? Ears? Books? Cars?

4-6 to Kindergarten

Question, When: *stars shine, eat breakfast, brush teeth, go to bed*	When do the stars shine? Do you eat breakfast? Brush teeth? Go to bed?
Action-Agent: *sails, floats, boils*	What sails? Floats? Boils?
Categories: vegetable	Name a vegetable.

Upon entry into kindergarten children can identify and name objects by function, identify category words, know and use many relational words as modifiers, define words, comprehend and use inflected words, such as possessives, *ing* and *ed*. They can answer what, where, why, and when questions. They have developed linguistic knowledge that will be basic to their reading-readiness program in kindergarten as well as the introduction to number facts in story problems. Their language system is approximating the adult model.

Kindergarten to First Grade

During kindergarten children use the knowledge they have about their world (concepts) and their linguistic code (language form) to gain more knowledge and to communicate in a variety of ways, particularly with their peer group but also with adults. Their understanding and use of complex sentence structures improve. They also comprehend verb tenses in the passive voice: The bus was hit by the car; The car was hit by the bus. In a study by Bangs (1980) children in private schools could give word opposites: What is the opposite of big? high? They knew the meaning of rhyming words: What rhymes with bat? with bed? Children in public schools, however, did not perform as well on these tasks because they were considered a first grade objective and not stressed in kindergarten. By the time of their entry into first grade children are ready for academic subjects. Their lexicons will have expanded and their sentence comprehension and production will have become increasingly complex and will include embedded clauses. Their language form is a close match to the adult model.

Reading Readiness

Reading-readiness programs, in general, begin at the kindergarten level, yet basic to any reading program is the child's acquisition of content and form of oral language commensurate with the behavioral criteria for entering kindergarten. Kindergarten curriculums differ depending on the goals and objectives of a school system. The following list of reading-readiness behaviors was taken from one school district.

Kindergarten to First Grade

Has developed a lexicon and sentence structure compatible at least with basal readers.

Can tell you the sound a letter makes, at least five.

Can point to the letter a sound makes, at least five.

Can name all letters of the alphabet, upper and lower case.

Recognizes own printed name from ten other printed names.

Sight reads at least five words not spelled phonetically.

Reads at least five words spelled phonetically.

Reads at least five words spelled phonetically that are not real words: *nis, bate, riz, nav.*

Arithmetic Readiness

Arithmetic readiness may be operationally defined as the accomplishment of skills that are basic to the operation of number facts: addition, subtraction, multiplication, and division as well as geometry and higher mathematics. These skills have been discussed in Chapter 3 and have been selected from criterion-referenced tests which provide an 80 percent cutoff point, that is, 80 percent of the children in the standardization process could perform the test item (Bangs 1975, Kraner 1976, and Bangs 1980).

2-6 to 3-0 Years

Comprehends *one, all*

3-0 to 3-6 Years

Count by rote to 3
Rational count to 2

3-6 to 4-0 Years

Count by rote to 4
Rational count to 4
Comprehends *more-less* (numeration)

4-0 to 4-6 Years

Count by rote to 10
Rational count to 10
Number concepts to 3
Comprehends *each*
Identifies a circle, triangle

4-6 to Kindergarten

Count by rote to at least 15
Rational count to at least 13
Number concepts to at least 6
Identifies a square

Can add 1 + 1 in a story problem
Can identify eight or more numbers

Kindergarten to First Grade

Comprehends ordinal numbers *first, last*
Counts by rote to at least 100
Can add 2 + 5 in a story problem
Can subtract 5-2 in a story problem
Comprehends *more than-less than*: Which set has more than this one?
Comprehends *same* number: Which set has the same number of objects as this one?

Problem Solving — Avenues of Learning

Problem solving in the age range birth to three years is operationally defined as the age level at which a child solves problems when no oral language is required to elicit the response. The behaviors represent those tasks that involve a means to an end. In the range three years to first grade the behaviors relate primarily to two avenues of learning, audition and vision. These avenues of learning or cognitive skills discussed in Chapter 4 include the modalities of audition and vision that are basic to the acquisition of both oral and written language and include sensation, attention, perception, motivation, memory-retrieval, and central processing. In Chapter 4 it was emphasized that the sensory-neural correlates of language learning do not function as independent factors, rather as a group of interactive mechanisms that contribute to the learning process. The fact that they are so closely interrelated points up the difficulty in attempting to identify a perceptual or memory task or a single learning attribute, such as motivation or attention (see Chapter 5). In the range three years to first grade only standardized items that are related to linguistic and nonlinguistic short-term memory and tasks that require no memory are listed. The problem solving tasks and the avenues of learning have been selected from Bangs and Dodson (1979) and Bangs (1979, 1980). These skills represent the age level at which 80 percent or more of the children could perform.

Problem Solving

0 to 6 Months

Visually follows object in horizontal, vertical, and circular movement.	(1-3)
Visually follows moving person.	(1-3)
Reaches persistently for object.	(4-6)

6 to 12 Months

Reaches for, grasps, and inspects object.
Looks for a fallen object.
Pulls a string to get object tied to it.
Uncovers a hidden toy.
Bangs things together or rings a bell purposefully.
Drops one of two objects when reaching for a third.
Touches object contained in a cup.

1-0 to 1-6 Years

Unwraps loosely wrapped toy.
Dumps object from a bottle.
Pushes a car along.
Pulls a string in vertical motion to obtain object at the end.
Opens and closes a round box after demonstration.
Places a round block in a form board.

1-6 to 2-0 Years

Searches for way to activate a toy.
Places three different shapes in a form board.
Uses spoon with little spilling.
Knows own clothing from others.
Leads adult to what is wanted.
Plays with several objects and misses one if taken.
Climbs on a chair to reach.
Places six pegs in a peg board.

2-0 to 2-6 Years

Pulls mat to get the object that is on it.
Completes a peg board without urging.
Builds a six block tower.
Places three different forms in a rotated form board.
Unscrews lid off small jar.
Places car at top of incline, then releases it to let it roll down. . . . . .

2-6 to 3-0 Years

Strings beads.
Builds a tower with eight cubes.
Copies examiner's train with a smoke stack using three blocks.
Places twelve blocks neatly in a box.

Avenues of Learning

MEMORY-LINGUISTIC

1. Test item: Auditory Memory for Pictures
   Procedure: From a set of nine pictures covered by a screen the examiner
              names one or more of the pictures: removes the screen,
              and asks the child to find pictures named.

Age	Score
3-6 to 4-0	Remembers two pictures, not necessarily in sequence.
4-0 to 4-6	Remembers two pictures, not necessarily in sequence.
4-6 to K	Remembers three pictures, not necessarily in sequence.
K to First Grade	Remembers four pictures, not necessarily in sequence.

2. Test Item: Visual Memory for Pictures
   Procedure: From a set of nine pictures covered by a screen the examiner shows one or more duplicate pictures, removes the screen, and asks the child to find pictures seen.

Age	Score
3-6 to 4-0	Remembers two pictures, not necessarily in sequence.
4-0 to 4-6	Remembers two pictures, not necessarily in sequence.
4-6 to K	Remembers three pictures, not necessarily in sequence.
K to First Grade	Remembers three pictures, not necessarily in sequence.

3. Test Item: Responds to Commands
   Procedure: Examiner gives a two-part command: Stand up, then give me the book. Three-part command: Give me a pencil, stand up, and sit down.

Age	Score
3-0 to 3-6	Responds to two-part command.
4-0 to 4-6	Responds to three-part command.

4. Test Item: Sentence Repetition
   Procedure: Child speaks sentence after examiner.

Age	Score	
3-6 to 4-0	Past Tense	The boy chased the cat.
4-0 to 4-6	Present Tense	The boy is climbing the tree.
	Future Tense	The horse will run the race.
	Negation	The mother is not cooking dinner.
	Time: After	After the rain stopped, the sun came out.
	Time: When	When the bell rang, he sat down.
	Tense: Passive	The dog was chased by the cat.
	Possessive	The girl's brother was tired.
4-6 to K	Time: Before	Before Mary ate dinner, she washed her hands.
	Modification	It was Daddy who ate the cookie.
	Attribution	The big, green hat was found.
K to First Grade	All of the above	

MEMORY-NONLINGUISTIC

1. Test Item: Paper Fold
   Procedure: Using a six-inch square of paper, examiner folds a pattern, gives child a square of paper and says, "Make one like it" or gestures to indicate the same.

Age	Score
3-0 to 3-6	Folds paper over once.
	Folds paper over once and then into a square.
3-6 to 4-0, and	Folds paper over once then over again.
4-0 to 4-6	

4-6 to K   Folds a triangle.
                        Folds a double triangle.
K to First Grade   Folds a square then a triangle.
                        Folds a square then a double triangle.

2. Test Item: Block tapping
   Procedure: Three sponge blocks are placed in a line in front of child. The blocks are tapped with a fourth sponge block and examiner indicates that the child is to tap the same pattern.

Age	Score
3-0 to 3-6, and 3-6 to 4-0	Taps each block in sequential order.
4-0 to 4-6	Taps block 1, taps table in front of block 1, taps block 2, taps block in front of block 2. Same for block 3.
4-6 to K	Taps block 1, taps the table twice in front of block 1. Same for blocks 2 and 3.
K to First Grade	Taps block 1, taps table in front of block 1, taps block 2, taps table behind block 2, taps block 3, taps table in front of block 3.

COPY-NO MEMORY

1. Test item: Copy Block Patterns
   Procedure: Three dimensional pictures of blocks stacked in different patterns are shown to the child who uses one-inch blocks to copy the picture.

Age	Score
3-0 to 3-6	Copies the bridge, two blocks separated at the base and one block on top covering the space.
3-6 to 4-0 and 4-0 to 4-6	Copies three blocks in vertical position. Copies three blocks in horizontal position with no space between blocks.
4-6 to K	Copies three blocks in a row, one block on top of left end block. Copies three blocks in a row, one block on top of right end block.
K to First Grade	Copies pyramid with three blocks at base with space between each. Copies five blocks in a row with no spaces, and one block on top of middle block.

2. Test Item: Copies Drawings
   Procedure: Child is shown a drawing and asked to copy it with pencil and paper.

Age	Score
3-0 to 3-6	Copies horizontal line. Copies vertical line.

3–6 to 4–0	Copies circle (fairly well formed).
and	Copies a slant line.
4–0 to 4–6	
4–6 to K	Copies a plus sign +.
	Copies a circle with vertical line at top and bottom ○̣.
	Copies circle with horizontal line at each side –○–.
K to First	Copies an X.
Grade	Copies a square.
	Copies a rectangle.

Social-Personal

The social and personal behaviors listed below are related primarily to inter-personal relations with peer group, younger children, and adults. The behaviors in the age range birth to three years are criterion referenced (Bangs 1979). Those behaviors listed in the three years to first grade levels were selected from a variety of references where one finds many overlapping behaviors (Gesell and others 1940, Frankenberg and others 1970, Elkind 1974, and Bluma and others 1976).

0 to 6 Months

Quiets when picked up.	(0–1)
Looks attentively at human face.	(1–3)
Responds with social smile.	(2–4)
Watches own hands.	(3–6)
Discovers own feet.	(4–6)
Discriminates strange face.	(4–6)
Smiles at mirror image.	(5–6)

6 to 12 Months

Playful response to mirror, pats self.
Holds arms out to be picked up when offered arms, followed by holding arms out to be picked up without caretaker's offering arms.
Gives affection.
Plays imaginative games, such as pat-a-cake, peek-a-boo.
Discriminates strangers and may retreat or cry. Later is only initially shy.
Likes frolic play.
Looks at pictures in book with a person.

1–0 to 1–6 Years

Interacts with other children by touching, pushing, taking toy.
Difficulty in obeying commands.
Takes favorite toys to bed.
Reacts to other people's emotions, such as anger or pleasure.
Wants adult to perform a task, such as winding a toy, if child cannot do it.

1–6 to 2–0 Years

Actively cooperates with person in dressing and undressing.
Looks for or recognizes a friend.

Dries own hands.

Helps with household tasks.

Solitary or onlooker play predominates.

Resistant to sudden change.

Participates in rough-and-tumble play.

Responds to familiar situations.

Watches other peoples' faces for cues.

Imitates another child's action. When one falls down, they all fall down.

Shows symptoms of pity or shame.

2-0 to 2-6 Years

Separates from caretaker without tantrums.

Dramatizes adult activities.

Warmly responsive to adults.

Able to wait a few minutes for gratification.

Does not like to share, finds a substitute toy for friend.

Parallel play.

Imagination enters into play.

Often offers object without wanting it back.

2-6 to 3-0 Years

Likes to perform for others.

Does not adapt easily to a new situation.

Sets up a rigid sequence of events that must follow each other.

Avoids dangerous or unpleasant situations.

3-0 to 4-0 Years

Three-year-olds are more like four than two-year-olds.

Outgoing, easy going, a delightful stage.

Usually obedient.

Gives as well as takes.

Is learning how to listen and learns from listening.

Takes pleasure in doing simple errands: getting Daddy's shoes, Mother's purse.

Talks to familiar person on telephone.

Laughs when adults laugh. Interest in things being funny.

Often silly in play and may purposefully do things wrong.

Fantasy play with imaginary companions begins, such as boxing.

More comfortable with adults than with children.

Needs extra attention and understanding.

Enjoys exclusive attention and may be jealous of attention given to others.

When upset child may be heard to say "Don't look" "Don't talk" "Don't laugh."

Occasional outbursts are usually brief.

Often whines.

Sucks thumb excessively.

Stuttering is common.

4-0 to Kindergarten

Demands detailed explanation with frequent use of "why."
Answers telephone calls and talks to familiar persons.
Likes to go on short errands outside of home.
Puts own toys away.
Seeks attention such as "Wanna see me?"
Demonstrates confidence in self.
Does not like to admit inability to perform.
Dramatizes, likes dress-up clothes.
Gives self-praise such as "I'm smart."
Engages in conversation but only for brief time.
Plays in group but often chooses companion of own sex.
Likes to criticize and boss others.
May hit, kick, throw stones, run away.
May engage in loud silly laughter.
May demonstrate rage with "I hate you."
May use "dirty" words.

Kindergarten to First Grade

Is satisfied with self.
Lives with the here and now.
Values friendship.
Usually offers apologies.
Behavior is socially acceptable in public.
Demonstrates willingness to conform.
Is dependable.
Is relatively calm when under stress.
Works alone at a task for twenty to thirty minutes.
Protects younger playmates.
Joins groups of children usually the same sex.
Plays with two or three children for twenty to thirty minutes in cooperative
 activity.
Will take turns with a group of children.
Enjoys being with own friends.
Often has a make-believe companion.
Often asks permission to use objects belonging to others.
Eager to comply in kindergarten class.
Contributes to adult conversation.

Motor and Self-Help Skills

Motor development includes gross motor skills, such as sitting and walking, and fine motor skills which are needed for picking up a pin, sewing, or writing. Closely related to motor development are the self-help skills that include feeding and dressing, both of which involve gross and fine motor coordination. It is difficult to assign gross motor and self-help activities to specific age categories due primarily to the variation in environmental experiences. The following developmental data in the age range birth to three years are recorded in Bangs (1979) and the age range from three years to first grade have been selected from various sources (Doll 1959, Bluma and others 1976, Frankenberg and others 1970, Gesell and others 1940).

0-6 Months

Moro Reflex (disappears four to five months).	(0-1)
Lifts head when held to shoulder.	(0-1)
Lateral head movements when prone.	(0-1)
Thrusts arms and legs vertically.	(0-1)
Rolls from side to back.	(1-2)
Lifts head when prone.	(2-3)
Head erect and steady.	(2-4)
Hands meet in midline.	(2-6)
Hands open most of the time.	(2-6)
Lifts head and chest when prone.	(3-4)
Rolls from back to side and returns.	(3-4)
Crawling movements, no forward movement.	(3-5)
Crumples tissue paper.	(4-5)
Head steady when propped for sitting.	(4-6)
Retains objects when placed in each hand.	(4-7)
Passes object from hand to hand.	(4-8)
Unilateral reaching.	(4-8)
Turns from back to stomach.	(4-10)

6 to 12 Months

Passes object from hand to hand.	(4-8)
Unilateral reaching.	(4-8)
Turns from stomach to back.	(4-10)
Sits alone with no support.	(6-8)
Crawls on stomach.	(6-8)
Stands while holding on to the furniture.	(6-12)
Gets to sitting position.	(6-12)
Crawls on all fours or scoots on buttocks.	(7-12)
Walks with help.	(7-12)
Picks object up with thumb and forefinger.	(7-12)
Sits down.	(7-14)
Sits steady and can rotate to pick up toys without tumbling over.	(9-12)
Gets to standing position with help.	(9-12)
Stands alone for short period of time.	(9-12)

1-0 to 1-6 Years

Throws a ball, poor direction.	(9-18)
Walks alone.	(9-18)

Walks upstairs and downstairs with help.	(12–18)
Chews solid food.	(12–18)
Turns groups of pages when looking at book.	(12–30)
Uses a spoon with much spilling.	(14–18)
Scribbles freely.	(14–18)
Stoops and returns to standing position.	(14–18)
Seats self on sofa or chair.	(14–18)
Can lick large area of lower lip to remove food.	(14–18)
Holds cup while drinking.	(16–18)

1-6 to 2-0 Years

Kicks a ball.
Walks upstairs alone, both feet on one step.
Descends stairs holding on.
Walks fast but stiffly.
Squats.
Pulls off own socks and shoes.

2-0 to 2-6 Years

Wiggles tongue or thumb in imitation.
Jumps in place two or more times.
Descends ladder, marks time.
Walks on line or circle, steps off frequently.
Walks on tiptoes for a few steps.
Walks downstairs alone, marks time.
Begins to lick upper lip.
Scribbling is confined to the page.
Opens doors.
Jumps from bottom step to floor.

2-6 to 3-0

Turns pages of a book, one by one.
Walks upstairs alternating feet.
Holds pencil with thumb and forefinger.
Throws ball overhead.
Catches large ball.
Stands on one foot for two seconds.

3-0 to 4-0 Years

Walks downstairs, one foot per tread.
Jumps from bottom stair.
Begins to ride a tricycle.
Climbs up and slides down four-to-six foot slide.
Swings on a swing when started in motion.
Turns a forward somersault.

Marches.

Catches a ball with hands rather than hands and arms.

Broad jumps.

Pours from a pitcher.

Dresses self with help on pullover clothes and fasteners.

Can button large buttons on button board or coat on table.

Brushes teeth with instruction and assistance.

Washes and dries hands and face.

Blows nose when reminded.

Feeds self entire meal. Likes to choose own menus and serve self.

4-0 to Kindergarten

Alternates feet up- and downstairs.

Is learning to skip, cannot hop.

Can change direction when running.

Jumps over a string approximately two inches from floor.

Jumps backward.

Bounces and catches large ball.

Rides tricycle with ease.

Brushes teeth.

Washes and dries face unassisted.

Dresses self, cannot tie.

Cares for self at toilet.

Goes about neighborhood unattended.

Kindergarten to First Grade

Skips smoothly.

Jumps backwards two or more jumps.

Bounces and catches a large ball.

Jumps over string two inches from floor.

Runs, changing direction.

Dresses and undresses self except ties.

Buttons and unbuttons, buckles and unbuckles.

Puts zipper in catch.

Laces shoes.

Hangs up clothes on hook.

Brushes teeth.

Bathes self except neck, ears, and back.

Wipes and blows nose most of the time without reminding.

Takes care of self after toileting, flushes.

Goes about neighborhood without constant supervision.

Combs or brushes hair.

Can safely cross street if not heavy traffic.

Serves self at table, parent holding dish.

Uses knife for spreading soft foods on toast.

appendix 2

CASE HISTORY FORM A: FOR PARENTS

Child's Name _____   Date _____

Examiner _____   Birth Date _____

C. A. _____

Chief Complaint:

_____

Note: The following questions are asked so that we can better understand your child. Please read them carefully and answer as fully as possible. If you are not sure how to answer some of the questions, please tell us and we will discuss them. If you need more space, use the back of the sheet.

SECTION I

1. Is mother Rh negative? _____ Did mother have any illnesses during her pregnancy with this child? _____ Did mother have to stay in bed? _____ Take medications (other than vitamins)? _____ If yes to any of these, explain _____
   Has mother had previous miscarriages? _____
2. Was labor very long or especially short? _____ If yes, estimate time _____
   Was the birth of this child normal? _____ If not, explain _____
   _____
   How much did child weigh? _____
3. Did child have any trouble breathing after birth? _____ Was child kept in an incubator or airlock over 12 hours? _____ Why? _____
   Did child look blue or yellow after birth? _____ For how long? _____
   Did child come home from hospital with the mother? _____ If not, why? _____
   _____
4. Is child adopted? _____ How old when adopted? _____

SECTION II

1. At what age did child sit alone? _____ Crawl? _____ Walk alone? _____
   Was child very active as a baby? _____
2. Was feeding the child a problem? _____ Why? _____

3. Is child a "picky" or fussy eater now? _____ Any trouble swallowing? _____
   Chewing? _____ Will eat meats, caramels, etc? _____ Does child eat with a
   spoon? _____ Fork? _____ Both? _____
4. Was toilet training a problem? _____ When was child completely trained? _____
   Does child wet the bed at night now? _____ How frequently? _____
   Does child wet or soil during the day? _____ How often? _____
5. Does child dress completely? _____ Partially? _____ Completely undress? _____
   Partially? _____ Button? _____ Tie shoes? _____
6. Does child fall frequently? _____ How well can child climb? _____
   Throw a ball? _____ Hit a ball? _____
   Ride a tricycle? _____
7. Which hand does child use to eat? _____ Draw or write? _____
   Throw a ball? _____

SECTION III

1. Has child been back in the hospital since birth? _____ If so, explain (operations, accidents, etc.) and give age at that time _____

   _____

2. Has child had other serious illnesses? _____ If so, describe _____

3. Has child ever fainted or passed out? _____ Ever had a convulsion? _____
   How many? _____ Describe _____

4. Does child have any problem hearing? _____ Ear infections? _____
   If so, explain _____

   Has child ever worn a hearing aid? _____
5. Does child see normally? _____ Wear glasses? _____
6. Is child allergic? _____
7. Does child take any medicine regularly except vitamins? _____
   Why? _____
8. Has child been seen by a neurologist? _____ Psychologist? _____
   Has speech or hearing been tested before now? _____ Has child had training in a speech,
   hearing, and language center? _____

SECTION IV

1. Was child very quiet as a baby (did not babble and coo as much as most babies)? _____
   Cry excessively? _____

2. How old when first words were used? _____ Began putting two or three words together? _____

3. How much does child talk now? _____ Understand? _____

4. How much of this speech can parents understand? All _____ Most _____ Some _____ None _____ How much can other adults understand? All _____ Most _____ Some _____ None _____

5. How much does child use gesture to help others understand? _____

6. Do parents feel child stutters or stammers? _____

7. Does child's voice sound like other children's voices? _____ If no, describe. Very soft _____ Very loud _____ Hoarse _____ Nasal _____ Other _____

8. Have parents done anything to improve child's speech? _____ Is so, explain _____

_____

SECTION V

1. Did child attend nursery school?_____ Kindergarten? _____ Any problems in nursery school or kindergarten? _____ If so, explain _____

_____

2. What program is child in at present? _____

3. Does child like to go to school? _____ Have friends at school? _____

SECTION VI

1. Below is a list of words which describe children's personalities and behaviors. Please circle those which you feel tend to describe your child.

sad	leader	happy	follower
moody	quiet	even tempered	very active
friendly	independent	prefers to be alone	dependent
hard to discipline		has trouble sleeping	
has temper tantrums		is unusually fearful	
how often? _____			
affectionate			

2. Describe any behavior which is a problem to parents _____

_____

_____

3. Does child enjoy books (being read to or reading)? _____ Does child like to watch TV? _____ For how long? _____

4. What are child's favorite activities? _____

_____

_____

5. How well does child play alone? _____ With younger children? _____
   With children own age? _____ With older children? _____
   With brothers and sisters? _____

SECTION VII

1. Are parents now separated? _____ Divorced? _____ If so, how old was child when
   this occurred? _____ Has either parent been married previously? _____
   Which one? _____ Is either parent deceased? _____
2. Father's occupation _____
   Father's level of education _____
   Mother's occupation _____
   Mother's level of education _____
   If parents work, who takes care of child? _____
3. Give names and ages of other children in the family _____
   _____
   _____

4. Are there persons living in the home other than the parents and children? _____
   Who? _____
5. Is any language other than English spoken at home? _____
6. Are there relatives, on either side of the family, who have had:
   Trouble speaking clearly? _____
   Trouble with their hearing? _____
   Trouble learning in school so that they left school or failed several grades, or who have had
   real trouble learning to read? _____
   If so, describe the problem _____
   _____
   _____

appendix 3

GENERAL CASE HISTORY FORM B

Child's Name _____   Date _____

Examiner _____   Birth Date _____

C. A. _____

Chief Complaint:

_____

Key: (+) significant
    (–) not significant
    (?) lack of information

I. BIRTH HISTORY
   Rh problems, other
   Miscarriages
   Gestation period
   Mother's health, attitude
   Previous pregnancies
   Labor
   Delivery
   Birth weight
   Trouble breathing, sucking
   Cyanosis, jaundice
   Oxygen

II. MOTOR DEVELOPMENT
   Sat alone
   Crawled
   Feeding, sucking, chewing
   Drooling
   Self-help skills
   Toilet training

III. MEDICAL HISTORY
   Convulsions
   Childhood diseases, fever
   Cerebral disease, meningitis, poisoning
   Glandular disturbances
   Excessive sweating

MEDICAL HISTORY (contd.)
   Allergies
   Drug therapy
   Tonsils, adenoids, palate
   Otological-audition problems
   Vision
   Operations
   Accidents
   Congenital deformities
   Name of physician(s)

IV LANGUAGE/SPEECH
   Comprehension
   Jargon
   Gestures
   Echolalia
   Onset of single words
   Current number of words
   Onset of phrases, sentences
   Examples of sentences
   Child's awareness of problem
   Previous assessments
   Previous training
   Voice
   Articulation
   Fluency

LANGUAGE/SPEECH (contd.)
- Oral anomalies
- % understood by parents
- % understood by other adults
- % understood by siblings

V. SCHOOLING
- Nursery School
- Kindergarten
- Attitude toward school
- Name of teacher

VI. INTERPERSONAL RELATIONSHIPS
- General disposition
- Playmates and play habits
- Parent-child relationships
- Other adult relationships
- In contact with environment
- Discipline
- Hyperactive

INTERPERSONAL RELATIONSHIPS (contd.)
- Hypoactive
- Tantrums
- Psychological assessments
- Psychological treatment
- Psychiatric assessment
- Psychiatric treatment

VII. FAMILY
- Parents' age, health
- Parents' occupation
- Parents' education
- Marital status
- Is child adopted?
- Siblings: age, health
- Others in home: age, health
- History of learning problems in family
- Other problems
- Language spoken in home

ADDITIONAL COMMENTS:

_____

_____

_____

_____

_____

_____

_____

_____

_____

_____

_____

_____

_____

_____

_____

_____

_____

_____

_____

_____

_____

_____

_____

_____

_____

appendix 4

FORM FOR RECORDING LANGUAGE SAMPLES[1]

Key to symbols

Name _____ Date _____   . . . = lapse of time in speech

Birth Date _____ C. A. _____   : = lapse of time: child active

Examiner _____ Test time _____   – – = unintelligible or unheard words

                                                  / = end of utterance: falling inflection

                                              ? = question: rising inflection

Total number of words _____

Number of utterances _____

Mean length of utterance _____

Setting for language sample

Persons present:

Speech event: Utterances:

(Note child's gestures, actions,
etc., which contribute to understanding utterances.)

[1]Lynch, 1978, p. 354.

appendix 5

TEACHER-MADE TEST

Identifying Pictures by Function

OBJECTIVE

By October 15 the children will identify by *function* eight out of nine of the following pictures — house, cat, needle, clock, scissors, piece of clothing, cow, toy, fish — as measured by a teacher-made test with a proficiency of two out of three correct responses for each picture.

MATERIALS

The following materials will be needed.

Test Forms. There are three test forms: Trial I, II, and III, each containing the nine pictures arranged differently on each sheet. The reader will note that the pictures may vary according to size or position (cat lying down, sitting), according to a class of objects (sock, shirt, coat) and subclass (alarm clock, cuckoo clock, and grandfather clock). (See pages 264–66.)

Score Sheet. A child receives a + for pass, a – for fail, and a blank if refused to respond or item was not administered. Criterion is met with two out of three correct responses. See page 267.

Pre- and Posttest Data Sheet for Prekindergarten Class. Each child's name, date tested, scores, and total correct responses are recorded for both pre- and post-tests. See page 267.

PROCEDURE

The child must be able to identify or name the objects on each page. If this is accomplished, Trial I form is placed in front of the child and the examiner proceeds with the instructions; Show me what: we wear, we cut with, we sew with, says meow, tells time, we live in, we play with, gives us milk, swims in the water. Scores are entered on the score sheet. Trial II form is placed in front of the child, and the instructions are repeated in random order. Scores are entered on the score sheet. Trial III form is used for those items that were correct only one time.

SCORE SHEET
IDENTIFYING PICTURES BY FUNCTION

Key

+ = Pass

Name _____

− = Fail

Date _____

Blank = No response

ITEMS	I	II	III		I	II	III		I	II	III
Live In	−	−	−	Tells Time	−	−	−	Gives Milk	−	−	−
Says Meow	−	−	−	Cut With	−	−	−	Play With	−	−	−
Sew With	−	−	−	Wear	−	−	−	Swims In Water	−	−	−

Criterion: 2 out of 3 correct responses

SCORE SHEET FOR PRE- AND POSTTEST DATA FOR
PREKINDERGARTEN CLASS

Student	Test Dates	Wear	Live In	Tells Time	Sew With	Ride In	Play With	Swims in Water	Meows	Gives Us Milk	Total Correct
K.M.	1/10	−	−	−	−	+	+	−	+	−	3/9
	3/11	+	+	+	−	+	+	+	+	−	7/9
F.T.	1/10	−	+	−	−	+	+	−	+	−	4/9
	3/12	+	+	+	+	+	+	+	+	+	9/9
L.G.	1/12	+	−	−	−	+	+	−	−	+	3/9
	3/10	+	+	−	+	+	+	+	+	+	8/9

appendix 6

BEHAVIOR MODIFICATION PROGRAM
FOR A KINDERGARTEN CLASS

Sometimes classrooms become hard to manage because of the disruptive behavior of two or more of the children in the class. One such class taught by Ms. Mauzy was disrupted persistently by four children who upset individual children and, needless to say, the teacher. Parents, in fact, who had observed some of the class sessions were concerned about their children's abilities to learn in such an environment. A one-on-one behavior modification program was not successful; therefore it was time to develop a group behavior modification program for this kindergarten class of fifteen children. A monetary reinforcement type model was planned to extend over a six-week period with social reinforcements provided throughout the remainder of the school year. Several steps had to be followed in order to eliminate the unwanted behaviors. Initially it was important to teach the concepts and meaning of the words *good citizen* and *earn.*

Step 1. To teach the meaning of the words good citizen, Ms. Mauzy, during the sequenced instruction period, asked the children to tell all of the things that they should not do in class and then all of the things they should do in class. One child said that you should not hit another child. Leanne said that you should not talk while the teacher is talking. The list became longer and included falling off your chair, lying across the table, tapping loudly on the table with a pencil, stomping feet, closing your eyes when the teacher asks you to look, pulling hair, pushing when in line for dismissal and all of the other disruptive behaviors that each class member readily could describe. It became apparent to the teacher early on that each child was aware of unwanted behaviors in a classroom. It was difficult for the children to shift from what not to do to what they should do, but finally came up with a list that included: pay attention to the teacher when she is talking, raise your hand when you have a question, sit straight in your seat, stand quietly in line. All of these attributes, then, were to be rewarded in the behavior modification program.

Step 2. The responses from the children were used to form behavioral categories and operational definitions of the unwanted behaviors and a coding system that could be used for charting behaviors. These categories included:

Ag = *Aggressiveness* (regarding people): pushing, hitting, kicking, pinching, taking something away from another child, throwing (at a child).

Op = *Oppositional Behavior:* deliberately disobeying a teacher's instruction (noncompliance or doing something different), defying teacher by saying "No," or putting hands over eyes or ears, or by turning away from teacher during or immediately after an instruction.

N = *Inappropriate Noisiness:* inappropriate banging, rattling objects (chairs, equipment, materials, and so on), clapping hands, slapping desk, stomping feet, kicking desk or chair, yelling or making other loud vocal noises.

Ina = *Inattention to Teacher's Signal for Attention:* ignoring the teacher when she signals for attention by holding her hand up (visual cue) and saying "boys and girls" (auditory cue).

Os = *Inappropriately out of Seat*: kneeling or squatting in chair or being on feet when supposed to be sitting, lying across desk, lying on floor when supposed to be sitting.

Dp = *Destroying Property*: pasting on desk, writing on books, tearing cards, tearing other children's paper work.

T = *Tantrum Behavior*: vehement crying, screaming, destructive acts toward self, others, or objects.

C = *Crying*: any instance of crying that is not of the "tantrum" variety.

After the behavioral categories were defined a score sheet for off-task behaviors was developed. The aide charted the unwanted behaviors of each child and these scores became the baseline data which presented the teacher with the challenge to decrease the scores of each child or to maintain low scores for those children who presented no problems.

Step 3. To teach the meaning of the word *earn*, Ms. Mauzy brought from her home pieces of silver that needed to be polished. When a child polished a piece, a penny was *earned* and dropped into the child's personalized paper cup clipped to the chalkboard. At the end of the week a play store was set up and before dismissal the children purchased gum, candy bars, and popcorn by reading the price tag and counting their pennies. When they returned home, they were to tell their parents that they *earned* what they had purchased. The concept and word for *earn* were quickly learned by all children.

Step 4. Now the children were ready to *earn* pennies for being a good citizen. The list of acceptable behaviors was read to them and they were told that the alarm would ring at the end of five minutes, and the teacher would put a penny into the cup of each child who was a good citizen during that period of time. Some of the children said they did not understand, but after the first two alarms they discovered how to get pennies into their cups. The teacher made such statements as, "Leanne, I liked the way you sat quietly in your chair. You get a penny." "Kenneth, I was pleased when you raised your hand to ask a question. You also get a penny." No mention was made of the children who did not follow the good citizen rules.

Step 5. Parents were asked to stock the store with small cars, hair bows, hair clips, gum, or any special trinkets they had at home. A price was placed on each item. The best item, perhaps a large balloon, would cost ten cents while three M & M's would cost a penny. During dismissal the teacher drew a name from the basket and the children lined up at the store counter in that order. If Joe, who was first in line, could not count his pennies, he was obliged to go to the end of the line. Or, if he could not read the price to be purchased, he went to the end of the line. This meant it was likely that someone else would purchase the very article he wanted. Needless to say the children learned very quickly to rational count and to read numbers. In addition, the unwanted behaviors were decreasing to the point where the class was becoming more manageable than it had ever been.

Another reinforcement technique was to allow all children who had earned a specified number of pennies during the week to go to a movie set up in another part of the building. Those who had not earned the appropriate amount stayed in the classroom at the work tables.

Step 6. To phase out the program the teacher replaced the pennies in the cup with nonverbal reinforcement such as a pat on the shoulder, touching, looking, and smiling. Once a week, until the end of the sixth week, the aide tallied the behaviors. At that time, it was found that the teacher's objectives had been met at her designated proficiency level, and the unwanted behaviors had disappeared or decreased.

HOME-TRAINING ACTIVITIES

Teachers should provide parents with suggestions for teaching or exposing their children to new concepts, vocabulary, and sentence structure during unstructured activities in the home. Parents, in turn, become creative in providing activities that help meet the school objectives.

Activities of Daily Living

The following ideas for parents include activities that occur every day in the home or periodically during the year.

COOKING

Teach children the sequence of making cookies from a prepared mix. Use a variety of cookie cutters to teach the names of shapes: *circle, square, rectangle, heart.*

For younger children, ask for the *big* measuring spoon, the *little* measuring spoon. Allow them to pour the ingredients into the bowl and to stir.

When making meatballs, give the child a sample of the size meatball to form. Assist him or her in taking only that amount of meat to form the *same size* meatball.

Help the child approximate the amount of butter and jelly needed to cover a slice of toast.

DRESSING

Talk about body parts as you help your child get dressed. "What goes into this sleeve? Does your leg go into this sleeve?"

As you assist your child in getting dressed, tell him or her what shirt or dress to get. Describe it as to color, buttons in front or back, short or long sleeves.

FAMILY FUN

Play "Guess Who" game with members of the family. Take turns hiding eyes while someone speaks, then the hider guesses who spoke, or say "I am thinking of something in this room that is bigger than a pillow, has four legs and a back."

Visit the park and use the following suggestion for teaching language related to the swings. "Hold on to the seat. Your hands get rusty from the chain. Is the swing too high for you? Can your feet touch the ground? Shall I push you? I'm going to run under you. Hold tight. Do you want the middle swing? Is the swing made of wood or cloth?" On the way home retell the events of the trip to the park in preparation for retelling it to other members of the family.

Take a walk with your child and bring back leaves, twigs, dried flowers, and rocks to show to other members of the family. With spray net, spray the delicate hairs found on some plants that have gone to seed. Make an arrangement with these and other grasses and seed pods. During the walk, teach safety rules related to crossing the street. Also observe the neighbors' homes to learn the following: What materials are used to make the houses? Are the addresses the same? Where is the street name located? Who lives next door?

Father may organize a leaf-raking party. He invites the neighborhood children and his own children to rake the leaves, place them in the wheelbarrow, and dispose of them in the usual way. When the job is completed, the children may be served cider and doughnuts and perhaps make a leaf person from special leaves that they have selected.

Mother may collect stamps from the mail. Each time a different stamp appears, it is cut from the envelope and saved. When a variety of different stamps are collected, the child is helped to place them in number configurations on filing cards. The finished product is brought to school for Show and Tell.

HOUSEKEEPING

Encourage your children to help with the housekeeping chores. Talk about the equipment: "Why do I need a broom?" Provide a different job for each day, and at the end of the week talk about the jobs and which pieces of equipment were used.

When folding clothes, show a sock and ask, "Where do you wear this?" or "Find something in the basket that you use to dry your hands." Teach the child to fold towels and wash cloths; the latter may be folded into triangles.

After the laundry has been folded ask your child to sort it according to the room in which it is stored. While putting the clothing away, give such directions as "Put the socks in the *top* drawer. Put the towels on the *bottom* shelf."

Keep tissues handy at home. Tour your house to decide where the boxes should be kept. Emphasize when tissues should be used and how to dispose of those that have been used.

READING

Use the family albums as books. Discuss actions of family members, their names, and what they are wearing.

If a new story book is being introduced, let your child look through the book before you begin, so he or she will be familiar with the pictures and ready to listen. On the first presentation, or even the first few, do not read the story word for word, rather tell it informally defining all new vocabulary. Have some props ready so that the story can be acted out, and ask other family members to participate. Ask questions such as "What did —— do first? What did she do next? What happened?" If a page of the book is torn, teach your child how to mend it with appropriate mending tape.

Visit the library on a regular schedule to check out books related to the school curriculum.

Special Events

Halloween, Valentine's Day, and birthday parties are examples of special days that provide a variety of experiences for concept and language development. Parents will add to the following list.

HALLOWEEN

Teach new vocabulary and encourage conversation by carving a jack-o-lantern at home. Seeds from the pumpkin are saved for another activity. Draw an outline of a pumpkin on paper and invite the neighborhood children in to decorate it with the seeds. Glue should be placed on appropriate spots to outline the lantern, to make the facial parts, or to cover the entire lantern.

You may help your child make jack-o-lanterns from oranges. Toothpicks hold raisins in place for eyes, nose, and mouth. The finished products are used for table decorations.

Let your child dress up in the Halloween costume in preparation for the school party. Remember that some children would rather carry a mask than wear it.

THANKSGIVING

Ask the children in the neighborhood to join in making table decorations. Turkeys are constructed from apples using toothpicks for legs: "How many legs does a turkey have?" Turkeys may also be constructed from pine cones.

Send a note to the teacher a week before Thanksgiving stating your plans for Thanksgiving Day, which your child will tell at a special Show and Tell time.

VALENTINE'S DAY

Mother draws several hearts on a large piece of paper, and her child outlines the hearts with various colored crayons. This activity is used to help develop hand skills.

Hand skills may be practiced also by helping to roll, cut, and frost valentine cookies.

Purchase a box of valentines well in advance of the party day. Each day choose two or three and read the verse helping the child interpret the humor in the written lines. Ask your child to make up simple stories about the pictures on the cards and to decide to whom they will be given.

BIRTHDAY

Invite the birthday child to help make the birthday cake. Employ many teaching techniques related to vocabulary, comprehension of sentence types, number concepts, and conversation.

When giving birthday gifts, parents might consider the language and communication skills that may result from a specific gift.

If a parent is asked to make favors for a birthday party at school, consideration should be given to decorating the favors in such a way that it will reinforce the school curriculum. The teacher may have suggestions.

Concluding Remarks

When parents are working on an activity at home which is designed to reinforce learning that has taken place at school, they should ask themselves three questions: (1) What did I do to secure interest in this activity? (2) What new thing did my child learn from this activity or what behaviors did I reinforce? (3) What did I do to encourage my child to talk about the activity, to communicate?

Parents of children with language and learning disorders were asked this question; How do you think you have changed since your child has been enrolled in the school program and you have become involved in the parent training program which included home training activities? A compilation of their answers stated that they had learned to:

1. Talk more slowly and use shorter phrases and sentences.
2. Become more encouraged with vocalizations and attempts to talk and not to be discouraged with substandard language and speech.
3. Use much more repetition when teaching a new idea.
4. Talk in more detail and expand on each idea.
5. Separate activities into individual steps: "I would have taught my child to write and mail a letter to Grandma all in one day. Now I know to take more than one day."
6. Make better use of my time in teaching my child: "Instead of telling my child to get out of my way while I'm cooking, I make use of my cooking time to build language. Now I don't have to sit across the table from my child for certain periods in a stereotyped situation. I teach Karl while doing the dishes, putting him to bed, or when driving the car."
7. Become more aware of what my child does not know: "I don't skip over these things like I used to."
8. Apply to my other children what I learned in parent classes. They have benefited a lot.
9. Observe my child and listen to what she says. This tells me what she does and doesn't know.
10. Keep encouraging my child until he gets "over the hump."

appendix 8

PICTURE FILE AND OTHER TRAINING MATERIALS

I. Units within the curriculum guide
   A. Appropriate pictures filed behind each unit
      1. Class words: shoes, coat, hat, sock, for clothing unit
      2. Sub class words: boot, sandal, loafer, moccasin, for clothing unit
      3. Scenes to be described: three rings at a circus for circus unit
      4. Pictures of incongruities: a dog holding a glass of milk for the pet unit
   B. Work sheets: "Completion of pictures" or "What's missing," such as a three-legged chair for furniture unit
II. Language: Content, Form, Use
   A. Lexicon
      1. Pictures of position: top–bottom of stairs, tree, house
      2. Pictures of direction: arrow pointing up–down, cars going toward–away from house
      3. Pictures of quantity: more–less cookies on plates, buttons on coats
      4. Pictures of quality: same–different dogs, chairs, birds
      5. Pictures of size: tall–short children, trees, tables
      6. Pictures of possession: the dog's bone, the mother's baby, the baby's mother
      7. Pictures of attribution: big red–little yellow balloons, cars, balls
      8. Pictures of negation: the cat is in the basket, not in the basket
      9. Pictures of pronouns: boy and girl, show me his hand, her hand.
      10. Pictures of colors; variety of colored dishes, clothing, cars
      11. Pictures of double meaning words: pair–pear, run–run, sail–sale
      12. Pictures of affective words: child crying, smiling, hitting.
      13. Pictures of verbs: The boy is climbing the tree, will climb the tree, climbed the tree
      14. Pictures assessing function: Pictures of household items. Which one do we drink out of? Sleep in? Sit on?
      15. Pictures for question words: Outdoor scene. Who is mowing the lawn? What is in the basket? When do we mow the lawn? Why do we mow the lawn?
   B. Describing: Picture of a birthday party showing children pinning tail on donkey
III. Arithmetic
   A. Number concepts: sets of pictures: three apples, three shoes, three trees
   B. Reading numbers: Number flash cards
IV. Reading
   A. Rhyming words: man, fan, pan
   B. Beginning sounds: pictures filed behind beginning sounds: /b/ boy, bat, bug
   C. Reading letters: letter flash cards.
V. Object Box: A collection of objects for teaching content, form, use of language

VI. Charts: Picture and word charts and picture and word cards for teaching content, form, use of language
VII. Patterns for hand-skill activities: Directions for making nut cups for party
VIII. Children's books
IX. Parent library
X. Parent handouts
XI. Recordings, film strips, and other audio-visual aids

bibliography

Aaronson, D., and R. W. Rieber, eds. *Developmental Psycholinguistics and Communication Disorders.* New York: Academy of Science, 1975.

Acredolo, L. P., H. L. Pick, Jr., and M. G. Olsen. "Environmental Differentiation and Familiarity as Determinants of Children's Memory for Spatial Location," *Developmental Psychology,* 11 (1975), pp. 495–501.

Ammons, R., and H. Ammons. *Full Range Picture Vocabulary Test.* Missoula, Mont.: Psychological Test Specialists, 1948.

Anthony, D., *Signing Essential English.* vol. 1, p. 110. Anaheim, Calif.: Educational Services Division, Anaheim School District, 1971.

Anthony, D. "Signing Essential English." Unpublished master's thesis, University of Michigan, 1966.

Auerbach, A. B. *Parents Learn through Discussion: Principles and Practices of Parent Group Education.* New York: John Wiley, 1968.

Austin, J. R. *How to Do Things with Words.* Cambridge, Mass.: Harvard University Press, 1962.

Ayres, A. J. "Sensorimotor Foundation of Academic Ability," in *Perceptual and Learning Disabilities in Children,* eds. W. M. Cruickshank and D. Hallahan. Syracuse, N.Y.: Syracuse University Press, 1975, pp. 361–393.

Bangs, T. E. "Language and Learning Assessment: For Training," Experimental copy, 7532 Chevy Chase, Houston, Tex., 1980.

Bangs, T. E. *Birth to Three: Developmental Learning and the Handicapped Child.* Boston, Mass.: Teaching Resources, 1979.

Bangs, T. E. *Vocabulary Comprehension Scale.* Boston, Mass.: Teaching Resources, 1975.

Bangs, T. E., and S. Dodson. *Birth to Three Developmental Scale.* Boston, Mass.: Teaching Resources, 1979.

Barsch, R. *Achieving Perceptual Motor Efficiency: A Space Oriented Approval to Learning.* Seattle, Washington: Special Child Publications, 1967.

Bates, E. "Pragmatics and Sociolinguistics in Child Language," in *Normal and Deficient Child Language,* eds., D. M. Morehead and A. E. Morehead. Baltimore, Md.: University Park Press, 1976a.

Bates, E. *Language in Context.* New York: Academic Press, New York, 1976b.

Bayley, N. *Bayley Scales of Infant Development.* New York: New York Psychological Corporation, 1969.

Berg, W. K. "Habilitation and Dishabilitation of Cardiac Responses in Awake, Four Month Old Infants," Unpublished doctoral dissertation. University of Wisconsin, 1971.

Berry, M. *Teaching Linguistically Handicapped Children.* Englewood Cliffs, N.J.: Prentice-Hall, 1980.

Bessell, H. and G. Ball. *Human Development Program: Preschool and Kindergarten Activity Guide.* San Diego, Calif.: Human Development Training Institute, 1972.

Bessell, H., and U. Palomares. *Methods in Human Development.* San Diego, Calif. Human Development Training Institute, 1967.

Bliss, C. K. *Semantography.* Sidney, Australia: Semantography Publications, 1965.

Blissymbolics Communication Institute, 350 Rumsey Rd., Toronto, Ont., M4G IR8 Canada

Bloom, L., ed. *Readings in Language Development.* New York: John Wiley, 1978.

Bloom, L. *One Word at a Time: The Use of Single Word Utterances before Syntax.* The Hague: Mouton, 1973.

Bloom, L. *Language Development: Form and Function in Emerging Grammars.* Cambridge, Mass.: MIT Press, 1970.

Bloom, L., and M. Lahey. *Language Development and Language Disorders.* New York: John Wiley, 1978.

Bloomfield, L., and C. L. Barnhart. *Let's Read: A Linguistic Approach.* Detroit, Mich.: Wayne State University Press, 1961.

Bluma, S.; M. Shearer; A. Frohman; and J. Hilliard. *Portage Guide to Early Education.* Portage, Wis.: Portage Project, 1976.

Bohn, W. "First Steps in Verbal Expression," *Pedalogical Seminary,* 21 (1914), pp. 578-595.

Bond, E. K. "Perception of Form by the Human Infant," *Psychological Bulletin,* 77 (1972), pp. 225-245.

Bornstein, H. *Reading the Manual Alphabet.* Washington, D.C.: Gallaudet College Press, 1965.

Bornstein, H.; L. Hamilton, H. Kannapell; and K. Saulnier, *Basic Pre-School Signed English Dictionary.* Washington, D.C.: Gallaudet College Press, 1973.

Bornstein, H.; L. Hamilton; K. Saulnier; and H. Roy. *The Signed English Dictionary for Pre-School and Elementary Levels.* Washington, D.C.: Gallaudet College Press, 1975.

Bortner, M. "Phrenology, Localization, and Learning Disabilities," *Journal of Special Education,* 5 (1971), pp. 23-29.

Bourne, L. E., R. L. Dominowski, and E. F. Loftus. *Cognitive Processes. Englewood Cliffs, N.J.: Prentice-Hall, 1979.*

Bowerman, M. "Structure Relationships in Children's Utterances: Syntactic or Semantic?" in *Cognitive Development and the Acquisition of Language,* ed. T. Moore. New York: Academic Press, New York, 1973.

Bridgman, P. *The Logic of Modern Physics.* New York: Macmillan, 1927.

Brown, R. *A First Language: The Early Stages.* Cambridge, Mass.: Howard University Press, 1973.

Brown, R. "The Development of Wh Questions in Child Speech," *Journal of Verbal Learning and Verbal Behavior,* 7 (1968), pp. 279-290.

Brownell, W. A. "Psychological Consideration in the Learning and Teaching of Arithmetic" in *Teaching of Arithmetic,* Tenth Yearbook of the National Council of Teachers of Mathematics, pp. 1-31. New York: Bureau of Publications, Teachers College of Columbia University, 1935.

Bruner, J. "The Ontogenesis of Speech Arts," *Journal of Child Language.* 2 (1975), pp. 1-19.

Bryan, J. H. "Children's Cooperation and Helping Behaviors," in *Review of Child Development Research,* ed. E. M. Hetherington. Chicago, Ill.: University of Chicago Press, 1975, pp. 127-181.

Caldwell, B. M., and D. J. Stedman, eds. *Infant Education: A Guide for Helping Handicapped Children in the First Three Years.* New York: Walker, 1977.

Carrier, J. K. *"Application of a Nonspeech Language System with the Severely Language Handicapped,"* in *Communication Assessment and Intervention Strategies,* ed., L. L. Lloyd, pp. 523-547. Baltimore, Md.: University Park Press, 1976.

Carrier, J. K., and T. Peak. *Non-Speech Language Initiation Program.* Lawrence, Kans.: H & H Enterprises, 1975.

Carrow, E. *Carrow Elicited Language Inventory.* Boston, Mass.: Teaching Resources, 1974.

Carrow, E. *Test for Auditory Comprehension of Language.* Boston, Mass.: Teaching Resources, 1973.

Castle, D. "The Rochester Method," *Journal of Academy of Rehabilitative Audiology.* 7 (1974), pp. 12-17.

Chomsky, N. *Aspects of the Theory of Syntax.* Cambridge, Mass.: M.I.T. Press, 1965.

Chomsky, N. "Review of 'Verbal Behavior,' by B. F. Skinner," *Language,* 35, (1959), pp. 26-58.

Chomsky, N. *Syntactic Structures.* The Hague: Mouton, 1957.

Clark, B., and D. Ling. "The Effects of Using Cued Speech: A Follow-up Study," *Volta Review,* 78 (1976), pp. 23-24.

Clark, C. R., and R. W. Woodcock. "Graphic Systems of Communication," in *Communication Assessment and Intervention Strategies,* ed. L. L. Lloyd. Baltimore, Md.: University Park Press, 1976.

Clark, C. R., D. F. Moores, and R. W. Woodcock. "The Minnesota Early Language Development Sequence," Research, Development and Demonstration Center in Education of Handicapped Children, Minneapolis, Minn.: University of Minnesota, 1975.

Clark, C. R., C. O. Davies, and R. W. Woodcock. *Standard Rebus Glossary.* Circle Pines, Minn.: American Guidance Service, 1974.

Clark, C. R., and J. A. Greco. *MELDS Glossary of Rebuses and Signs.* Research, Development and Demonstration Center in Education of Handicapped Children, Minneapolis, Minn.: University of Minnesota, 1973.

Clark, E. "What's in a Word? On the Child's Acquisition of Semantics in His First Language," in *Cognitive Development and the Acquisition of Language,* ed. T. Moore. New York: Academic Press, New York, 1973.

Clark, E. "On the Child's Acquisition of Antonyms in Two Semantic Fields," *Journal of Verbal Learning and Verbal Behavior,* 11 (1972), pp. 750-758.

Clarke, H. "Linguistic Processes in Deductive Reasoning," *Psychology Review,* 76 (1969), pp. 387-404.

Copeland, R. W. *How Children Learn Mathematics.* New York: Macmillan, 1979.

Cornett, R. O. "Cued Speech," *American Annals of the Deaf,* 121 (1967), pp. 3-13.

Crammattee, A. B. "Comments, Questions, and Answers," *American Annals of the Deaf,* 121 (1967), p. 358.

Cromer, R. "The Development of Language and Cognition: The Cognition Hypothesis," in *New Perspectives in Child Development,* ed. B. Foss. New York: Penguin Books, 1974, pp. 184-252.

Cruickshank, W. M.; F. A. Bentsen; F. H. Retzburg; and M. T. Tannhauser, *A Teaching Method for Brain Injured and Hyperactive Children*. Syracuse, N.Y.: Syracuse University Press, 1961.

Crystal, D., P. Fletcher, and M. Garman. *The Grammatical Analysis of Language Disability: A Procedure for Assessment and Remediation*. New York: American Elsevier, 1976.

Dale, P. S. *Language Development: Structure and Function* (2nd ed). New York: Holt, Rinehart & Winston, 1976.

deAjuriaguerra, J.; A. Jaeggi; F. Guignard; F. Kocher; M. Maquard; S. Roth; and E. Schmid. "The Development and Prognosis of Dysphasia in Children," in *Normal and Deficient Child Language*, eds. D. Morehead and A. Morehead, Baltimore, Md.: University Park Press, 1976.

Delack, J. B. "Aspects of Infant Speech Development in the First Year of Life," *Canadian Journal of Linguistics*, 21 (1976), pp. 17-37.

Doll, E. *Vineland Social Maturity Scale*. Circle Pines, Minn.: American Guidance Service, 1959.

Donaldson, M., and G. Balfour. "Less is More: A Study of Language Comprehension in Children," *British Journal of Psychology*, 59, no. 4, (1968), pp. 461-471.

Dore, J. *The Development of the Speech Acts*, The Hague: Mouton, 1977.

Dore, J. *Children's Illocutionary Acts in Discourse Relations: Comprehension and Production*. Hillsdale, N.J.: Lawrence Erlbaum, 1976.

Dore, J. "Holophrases, Speech Acts, and Language Universals," *Journal of Child Language*, 2 (1975), pp. 21-40.

Dore, J. "A Pragmatic Description of Early Language Development," *Journal of Psycholinguistic Research*, 3 (1974), pp. 343-350.

Dunn, L. *Expanded Manual Peabody Picture Vocabulary Test*. Circle Pines, Minn.: American Guidance Service, 1965.

Dunn, L. *Peabody Picture Vocabulary Test (PPVT)*. Circle Pines, Minn.: American Guidance Service, 1959.

Eilers, R. E., and F. D. Minifie. "Fricative Discrimination in Early Infancy," *Journal of Speech and Hearing Research*, 18 (1975), pp. 158-167.

Eimas, P.; E. Siqueland; P. Jusczyk; and J. Vigorito. "Speech Perception in Infants," *Science*, 171 (1971), pp. 303-306.

Elkind, D. *A Sympathetic Understanding of the Child: Birth to Sixteen*. Boston, Mass.: Allyn & Bacon, 1974.

Erikson, E. *Childhood and Society*. New York: W. W. Norton & Co., Inc., 1963.

Ervin-Tripp, S. "Discourse Agreement: How Children Answer Questions," in *Cognition and the Development of Language*, ed. J. R. Hayes. New York: John Wiley, 1970.

Evans, E. D. *Contemporary Influences in Early Childhood Education*. New York: Holt, Rinehart & Winston, 1975.

Evans, J., and T. Bangs. "Effects of Preschool Language Training on Later Academic Achievement of Children with Language and Learning Disabilities: A Descriptive Analysis," *Journal of Learning Disabilities*, 5, no. 10, (December 1972).

Fantz, R. L. "The Origin of Form Perception," *Scientific American*, 204, no. 5 (1961), pp. 66-72.

Ferguson, C. A., and C. Farwell. "Words and Sounds in Early Language Acquisition," *Language*, 51 (1975), pp. 419-439.

Flavell, J. H. "What Is Memory Development the Development of?" *Human Development*, 14 (1971), pp. 225-286.

Flavell, J. H., and H. M. Wellman. "Metamemory," in *Perspectives on the Development of Memory and Cognition*, eds. R. V. Kail, Jr., and J. W. Hagen. Hillsdale, N.J.: Lawrence Erlbaum, 1977.

Foster, R., J. J. Gidden, and J. Stark. *Assessment of Children's Language Comprehension*. Palo Alto, Calif.: Consulting Psychologists Press, 1972.

Frankenberg, W. K., J. B. Dodds, and A. W. Fandal. *Denver Developmental Screening Test* (rev. ed.). Denver, Colo.:, Denver Ladoca Project and Publishing Foundation, 1970.

Frith, U. "Why Do Children Reverse Letters?" *British Journal of Psychology, 62 (1971), pp. 459-568.*

Gagne, R. M. *The Conditions of Learning*. New York: Holt, Rinehart & Winston, 1965.

Garvey, C. "Requests and Responses in Children's Speech," *Journal of Child Language*, 2 (1975), pp. 41-63.

Garvey, M., and N. Gordon. "A Follow-Up Study of Children with Disorders of Speech and Language Development," *British Journal of Disorders of Communication*, 8 (1973), pp. 17-28.

Gesell, A.; M. Halverson; H. Thompson; F. L. Illg; M. Castner; L. B. Ames; and S. Amatruda. *The First Five Years of Life*, New York: Harper and Brothers, 1940.

Gillingham, A., and B. Stillman. *Remedial Training for Children with Specific Disability in Reading, Spelling and Penmanship*. Cambridge, Mass.: Educators Publishing Service, 1960.

Gordon, T. *P.E.T. Parent Effectiveness Training*. New York: Wyden, 1970.

Greenfield, P.M., and P. G. Zukow. "Why Do Children Say What They Say When They Say It?" in *Children's Language*, ed. K. Nelson, vol. 1, pp. 287-336. New York: Gardner Press, 1978.

Gustason, G., D. Pfetzing and E. Zawolkow. *Signing Exact English* (rev. and enlarged ed.). Rossmoor, Calif.: Modern Sign Press, 1972.

Gwynne, F. *The King Who Rained*. New York: Windmill Books and Dutton, 1970.

Hagen, J. W., R. H. Jongeward, and R. V. Kail. "Cognitive Perspectives on the Development of Memory," in *Advances in Child Development and Behavior*, Vol. 10, ed. H. W. Reese. New York: Academic Press, New York, 1975.

Hall, P. K., and B. J. Tomblin. "A Follow-Up Study of Children with Articulation and Language Disorders," *Journal of Speech and Hearing Disorders*, 43, no. 2, (May 1978), pp. 227-241.

Halliday, M. A. K. *Learning How to Mean: Explorations in the Development of Language*. London: Edward Arnold, 1975.

Hammill, D., and S. Larsen. "The Effectiveness of Psycholinguistic Training," *Exceptional Children*, 40 (1974), pp. 5-13.

Hayden, A. H., and E. Gotts. "Multiple Staffing Patterns," in *Early Childhood Education for Exceptional Children*, eds. J. B. Jordan, A. Hayden, M. B. Karnes, and M. M. Wood. Reston, Va.: The Council for Exceptional Children, 1977.

Heider, E. R. "Focal Color Areas and the Development of Color Names," *Developmental Psychology*, 4 (1971), pp. 447-455.

Hiskey, M. S. *Hiskey-Nebraska Test of Learning Aptitude.* Lincoln, Neb.: Union College Press, 1966.

Holt, C., and G. C. Vanderheiden. "Masterchart of Communication Aids," in *Non-Vocal Communication Techniques and Aids for Severely Physically Handicapped,* eds. G. C. Vanderheiden and K. Grilley, pp. 174-210. Baltimore, Md.: University Park Press, 1976.

Hood, L.; M. Lahey; K. Lifter, and L. Bloom. "Observational Descriptive Methodology in Studying Child Language: Preliminary Results on the Development of Complex Sentences," in *Observing Behavior: Theory and Applications in Mental Retardation,* ed. G. P. Sackett, vol. 1, pp. 239-263. Baltimore, Md.: University Park Press, 1978.

Hymes, D. "Competence and Performance in Linguistic Theory," in *Language Acquisition: Models and Methods,* eds. R. Huxley and E. Ingram, pp. 3-24. New York: Academic Press, New York, 1971.

Irwin, O. "Infant Speech: Consonant Sounds According to the Manner of Articulation," *Journal of Speech Disorders,* 12 (1947), pp. 397-401.

Jordan, I. K., F. Gustason, and R. Rosen. "Current Communication Trends in Programs for the Deaf," *American Annals of the Deaf,* 121 (1976), pp. 527-532.

Jordan, J.; A. Hayden; M. Karnes; and M. Wood. *Early Childhood Education for Exceptional Children.* Reston, Va: The Council for Exceptional Children, 1977.

Kail, R. V., Jr., and J. W. Hagen, eds. *Perspectives on the Development of Memory and Cognition.* Hillsdale, N.J.: Lawrence Erlbaum, 1977.

Katz, J. J., and D. T. Langendoen. "Pragmatics and Presupposition," *Language,* 52, no. 1 (1976), pp. 1-17.

Kephart, N. C. *The Slow Learner in the Classroom.* Columbus, Ohio: Chas. E. Merrill, 1960.

Kirk, S., J. McCarthy, and W. Kirk. *The Illinois Test of Psycholinguistic Abilities,* (rev. ed.). Urbana, Ill.: University of Illinois Press, 1968.

Klatzky, R. L., V. E. Clark, and M. Macken. "Assymmetries in Acquisition of Polar Adjectives, Linguistic or Conceptual?" *Journal of Experimental Child Psychology,* 16 (1973), pp. 32-46.

Klima, E. "Negation in English," in *The Structure of Language,* eds. J. Fodor and J. Katz. Englewood Cliffs, N.J.: Prentice-Hall, 1964.

Kobasigawa, A., and R. Orr. "Free Recall and Retrieval Speed of Categorized Items by Kindergarten Children," *Journal of Experimental Child Psychology,* 15 (1973), pp. 187-192.

Kraner, R. E.. *Preschool Math Inventory.* Boston, Mass.: Teaching Resources, 1976.

Kraynak, A. R., and L. M. Raskin. "The Influence of Age and Stimulus Dimensionality on Form Perception by Preschool Children," *Developmental Psychology,* 4 (1971), pp. 389-393.

Lackner, J. R. "A Developmental Study of Language Behavior in Retarded Children," in *Normal and Deficient Language,* eds. D. M. Moorhead and A. E. Moorhead. Baltimore, Md.: University Park Press, 1976.

Lee, L. *Developmental Sentence Analyses.* Evanston, Ill.: Northwestern University Press, 1974.

Lee, L. *Northwestern Syntax Screening Test.* Evanston, Ill.: Northwestern University Press, 1971.

Leiter, R. G. *Examiner's Manual for the Leiter International Performance Scale.* Chicago, Ill.: Stoelting, 1969.

Lenneberg, E. *Biological Foundations of Language.* New York: John Wiley, 1967.

Leonard, L., J. G. Bolders, and J. A. Miller. "An Examination of the Semantic Relations Reflected in the Language Usage of Normal and Language-Disordered Children," *Journal of Speech and Hearing Research,* 19 (1976), pp. 371–392.

Lewis, M., and R. Freedle. "Mother-Infant Dyad: The Cradle of Meaning," in *Communication and Affect,* ed. P. Piner, New York: Academic Press, 1973.

Lewis, S. B. *Parent Participation in Vocabulary Development: A Model Program.* Unpublished report. Speech and Hearing Institute, The University of Texas Health Science Center at Houston, 1976.

Libby, E. R., ed. *Binaural Hearing and Amplification,* vols. 1 and 2. Chicago, Ill.: Zenetron, 1980.

Lieberman, P. *Intonation, Perception and Language.* Cambridge, Mass.: MIT Press, 1967.

Lloyd, L. L., ed. *Communicative, Assessment and Intervention Strategies.* Baltimore, Md.: University Park Press, 1976.

Longhurst, T., and T. Schrandt. "Linguistic Analysis of Children's Speech: A Comparison of Four Procedures," *Journal of Speech and Hearing Disorders,* 38 (1973), pp. 240–249.

Lynch, J. "Evaluation of Linguistic Disorders in Children," in *Diagnostic Procedures in Hearing, Speech, and Language,* eds. S. Singh and J. Lynch, pp. 327–378. Baltimore, Md.: University Park Press, 1978.

Lyons, J. *Introduction to Theoretical Linguistics.* Cambridge, Mass.: Cambridge University Press, 1968.

McDonald, E. T. "Design and Application of Communication Boards," in *Non-Vocal Communication Techniques and Aids for the Severely Physically Handicapped,* eds. G. C. Vanderheiden and K. Grilley, pp. 105–120. Baltimore, Md.: University Park Press, 1976.

McLean, L., and J. McLean. "A Language Training Program for Nonverbal Autistic Children," *Journal of Speech and Hearing Research,* 35 (1974), pp. 186–193.

McNaughton, S. "Bliss Symbols — An Alternate Symbol System For The Non-Vocal Pre-Reading Child," in *Non-Vocal Communication Techniques and Aids For The Severely Physically Handicapped,* eds. G. Vanderheiden and K. Grilley, pp. 85–143. Baltimore, Md.: University Park Press, 1976.

McNeil, D. "Developmental Psycholinguistics," in *The Genesis of Language: A Psycholinguistic Approach,* eds., F. Smith and G. Miller. Cambridge, Mass.: MIT Press, 1966.

Maratsos, M. "Nonegocentric Communication Abilities in Preschool Children," *Child Development,* 44 (1973), pp. 697–700.

Menig-Peterson, C. "The Modification of Communicative Behavior in Preschool Aged Children as a Function of the Listener's Perspective," *Child Development,* 46 (1975), pp. 1,015–1,018.

Moffit, A. R. "Consonant Cue Perception by Twenty to Twenty-Four Week Old Infants," *Child Development,* 42 (1971), pp. 717–731.

Moorhead, D., and D. Ingram. "The Development of Base Syntax in Normal and

Linguistically Deviant Children," *Journal of Speech and Hearing Research,* 16 (1973), pp. 330-352.

Morrison, F. J., D. L. Holmes, and H. M. Haith. "A Developmental Study of the Effect of Familiarity: A Short Term Visual Memory," *Journal of Experimental Child Psychology,* 18 (1974), pp. 412-425.

Morse, P. A. "The Discrimination of Speech and Nonspeech Stimuli in Early Infancy," *Journal of Experimental Child Psychology,* 14 (1972), pp. 477-492.

Morton, R. L. "The National Council Committee on Arithmetic," *Mathematics Teacher,* 31 (October 1938), pp. 267-272.

Moynahan, E. D. "The Development of Knowledge Concerning the Effect of Categorizing upon Free Recall," *Child Development,* 44 (1973), pp. 238-246.

Muma, J. "Language Assessment: The Co-Occurring and the Restricted Structure Procedure," *ACTA Symbolica,* 4 (1973), pp. 12-29.

Nelson, K. "Structure and Strategy in Learning to Talk," *Monographs of the Society for Research in Child Development,* 38 no. 149, 1973.

Nix, G. W. "Total Communication: A Review of the Studies Offered in Its Support," *The Volta Review,* 77 (1975), pp. 470-494.

Northern, J. L., and M. Downs. *Hearing in Children,* (rev. ed.). Baltimore, Md.: Williams & Wilkins, 1978.

Ornstein, P. A., ed. *Memory Development in Children.* Hillsdale, N.J.: Lawrence Erlbaum, 1978.

Orton, S. T. *Reading, Writing, and Speech Problems in Children.* New York: W. W. Norton & Co., Inc., 1937.

Palermo, D. S. "More About Less: A Study of Language Comprehension," *Journal of Verbal Learning and Verbal Behavior,* 12 (1973), pp. 211-21.

Peeples, D. R., and D. Y. Teller. "Color Vision and Brightness Discrimination in Two Month Old Infants," *Science,* 189 (1975), pp. 1,102-1,103.

Piaget, J. *The Psychology of Intelligence.* Paterson, N.J., Littlefield and Adams, 1960.

Piaget, J. *The Language and Thought of the Child.* Cleveland, Ohio: World Publishing Co., rpt. 1955.

Piaget, J. *The Construction of Reality in the Child.* New York: Basic Books, 1954.

Piaget, J. *Judgment and Reasoning in the Child.* New York: Harcourt, Brace, and Co., 1928.

Premack, D., and A. J. Premack. "Teaching Visual Language to Apes and Language Deficient Persons," in *Language Perspectives: Acquisition, Retardation, and Intervention,* ed., R. L. Schiefelbusch and L. L. Lloyd. Baltimore, Md.: University Park Press, 1974.

Premack, A. J., and D. Premack. "Teaching Language to an Ape," *Scientific American,* 277, (1972), pp. 92-99.

Premack, D. "Language in Chimpanzee?" *Science,* 172 (1971), pp. 808-822.

Premack, D. "A Functional Analysis of Language," *Journal of Experimental Analytic Behavior,* 14 (1970), pp. 107-125.

Public Law 94-142: The Education for All Handicapped Children Act. For copies of the law and further information, write to NEA Instruction and Professional Development, 1201 16th Street, N.W., Washington, D. C. 20036.

Reynolds, M. C. *Delphi Survey: A Report of Rounds I and II,* ERIC ED 087-734. Reston, Va.: Council for Exceptional Children, September, 1973.

Rister, A. "Deaf Children in Mainstream Education," *The Volta Review,* 77, no. 5 (1975), pp. 279-290.

Roe, V., and R. Milisen. "The Effect of Maturation Upon Defective Articulation in Elementary Grades," *Journal of Speech Disorders,* 1942, pp. 37-50.

Ruder, K., and M. Smith. "Children's Imitations of Parents' Speaking Fundamental Frequency." Unpublished manuscript, Bureau of Child Research, Working Paper, University of Kansas, 1972.

Ryan, J. "Mental Subnormality and Language Development," in *Foundations of Language Development: A Multi-Disciplinary Approach,* vol. 2, eds. I. Lenneberg and E. Lenneberg. New York: Academic Press, New York, 1975.

Schaefer, E. S. "Family Relationships," in *The Application of Child Development Research to Exceptional Children,* ed. J. J. Gallagher. Reston, Va.: Council for Exceptional Children, 1975.

Schiefelbusch, R. L, ed. *Bases of Language Intervention.* Baltimore, Md.: University Park Press, 1978.

Schiefelbusch, R. L. *Language Intervention Strategies.* Baltimore, Md.: University Park Press, 1978.

Schlesinger, H. S., and K. P. Meadow. *Sound and Sign: Childhood Deafness and Mental Health.* Berkeley, Calif.: University of California Press, 1972.

Scouten, E. L. "The Rochester Method: An Oral Multi-Sensory Approach for Instructing Prelingual Deaf Children," *American Annals of the Deaf,* 112, no. 2 (1967), pp. 50-55.

Searle, J. R. "Speech Acts and Recent Linguistics," in *Developmental Psycholinguistics and Communication Disorders,* eds. D. Aaronson and R. W. Rieber. New York: Academy of Sciences, 1975.

Searle, J. R. *Speech Acts.* Cambridge, Mass.: University Park Press, 1969.

Shantz, C. U. "The Development of Social Cognition," in *Review of Child Development Research,* ed. E. M. Hetherington, vol. 5, pp. 257-323, 1975.

Shatz, M., and R. Gelman. "The Development of Communication Skills: Modification in the Speech of Young Children as a Function of the Listener," *Monographs of the Society for Research in Child Development,* 38, no. 152, (1973).

Skinner, B. F. *Verbal Behavior.* Englewood Cliffs, N.J.: Prentice-Hall, 1957.

Smirnov, A. A., and P. I. Zinchenko. "Problems in the Psychology of Memory," in *A Handbook of Contemporary Soviet Psychology,* eds. M. Cole and L. Maltzman. New York: Bosie Books, 1969.

Smith, E. B., K. S. Goodman, and R. Meredith. *Language and Thinking in School.* New York; Holt, Rinehart and Winston, 1976.

Smith, M. "The Influence of Age, Sex, and Situation on the Frequency, Form and Function of Questions Asked by Preschool Children," *Child Development,* 4 (1933), pp. 201-213.

Spalding, R. B., and W. F. Spalding. *The Writing Road to Reading.* New York: Morrow, 1972.

Spring, D. R. "Linguistic Stress Discrimination in One-to-Four-Month-Old Infants." Unpublished doctoral dissertation, University of Washington, 1975.

Stern, D.; J. Jaffe; B. Beebe; and S. Bennett. "Vocalizing in Unison and in Alternation: Two Modes of Communication Within the Mother-Infant Dyad," in *Developmental Psycholinguistics and Communication Disorders,* eds. D. Aaronson and R. Rieber, *Annals of the New York Academy of Sciences,* 263 (1975), pp. 89-100.

Strauss, A. A., and L. E. Lehtinen. *Psychology and Education of the Brain Injured Child.* New York: Grune and Stratton, 1947.

Templin, M. *Certain Language Skills in Children: Their Development and Interrelationships.* Minneapolis, Minn.: University of Minnesota Press, 1957.

Terman, L. M., and M. A. Merrill. *Stanford-Binet Intelligence Scale: Manual for the Third Revision Form L-M.* Boston, Mass.: Houghton Mifflin, 1973.

Terman, L. M. and M. A. Merrill. *Stanford-Binet Intelligence Scale.* Boston, Mass.: Houghton Mifflin, 1960.

Terman, L. M., and M. A. Merrill. *Measuring Intelligence.* Cambridge, Mass.: Riverside Press, 1937.

Tobin, H. "Disordered Functions Approach to Audiological Diagnosis: The Sixth Year Through Adulthood," in *Diagnostic Procedures in Hearing, Speech, and Language,* eds. S. Singh and J. Lynch, Baltimore, MD.: University Park Press, 1978.

Trehub, S. E. "Infant's Sensitivity to Tonal Contrasts," *Developmental Psychology,* 9 (1973), pp. 91-96.

Tyack, D., and R. Gottsleben, *Language Sampling Analysis and Training: A Handbook for Teachers and Clinicians.* Palo Alto, Calif.: Consulting Psychological Press, 1974.

Vanderheiden, G. C., and K. Grilley, eds. *Non-vocal Communication Techniques and Aids for the Physically Handicapped.* Baltimore, Md.: University Park Press, 1976.

Vanderheiden, G. C., and D. R. Harris-Vanderheiden. "Communication Techniques and Aids for the Nonvocal Severely Handicapped," in *Communication Assessment and Intervention Strategies,* ed. L. L. Lloyd. Baltimore, Md.: University Park Press, 1976.

Vernon, M., and S. Koh. "Effects of Oral Preschool Compared to Early Manual Communication on Education and Communication in Deaf Children," *American Annals of the Deaf,* 116 (1971), pp. 569-574.

Von Haden, H. I., and J. M. King. *Educational Innovation Guide.* Worthington, Ohio: Charles A. Jones, 1974.

Wechsler, D. *Intelligence Scale for Children,* (rev. ed.), New York: Psychological Corp., 1974.

Wechsler, D. *Preschool and Primary Scale of Intelligence (WIPSI).* New York: Psychological Corp., 1967.

Weiner, P. S. "A Language Delayed Child in Adolescence," *Journal of Speech and Hearing Disorders,* 39, (1974), pp. 202-212.

Whatmough, J. *"Language"—A Modern Synthesis,* New York: St. Martin's Press, 1956.

Wilbur, R. B. *The Linguistics of Manual Language and Manual Systems in Communication Assessment and Intervention Strategies,* ed., L. L. Lloyd. Baltimore, Md.: University Park Press, 1976, pp. 423-500.

Winitz, H. *Articulatory Acquisition and Behavior.* New York: Appleton-Century-Crofts, 1969.

Woodcock, R. W., C. R. Clark, and C. O. Davies. *Peabody Rebus Reading Program.* Circle Pines, Minn.: American Guidance Service, 1968.

Woodcock, R. W., ed. *The Rebus Reading Series Institute on Mental Retardation and Intellectual Development.* Nashville, Tenn.: George Peabody College, 1965.

index

Accountability, program design, 8, 122
Acredelo, L. P., 79
Action-Agent test, 31
Active reform, 56
Activities, 129
    critiquing parent's, 144
    home training, 270-73
    varying, 132
Admission, Review, and Dismissal
    Committee (ARD), 114
Affective education, 63-67
    method, 64-67
    objectives, 66-67
Affective words, 30, 65
    acquiring a vocabulary of, 65
    effective use of, 65
Alphabet, initial teaching, 224
Alternate communication system,
    219-30
    augmentative devices, 231-32
    criteria for selecting, 233-36
    research, 236
    technical aids, 230-32
American Sign Language (ASL), 221-22
Ameslan. See American Sign Language
Anthony, D., 222
Arithmetic
    meaningful, 55-56
    methods of teaching, 55-56
    testing, 92
Arithmetic readiness, 245-46
Arousal techniques, 128
Articulation, 20
Art project, 153-55
Assessment, 90
    parent's observation of, 104-5
    reporting results, 110-14
    room, appearance of, 103-4
    time allotment, 106
Attention, 70-72
    procuring and maintaining, 128-30
Attributes, quantifiable, 56-59
Audition and vision, 128
Auditory matching skills, 49
Augmentative devices, 231-32
Aural and oral method of communi-
    cation, 221
Austin, J. R., 38
Ayres, A. J., 123

Babbling, 19, 22
Balfour, G., 26

Ball, G., 65, 135
Bangs, T. E., 6, 21, 24, 26, 28, 29, 30,
    31, 34, 88, 94, 102, 119, 122, 125,
    140, 238, 244, 245, 246, 250, 253
Barnhart, C. L., 45
Barsch, R., 123
Bates, E., 36
Bayley, N., 88
Bayley Scales of Infant Development,
    88
Behavior, developmental, 148,
    238-55
    avenues of learning, 247-50
    language comprehension, 238-41
    language expression, 241-44
    motor, 252-55
    problem solving, 246-47
    self help, 252-55
    social-personal, 250-52
Behavior modification program, kinder-
    garten class, 268-69
Berg, W. K., 21, 73
Berry, M., 69
Bessell, H., 64, 65, 135
Birth to Three Developmental Scale, 88
Blissymbolics, 225-28
Block patterns, 109
Bloom, L., 2, 17, 18, 19, 23, 30, 101,
    124, 146
Bloomfield, L., 45
Bluma, S., 101, 250, 253
Bohn, W., 35
Bond, E. K., 73
Bornstein, H., 222
Bowerman, M., 17
Braille, 224
Braille, L., 224
Bridgman, P., 15
Brown, R., 17, 30, 35
Brownell, W. A., 55
Buddy system, 144
Bulletin board projects, 155-56

Calendar project, 156-57
Capacity and volume, concept of,
    57-58
Carrier, J. K., 228
Case histories, 95-100
    Form A, for parents, 256-59
    Form B, general, 260-61
Castle, D., 222

Categorizing, 80
Category words, 24
Center of Applied Linguistics (Washington), 11
Central processing integration, 83-84
Charts project, 157-59, 188
Checklists, 101
Chomsky, N., 17
Clark, B., 221
Clark, C. R., 224, 225, 228, 230
Clark, E., 26, 27
Clarke, H., 26
Class levels, 148-49
Class placement, 136-38
Class words, 24
Club day project, 159-61
Cognitive skills, 69-84, 93, 235
Color words, 29
Communication
    alternate systems of, 219-30
    on child's level, 130
    oral and aural method, 221
    oral and manual systems, 220-23
    presupposition, 40
    relating new to old, 39-40
    total, 222-23
Conferences, group, 140-43
Constant words, 24
Contrast words, 25-26
Cooing, 36
Cooking projects, 161-62
Cornett, R. O., 221
Crammatee, A. B., 222
Creative teaching, 131-33
Creativity, 105
Criterion-referenced tests, 94-95
Cromer, R., 17
Cruickshank, W. M., 123, 138
Crying, 36, 37
Crystal, D. P., 101
Cued speech, 221
Cuing, 79
Curriculum
    long term objectives, 149-50
    schedule of events, 187-90
Curriculum-based test, 147-48
Curriculum guide, 122-27, 149-50,
    186-217
    kindergarten level, 190-99
    nursery level, 208-17
    prekindergarten level, 200-208
Curriculum lesson plans, 150
Curriculum units, 149

DeAjuriaguerra, J., 118
Deaf, manual language for, 221-22
Defining, 109
Delphi Survey, 120-21

Delack, J. B., 37
Denver Developmental Screening
    Test, 88-89
Designs, copying, with pencil and paper,
    109
Developmental behaviors, 148, 238-55.
    See also Behavior.
Diagnostic teaching, 103
Diaries, 100
Digit Span, 78
Digraph, 45-46
Dodson, S., 6, 21, 88, 238, 246
Doll, E., 253
Donaldson, M., 26
Dore, J., 38
Downs, M., 221, 234
Drill theory, 55
Dunn, L., 90
Dyslexia, 44-45

Early training, 118-20
Echolalia, 19, 22-23, 37
Education
    affective, 63-67
    preacademic 43-62
Educational philosophy, 117-22
Education for All Handicapped Children
    Act. *See* Public Law 94-142
Eilers, R. E., 21
Eimas, P., 20, 73
Elkind, D., 250
Environment
    language development, 18-19
    learning, 138-40
    test, 103-7
Ervin-Tripp, S., 31
Evaluation, 90. *See also* Testing.
Evans, E. D., 119
Expansion picture file project, 162-63,
    188
Experience story projects, 163
Extrinsic rewards, 76. *See also* Learning,
    requirements

Fantz, R. L., 73
Farwell, C., 22
Feedback techniques, 132
Ferguson, C. A., 22
Field trip projects, 163-65
Finger play projects, 165
Finger spelling, 224
First Chance programs, 4-12
    problems encountered in, 9-12
Flavell, J. H., 80
Frankenburg, W. K., 89, 250, 253
Freedle, R., 37
Frith, U., 75

Gagne, R. M., 141
Game projects, 165–67
Garvey, C., 39
Garvey, M., 119
Gelman, R., 40
Generic programs, 120–21
Gesell, A., 31, 250, 253
Gillingham, A., 44, 45
Glossary of signs
   MELDS, 230
   Standard Rebus, 225
Gordon, N., 119
Gotts, E., 6
Gottsleben, R., 101
Grapheme, 45
Greco, J. A., 230
Greenfield, P. M., 40
Gustason, G. D., 222
Gwynne, F., 32

Hagen, J. W., 78, 79
Hall, P. K., 118
Halliday, M. A. K., 37
Hammill, D., 124
Handedness, 52–53
Handicapped Children's Early Educa-
   tion Assistance Act. *See* Public
   Law 90–538
Handwriting, 50–54
   methods, 51–53
   objectives, 53
Harris-Vanderheiden, D. R., 231
Hayden, A., 6
Heider, E. R., 74
Height, concept of, 58
Holt, C., 232
Home training activities, 270–73
Home visit projects, 167
Hood, L. M., 35
Hymes, D., 36

Illinois Test of Psycholinguistic
   Abilities (ITPA), 123–24
Individual educational plan (IEP), 90
Inflections, 33–36
Information, relating new to old, 39–40
Ingram, D., 119
Initial teaching alphabet, 224
Instruction, sequenced, 188–89
Instructional projects, 152–85. *See also*
   Projects.
Integration, central processing, 83–84
Intelligence Quotient (IQ), 90, 94
International Commission on Technical
   Aids, (ICTA), 232
Intrinsic rewards, 76–77
Irwin, O., 21

Jargon, 19, 22, 37
Jordan, I. K., 222

Kail, R. V., Jr., 78
Katz, J. J., 40
Kephart, N. C., 123
Key word projects, 167–68, 188
Kindergarten,
   class description, 190–91
   long-range objectives, 192
   sample lesson plans, 192–99
   units, 191
Kindergarten class, behavior modifica-
   tion program, 268–69
Kindergarten level curriculum guide,
   190–99
King, J. M., 123
King Who Rained, The (Gwynne), 32
Kirk, S., 123
Klatsky, R. L., 26
Klima, E., 30
Kobasigawa, A., 80
Koh, S., 222
Kraner, R. E., 28, 29, 59, 238, 245
Kraynak, A. R., 75

Lackner, J. R., 119
Lahey, M., 2, 17, 18, 23, 101, 124, 146
Language
   acquisition, 15–41
   American sign, 221–22
   comprehension, 238–241
   content, 18–19
   definition of, 16
   disorder, 2
   expression, 241–44
   major components of, 17–40; con-
      tent, 17–19; form, 17, 19–36;
      use, 18, 36–40, 91–92
   oral, 91–92
   prelinguistic, 36–37
Language development, theories of,
   16–17
Language samples, 101–2
   recording form, 262
Larsen, S., 124
Learning
   avenues of, 93, 246–50
   copy–no memory, 249–50
   environment, 138–40
   memory-linguistic, 247–48
   memory-nonlinguistic, 248–49
   requirements, 69–84
Lee, L., 101
Lehtinen, L. E., 138
Length, concept of, 58
Lenneberg, E., 17

Leonard, L., 119
Lesson plans, curriculum, 150
  kindergarten, 192–99
  nursery level, 210–17
  prekindergarten, 201–8
Lexicon, 23–33, 91. *See also* Words.
Lewis, M., 37
Lewis, S. B., 141
Libby, E. R., 221
Library books project, 168–69
Lieberman, P., 22
Ling, D., 221
Linguistic model program, 124–27
Linguistic skills, effective use of, 65–66
Lloyd, L. L., 219
Logographic systems, 224–30
Longhurst, T., 101
Long-term objectives, 149–50
  kindergarten, 192
  nursery level, 209
  prekindergarten, 200–201
Long-term memory, 78–79
Look and Say Method, 46–47
Lunch projects, 169
Lynch, J., 102
Lyons, J., 26

McDonald, E. T., 234
McLean, J., 228
McLean, L., 228
McNeill, D., 17
Magic Circle Program, 65, 135
Mainstreaming, 137–38
Manuscript writing, 51–52
Maratsos, M., 40
"Masterchart of Communication Aids,"
  232
Mathematics, 54–62
  modern, 56
  quantifiable attributes, 56–59
Mauzy, A., 6, 124
Meadow, K. P., 223
Mean length of utterance (MLU), 35
Measurement, concept of, 57
Me Book project, 169–71
MELDS. *See* Minnesota Early Language
  Development Sequence
MELDS Glossary of Rebuses and
  Signs, 230
Memory
  long-term, 78–79
  retrieval, 77–84
  short-term, 78
Memory development, structural vs.
  functional, 80–81
Memory, educational implications,
  81–82
Memory-linguistic learning, 247–48

Memory-mnemonic devices, strategies
  in, 79–80
Memory-nonlinguistic learning, 248–49
Menig-Peterson, C., 40
Merrill, M. A., 78, 90, 94
Metalinguistics, 40–41
Milisen, R., 21
Minifie, F. D., 21
Minnesota Early Language Develop-
  ment Sequence (MELDS), 225,
  228, 229
Moffitt, A. R., 21, 73
Moores, D. F., 228
Moorhead, D., 119
Morphology, 23, 44
Morrison, F. J., 80
Morse, P. A., 21
Morse Code, 16
Morton, R. L., 55
Motivation, 75. *See also* Learning
  requirements
Motor skills, 233, 252–55
Motor testing, 93
Mount Carmel Guide Diagnostic Center
  for Hearing, Speech and Communi-
  cation Disorders, 10
Moynahan, E. D., 80
Multi-meaning words, 32
Muma, J., 101

National Council of Teachers of Mathe-
  matics, 55
Negation, 30
Nelson, K., 35
Newspaper project, 171
Nix, G. W., 223
Non-Speech Language Initiation Pro-
  gram, 225, 228, 229
  goal of, 228
Nonstandardized tests, 95–103
Norm-referenced tests, 94
Northern, J. L., 221, 234
Number skills, 60
Nursery level
  class description, 209
  long-range objectives, 209
  sample lesson plans, 210–17
  units, 209
Nursery rhymes project, 171–72

Object(s)
  identify by category, 108
  names by function, 108
  recognition by function, 108
Object box project, 172–73, 188
One-to-one correspondence, 60, 61
Open House for Parents, 173–75

Oral and aural method, 221
Oral and manual systems, 220-23
Oral language, 16
Oral language testing, 91-92
Ornstein, P. A., 78
Orr, R., 80
Orthography, 223-24
Orton, S. T., 44
Orton Society, 44
Otitis media, 11

Palermo, D. S., 26
Palomares, U., 64, 65
Paper folding, 109
Parent involvement, 140-44
Peabody Picture Vocabulary Test, 90
Peabody Reading Program, 225
Peak, T., 228
Peeples, D. R., 73
Perception, 72-75, *See also* Learning
    requirements
  self, 73
  speech, 20-21
Perceptual-motor program, 123
Personnel utilization, 134-36
Philosophy, educational, 117-22
Phonics, 45-46, 48-49
Phonics Box project, 175
Phonology, 20
Physical health, 128
Piagetian concept of conservation, 29
Pitman, I., 224
Plural words, 33
Portage Guide to Early Education, 101
Position words, 28
Pragmatics, 36-40, 91-92
Preacademic education, 43-62
Prekindergarten
  class description, 200
  long-range objectives, 200-201
  sample lesson plans, 201-208
  units, 200
Premack, A. J., 228
Premack, D., 228
Preschool handicapped children, early
    training of, 118-20
Presupposition, 40
Problem solving, 246-47
Program(s)
  generic, 120-21
  linguistic model, 124-27
  perceptual-motor model, 123
  specific disabilities model, 123-24
Program design, 117-45
  organization, 133-44
  process, 146-51
Project(s)
  art, 153-55

bulletin boards, 155-56
calendar, 156-57
charts, 157-59
club day, 159-61
cooking, 161-62
expansion picture file, 162-63
experience story, 163
field trips, 163-65
finger plays, 165
games, 165-67
home visits, 167
key words, 167-68
library books, 168-69
lunch, 169
Me Book, 169-71
newspaper, 171
nursery rhymes, 171-72
object box, 172-73
open house for parents, 173-75
phonics box, 175
records, 175-76
roll call, 176
scrapbook, 176-77
self concept, 177-78
show and tell, 178-79
songs, 179
special events, 179-80
stations, 181-83
stories, 183
vocabulary box, 184
voting, 184
work tables, 184
Pronouns, 31
Prosody, 129
Public Law 90-538, 3-12
  goals of, 4-9
Public Law 94-142, 3, 12-14, 89, 90,
    114, 118, 122, 135, 137, 219, 237

Quality words, 28-29
Quantifiable attributes, 56-59
Quantitative vocabulary, 59-62
Quantity words, 28-29
Questions acquisition, 30-31

Rapport, 104, 110
Raskin, L. M., 75
Reading, 43-50
Reading failures, 44-45. *See also*
    Dyslexia
Reading methods, 45-47
  experience stories, 47
  look and say, 46-47
  phonics, 45-46
Reading readiness, 244-45
  objectives, 47-50
Reading testing, 92

Rebus Glossary, 225
Rebus Reading Series, 225
Records project, 175–76
Rehearsal techniques, 79–80
Relational words, 25–27, 109
Resource room, 137
Retrieval, memory, 77–84
Rewards
  extrinsic, 76
  intrinsic, 76–77
Reynolds, M. C., 119
Rister, A., 222
Rochester Method, 222
Roe, V., 21
Roll call project, 176
Ruder, K., 22
Ryan, J., 119

Sample lesson plans
  kindergarten, 192–99
  nursery level, 210–17
  prekindergarten, 201–8
Schaefer, E. S., 140
Schedule of classroom events
  arrival, 187
  assembly, 188
  dismissal, 190
  fine arts, 189–90
  follow-up activities, 189
  projects, 189
  sequenced instruction, 188–89
Schlesinger, H. S., 223
Schrandt, T., 101
Scouten, E. L., 222
Scrapbook project, 176–77
Searle, J. R., 38
SEE 1. *See* Seeing Essential English
SEE 2. *See* Signing Exact English
Seeing Essential English, 222
Self-concept, 63, 64, 66
Self-concept project, 177–78
Self-contained classroom, 136
Self-help skills, 252–55
Self-perception, 73
Semantography. *See* Blissymbolics
Sensation, 70
Sensory input, assessing, 233
Sensory skills, 233–35
Sentences. *See also* Syntax.
  direct-indirect forms of, 38–39
  repetition of, 109
Sequenced instruction, 188–89
Shantz, C. U., 67
Shape, concept of, 58
Shape words, 29
Shatz, M., 40
Short-term memory, 78
Show and Tell project, 178–79

Sight word training, 48
Signing Exact English, 222
Sign language, American, 221–22
Size words, 29
Skills
  auditory matching, 49
  cognitive, 235
  language, 235
  motor, 233
  motor and self-help, 252–55
  number, 60
  prehandwriting, 51
  prespelling, 53–54
  sensory, 233–35
  visual matching, 49
  word-attack, 48–49
Skinner, B. F., 17
Smirnov, A. A., 80
Smith, E. B., 45, 46
Smith, M., 22, 40
Social-Personal behavior, 250–52
Social-Personal testing, 92
Social words, 32–33
Sociograms, 102–103
Songs project, 179
Sound perception, 36
Sound production, 36
Sound system, 20–23, 44
Spalding, R. B., 45
Spalding, W. F., 45
Special events projects, 179–80
Specific disabilities program,
  123–24
Speech acts, 38
Speech perception, 20–21
Speech production, 21–23
Spelling, 53–54
  finger, 224
Spring, D. R., 21
Standardized tests, 93–95
Standard Rebus Glossary, 225
Stanford-Binet Intelligence Scale, 90
Stations projects, 181–83, 188
Stern, D., 37
Stillman, B., 44, 45
Story projects, 183
Strauss, A. A., 138
Stuttering, 134
Substantive words, 23
Success, feelings of, 129
Syntax, 34–36, 91
Systems
  logographic, 224–30
  orthographic, 223–24

Tape recordings, 133
Teacher-made tests, 102, 263–67

Teaching
  creative, 131–33
  diagnostic, 103
  strategies, 127–33
Technical aids, alternative systems of
    communication, 230–32
Teller, D. Y., 73
Temperature, concept of, 58
Templin, M., 21
Terman, L. M., 78, 90, 94
Test environment, 103–107
Testing, 86–115
  arithmetic, 92
  assessment, 90
  avenues of learning, 93
  evaluation, 90
  identification, 88–89
  motor, 93
  oral language, 91–92
  purpose of, 87–88
  reading, 92
  screening, 88–89
  social and personal, 92

Tests
  criterion-referenced, 94–95
  curriculum-based, 147–48
  nonstandardized, 95–103
  norm-referenced, 94
  qualitative interpretation, 108–109
  quantitative interpretation, 107–108
  results reporting, 110–14
  standardized, 93–95
  teacher-made, 102, 263–67
Test scoring, 107–109
Test selection, 93–103
Time, concept of, 58
Tobin, H., 86
Tomblin, B. J., 118
Total communication, 222–23
Traditional orthography (T.O.), 50,
    223–24
Training
  early, 118–20
  materials, 274–75
Trehub, S. E., 21
Tyack, D., 101

Units, curriculum, 129, 149
Use, language, 36–40, 91–92

Vanderheiden, G. C., 231, 232
Verbal response, eliciting from children,
    130–31
Verbs, 33
Vernon, M., 222
Visual matching skills, 49
Vocabulary, 48. *See also* Words.
Vocabulary Comprehension Scale, 94,
    141
Vocabulary box project, 184
Von Haden, H. I., 123
Voting projects, 184

Wechsler, D., 78
Weight, concept of, 58
Weiner, P. S., 119
Whatmough, J., 15
Wilbur, R. B., 222
Winitz, H., 22
Woodcock, R. W., 224, 225, 228
Word-attack skills, 48–49
Words
  affective, 30, 65
  category, 24
  class, 24
  color, 29
  constant, 24
  contrast, 25–26
  multimeaning, 32
  position, 28
  pronouns, 31
  quality, 28–29
  quantity, 28–29; plurals, 33, verbs,
    33, possessive, 34
  relational, 25–27
  shape, 29
  size, 29
  social, 32–33
  substantive, 23
Work table projects, 184
Writing
  cursive, 51–52
  manuscript, 51–52
  Palmer method, 52
  prehandwriting skills, 51

Zinchenko, P. I., 80
Zukow, P. G., 40